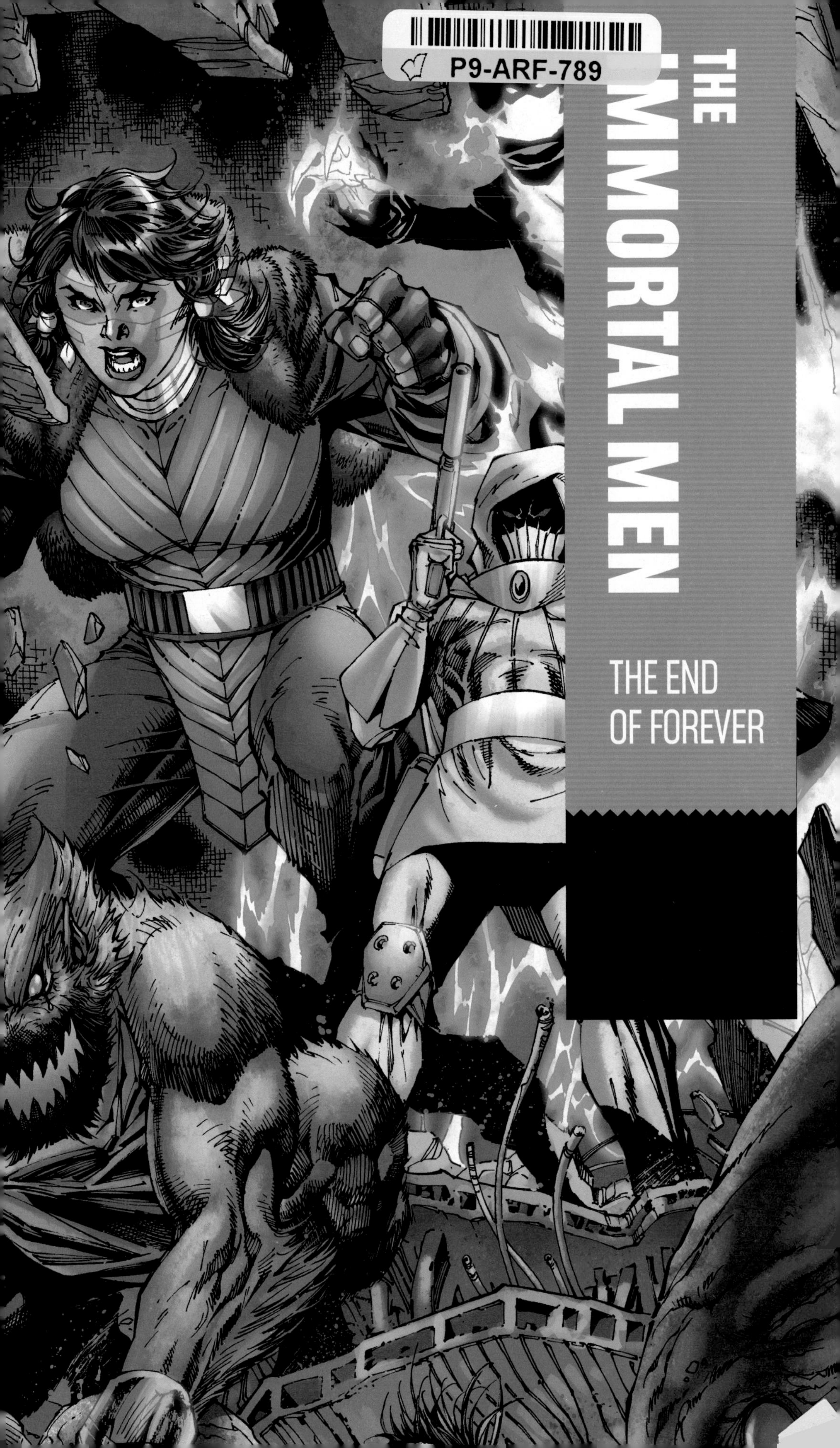
THE IMMORTAL MEN
THE END OF FOREVER

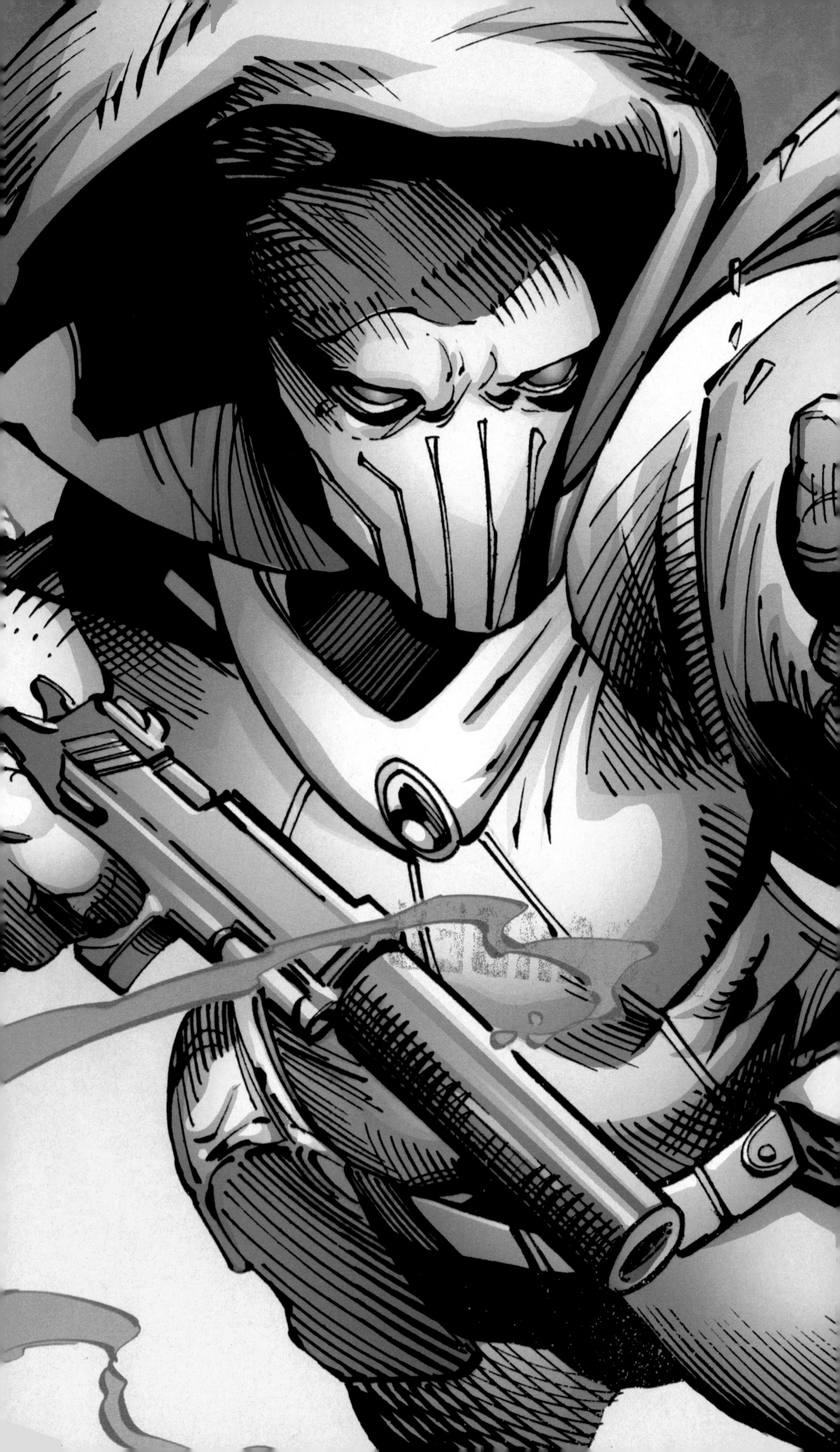

THE
IMMORTAL MEN
THE END OF FOREVER

artists

JIM LEE
RYAN BENJAMIN
TYLER KIRKHAM

writer

JAMES TYNION IV

inkers

SCOTT WILLIAMS
RICHARD FRIEND

colorists

ALEX SINCLAIR \ JEREMIAH SKIPPER
DAVID BARON \ ARIF PRIANTO

letterer

CARLOS M. MANGUAL

collection cover artists

JIM LEE, SCOTT WILLIAMS
& ALEX SINCLAIR

IMMORTAL MEN created by **JIM LEE** and **JAMES TYNION IV**

SUPERMAN created by **JERRY SIEGEL** and **JOE SHUSTER**
By special arrangement with the Jerry Siegel family

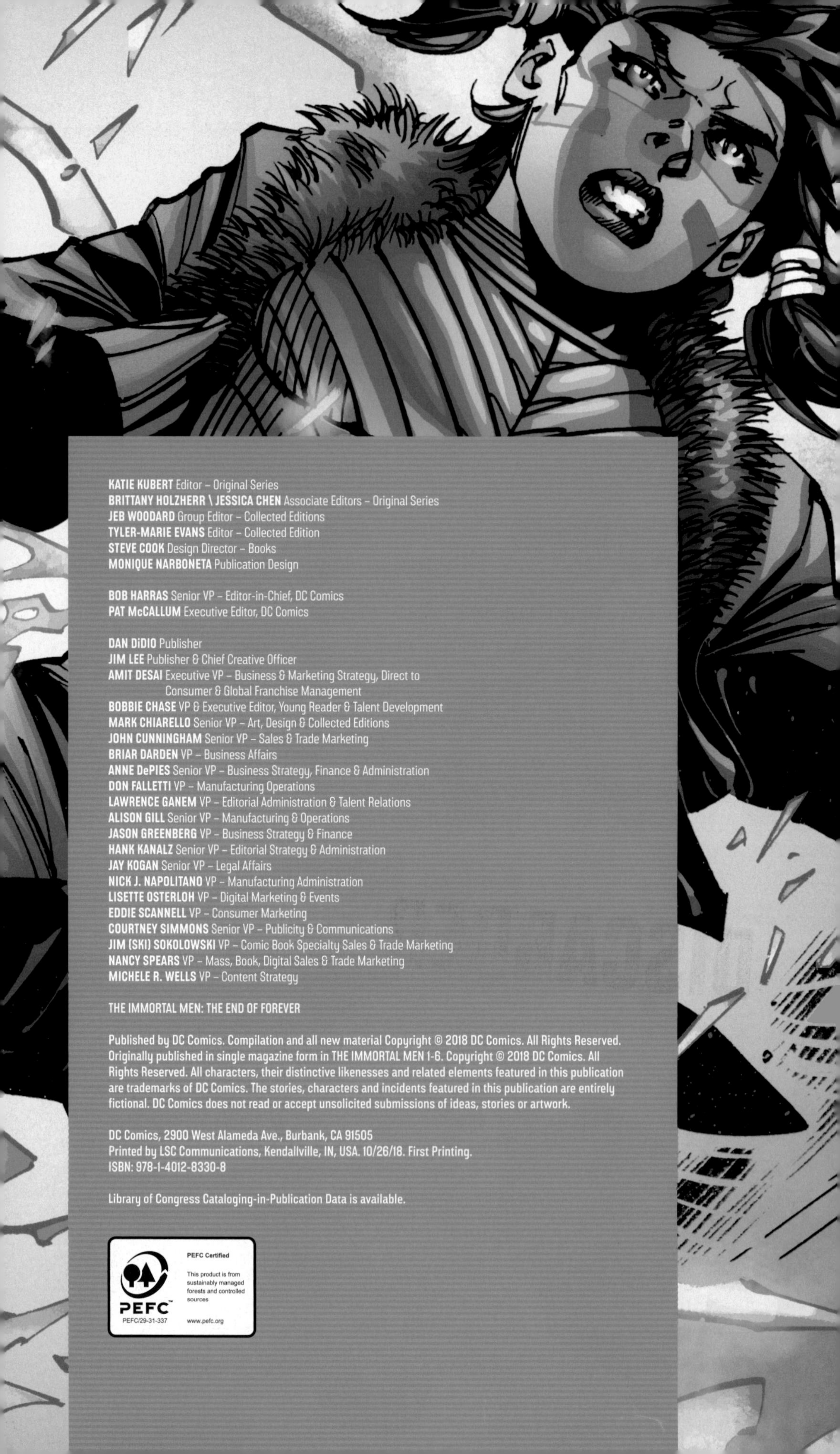

KATIE KUBERT Editor – Original Series
BRITTANY HOLZHERR \ JESSICA CHEN Associate Editors – Original Series
JEB WOODARD Group Editor – Collected Editions
TYLER-MARIE EVANS Editor – Collected Edition
STEVE COOK Design Director – Books
MONIQUE NARBONETA Publication Design

BOB HARRAS Senior VP – Editor-in-Chief, DC Comics
PAT McCALLUM Executive Editor, DC Comics

DAN DiDIO Publisher
JIM LEE Publisher & Chief Creative Officer
AMIT DESAI Executive VP – Business & Marketing Strategy, Direct to Consumer & Global Franchise Management
BOBBIE CHASE VP & Executive Editor, Young Reader & Talent Development
MARK CHIARELLO Senior VP – Art, Design & Collected Editions
JOHN CUNNINGHAM Senior VP – Sales & Trade Marketing
BRIAR DARDEN VP – Business Affairs
ANNE DePIES Senior VP – Business Strategy, Finance & Administration
DON FALLETTI VP – Manufacturing Operations
LAWRENCE GANEM VP – Editorial Administration & Talent Relations
ALISON GILL Senior VP – Manufacturing & Operations
JASON GREENBERG VP – Business Strategy & Finance
HANK KANALZ Senior VP – Editorial Strategy & Administration
JAY KOGAN Senior VP – Legal Affairs
NICK J. NAPOLITANO VP – Manufacturing Administration
LISETTE OSTERLOH VP – Digital Marketing & Events
EDDIE SCANNELL VP – Consumer Marketing
COURTNEY SIMMONS Senior VP – Publicity & Communications
JIM (SKI) SOKOLOWSKI VP – Comic Book Specialty Sales & Trade Marketing
NANCY SPEARS VP – Mass, Book, Digital Sales & Trade Marketing
MICHELE R. WELLS VP – Content Strategy

THE IMMORTAL MEN: THE END OF FOREVER

DC Comics, 2900 West Alameda Ave., Burbank, CA 91505
Printed by LSC Communications, Kendallville, IN, USA. 10/26/18. First Printing.
ISBN: 978-1-4012-8330-8

Library of Congress Cataloging-in-Publication Data is available.

PEFC Certified

This product is from sustainably managed forests and controlled sources

PEFC
PEFC/29-31-337

www.pefc.org

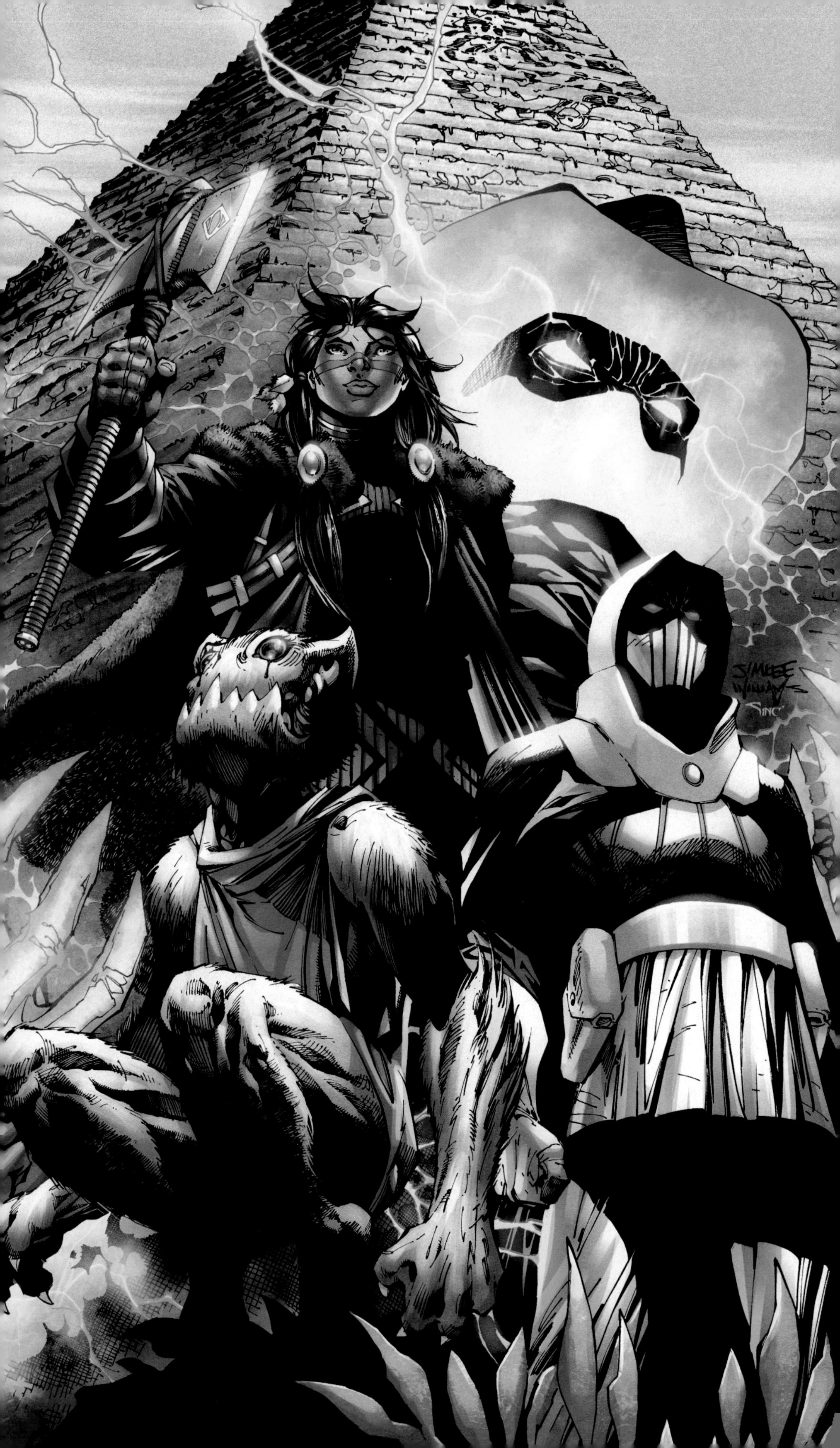

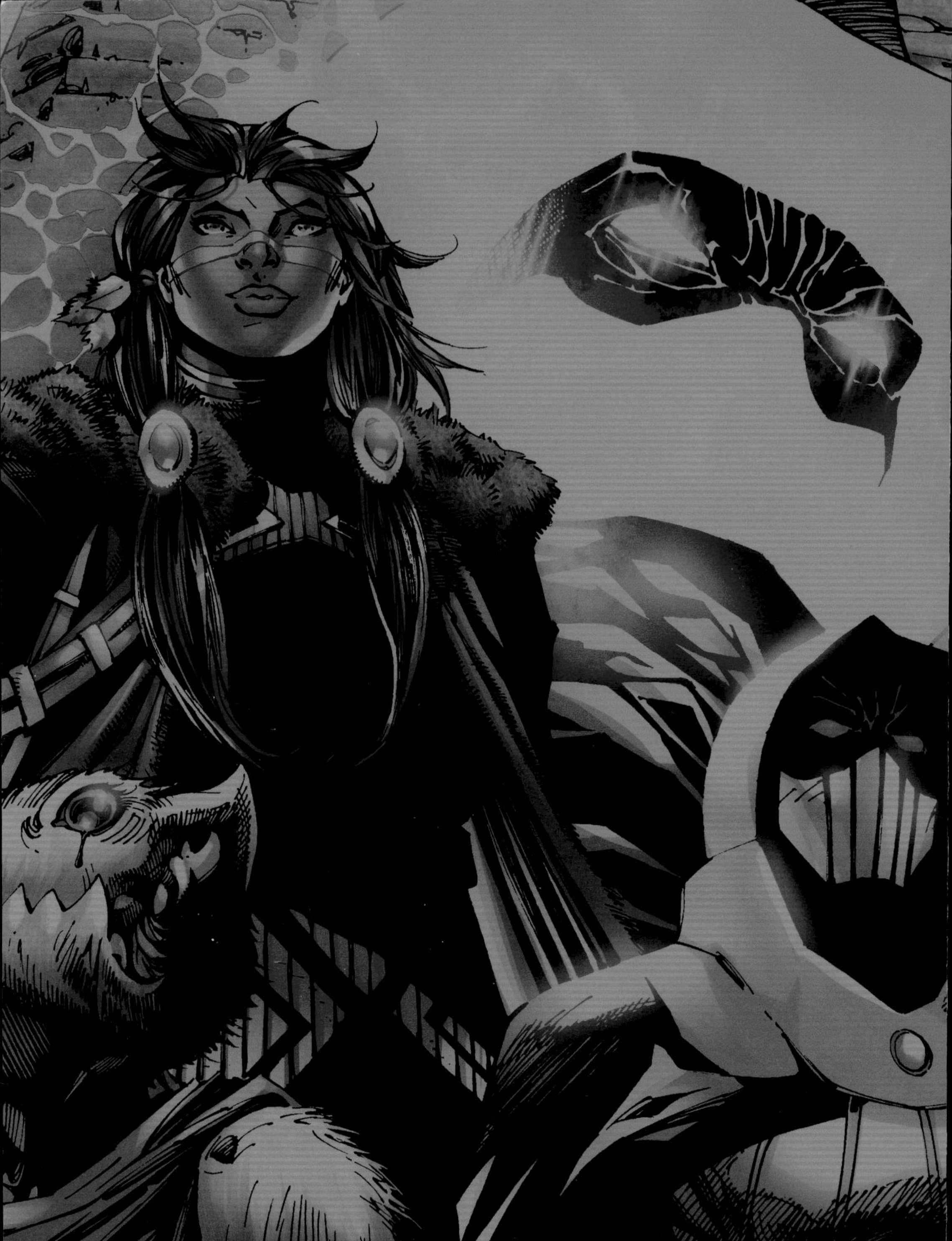

THE
IMMORTAL MEN
#1

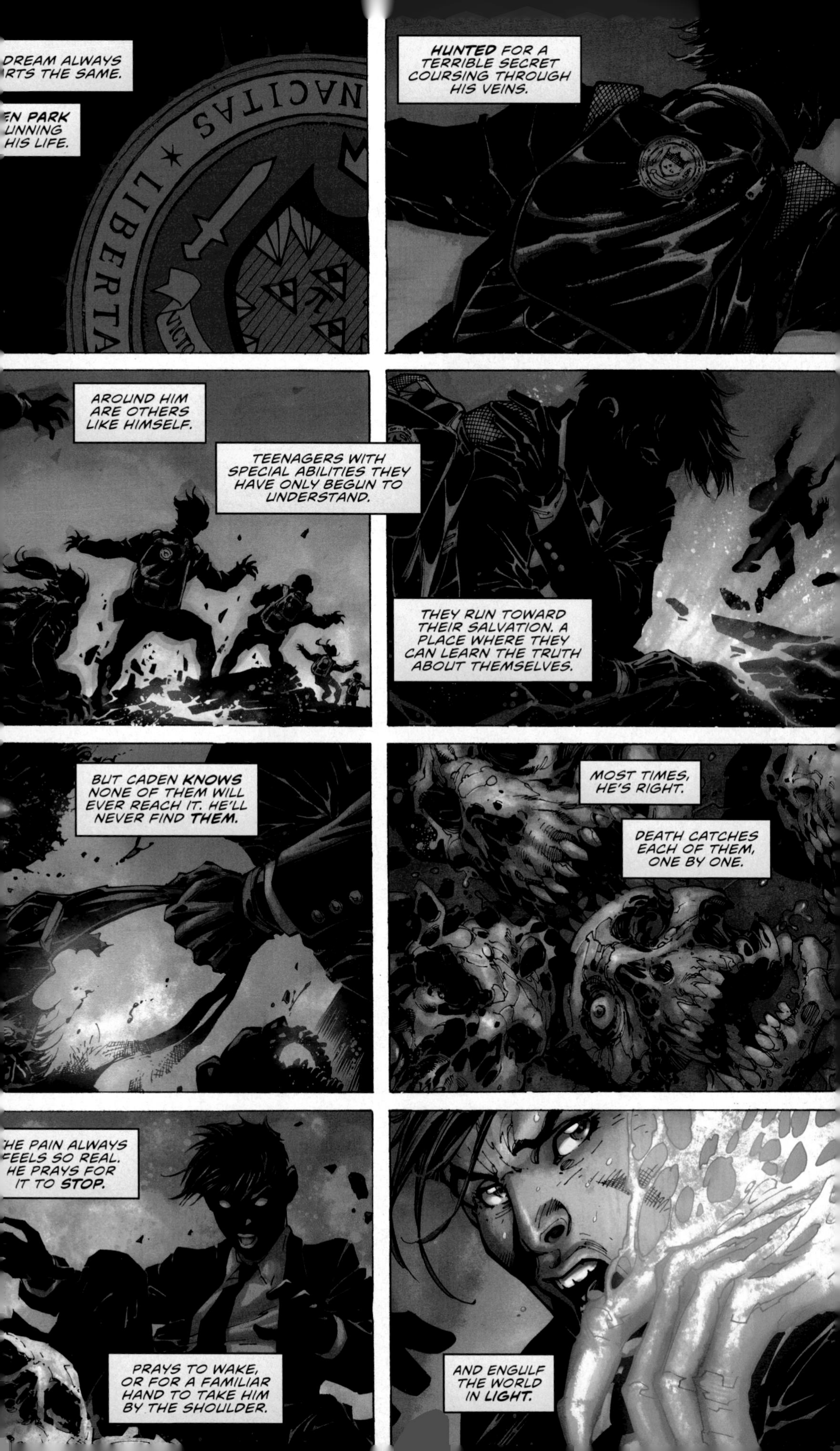

DREAM ALWAYS
RTS THE SAME.
EN PARK
UNNING
HIS LIFE.
HUNTED FOR A TERRIBLE SECRET COURSING THROUGH HIS VEINS.
AROUND HIM ARE OTHERS LIKE HIMSELF.
TEENAGERS WITH SPECIAL ABILITIES THEY HAVE ONLY BEGUN TO UNDERSTAND.
THEY RUN TOWARD THEIR SALVATION. A PLACE WHERE THEY CAN LEARN THE TRUTH ABOUT THEMSELVES.
BUT CADEN KNOWS NONE OF THEM WILL EVER REACH IT. HE'LL NEVER FIND THEM.
MOST TIMES, HE'S RIGHT.
DEATH CATCHES EACH OF THEM, ONE BY ONE.
HE PAIN ALWAYS
FEELS SO REAL.
HE PRAYS FOR
IT TO STOP.
PRAYS TO WAKE, OR FOR A FAMILIAR HAND TO TAKE HIM BY THE SHOULDER.
AND ENGULF THE WORLD IN LIGHT.

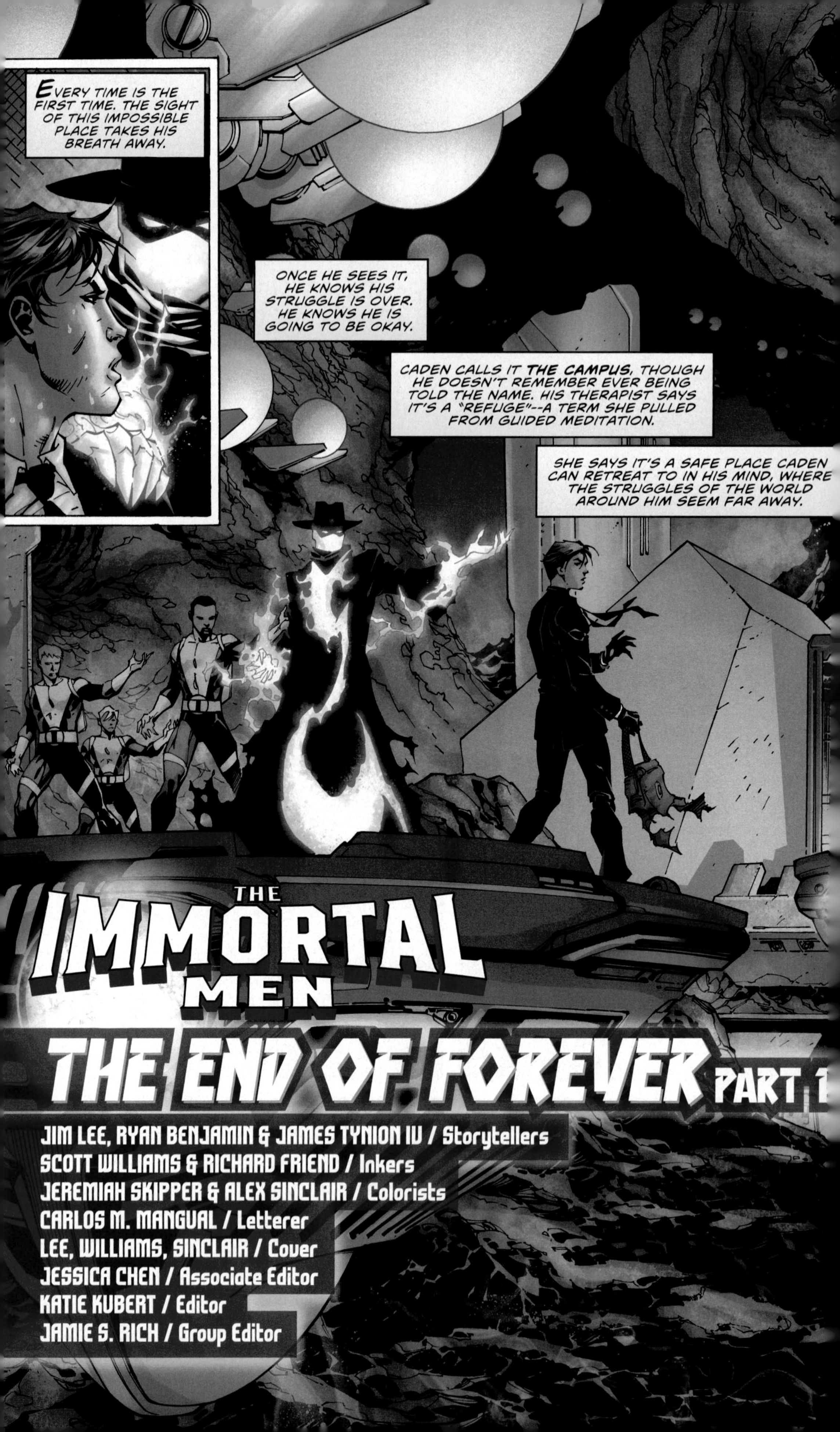
EVERY TIME IS THE FIRST TIME. THE SIGHT OF THIS IMPOSSIBLE PLACE TAKES HIS BREATH AWAY.
ONCE HE SEES IT, HE KNOWS HIS STRUGGLE IS OVER. HE KNOWS HE IS GOING TO BE OKAY.
CADEN CALLS IT THE CAMPUS, THOUGH HE DOESN'T REMEMBER EVER BEING TOLD THE NAME. HIS THERAPIST SAYS IT'S A "REFUGE"--A TERM SHE PULLED FROM GUIDED MEDITATION.
SHE SAYS IT'S A SAFE PLACE CADEN CAN RETREAT TO IN HIS MIND, WHERE THE STRUGGLES OF THE WORLD AROUND HIM SEEM FAR AWAY.
THE IMMORTAL MEN
THE END OF FOREVER PART 1
JIM LEE, RYAN BENJAMIN & JAMES TYNION IV / Storytellers
SCOTT WILLIAMS & RICHARD FRIEND / Inkers
JEREMIAH SKIPPER & ALEX SINCLAIR / Colorists
CARLOS M. MANGUAL / Letterer
LEE, WILLIAMS, SINCLAIR / Cover
JESSICA CHEN / Associate Editor
KATIE KUBERT / Editor
JAMIE S. RICH / Group Editor

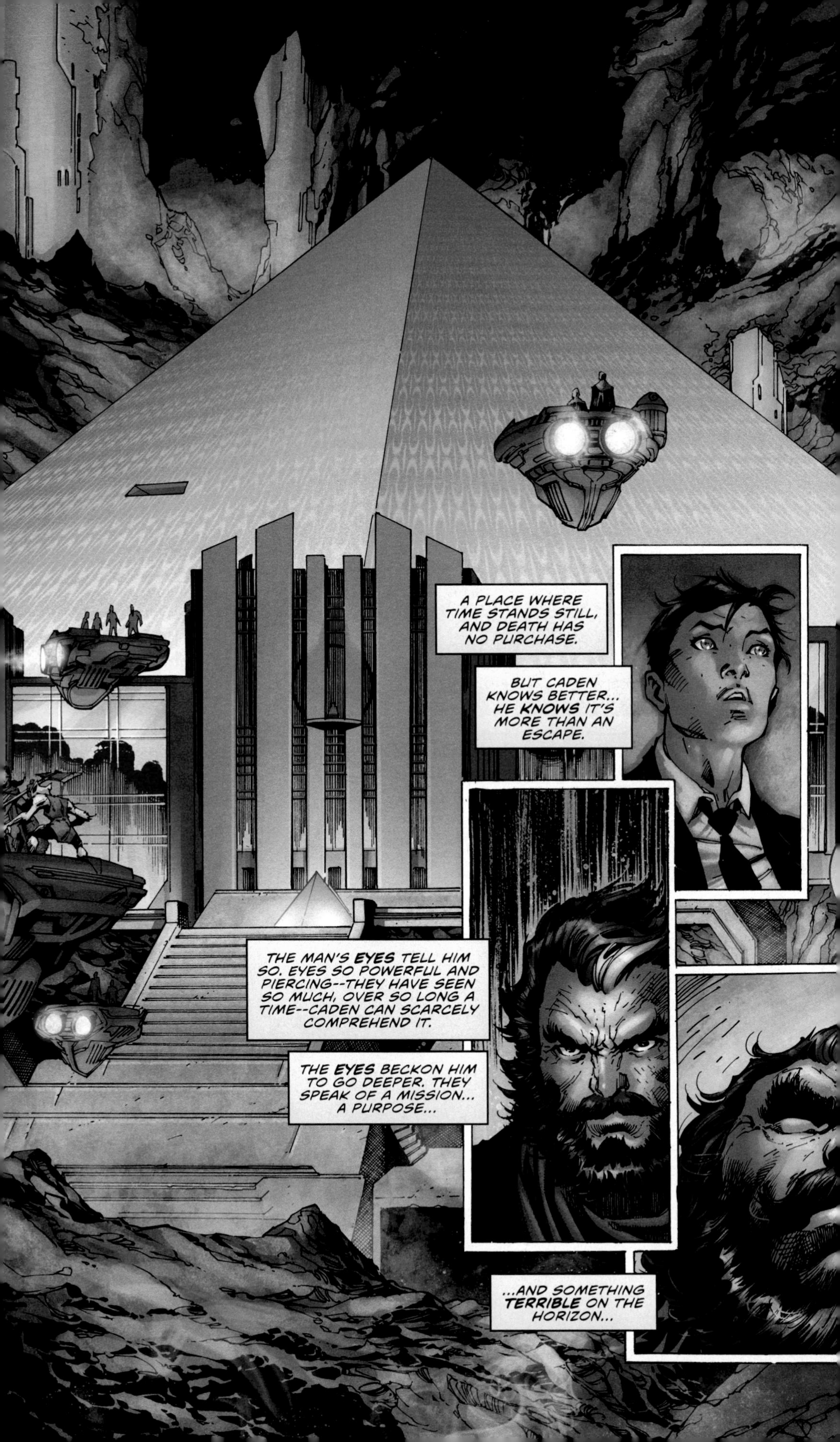
A PLACE WHERE TIME STANDS STILL, AND DEATH HAS NO PURCHASE.
BUT CADEN KNOWS BETTER... HE KNOWS IT'S MORE THAN AN ESCAPE.
THE MAN'S EYES TELL HIM SO. EYES SO POWERFUL AND PIERCING--THEY HAVE SEEN SO MUCH, OVER SO LONG A TIME--CADEN CAN SCARCELY COMPREHEND IT.
THE EYES BECKON HIM TO GO DEEPER. THEY SPEAK OF A MISSION... A PURPOSE...
...AND SOMETHING TERRIBLE ON THE HORIZON...

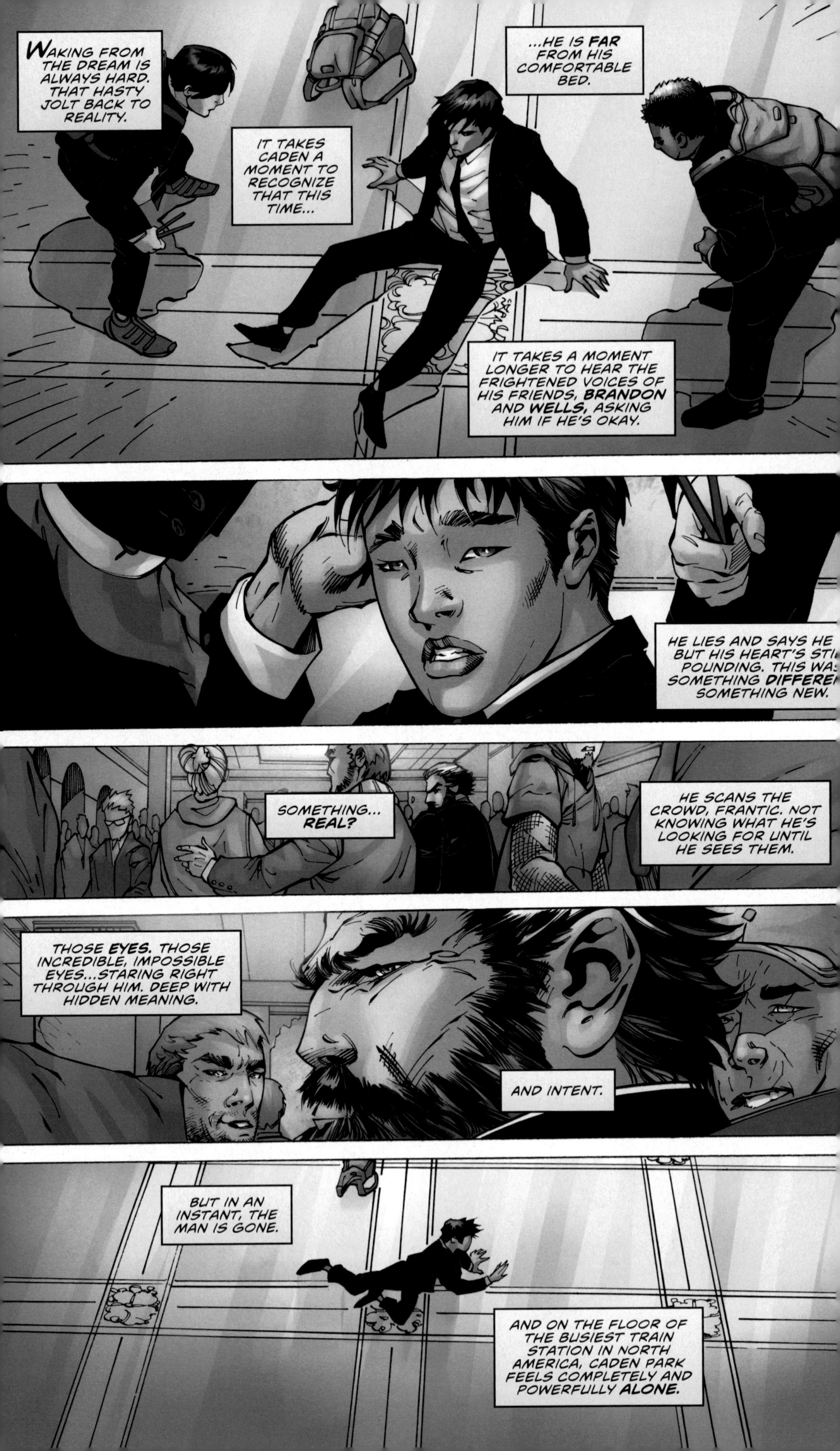
WAKING FROM THE DREAM IS ALWAYS HARD. THAT HASTY JOLT BACK TO REALITY.
IT TAKES CADEN A MOMENT TO RECOGNIZE THAT THIS TIME...
...HE IS FAR FROM HIS COMFORTABLE BED.
IT TAKES A MOMENT LONGER TO HEAR THE FRIGHTENED VOICES OF HIS FRIENDS, BRANDON AND WELLS, ASKING HIM IF HE'S OKAY.
HE LIES AND SAYS HE BUT HIS HEART'S STI POUNDING. THIS WAS SOMETHING DIFFERE SOMETHING NEW.
SOMETHING... REAL?
HE SCANS THE CROWD, FRANTIC. NOT KNOWING WHAT HE'S LOOKING FOR UNTIL HE SEES THEM.
THOSE EYES. THOSE INCREDIBLE, IMPOSSIBLE EYES...STARING RIGHT THROUGH HIM. DEEP WITH HIDDEN MEANING.
AND INTENT.
BUT IN AN INSTANT, THE MAN IS GONE.
AND ON THE FLOOR OF THE BUSIEST TRAIN STATION IN NORTH AMERICA, CADEN PARK FEELS COMPLETELY AND POWERFULLY ALONE.

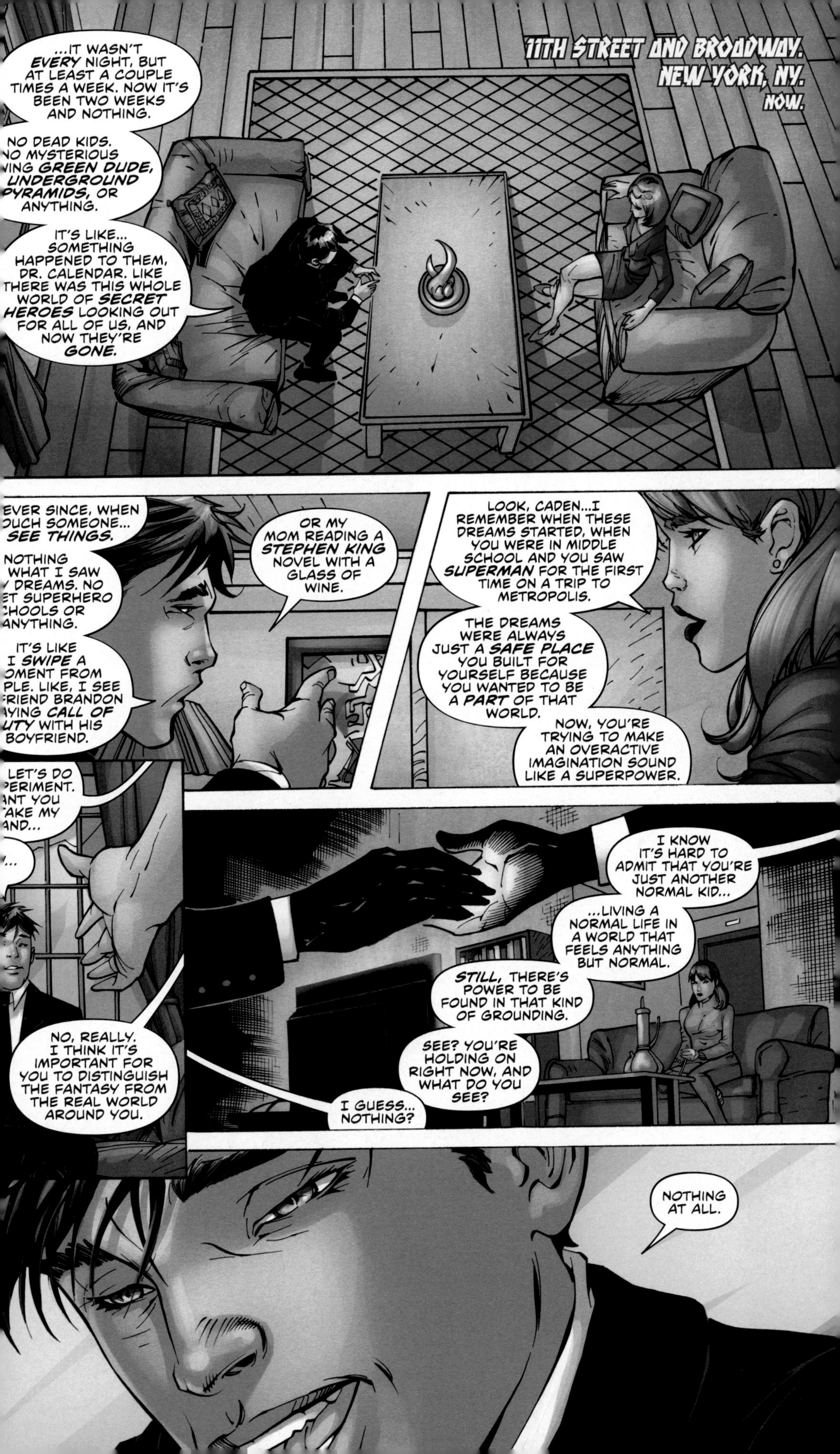
11TH STREET AND BROADWAY. NEW YORK, NY. NOW.
...IT WASN'T EVERY NIGHT, BUT AT LEAST A COUPLE TIMES A WEEK. NOW IT'S BEEN TWO WEEKS AND NOTHING.
NO DEAD KIDS. NO MYSTERIOUS WING GREEN DUDE, UNDERGROUND PYRAMIDS, OR ANYTHING.
IT'S LIKE... SOMETHING HAPPENED TO THEM, DR. CALENDAR. LIKE THERE WAS THIS WHOLE WORLD OF SECRET HEROES LOOKING OUT FOR ALL OF US, AND NOW THEY'RE GONE.
EVER SINCE, WHEN OUCH SOMEONE... SEE THINGS.
NOTHING WHAT I SAW DREAMS. NO ET SUPERHERO CHOOLS OR ANYTHING.
IT'S LIKE I SWIPE A OMENT FROM PLE. LIKE, I SEE FRIEND BRANDON AYING CALL OF UTY WITH HIS BOYFRIEND.
OR MY MOM READING A STEPHEN KING NOVEL WITH A GLASS OF WINE.
LOOK, CADEN...I REMEMBER WHEN THESE DREAMS STARTED, WHEN YOU WERE IN MIDDLE SCHOOL AND YOU SAW SUPERMAN FOR THE FIRST TIME ON A TRIP TO METROPOLIS.
THE DREAMS WERE ALWAYS JUST A SAFE PLACE YOU BUILT FOR YOURSELF BECAUSE YOU WANTED TO BE A PART OF THAT WORLD.
NOW, YOU'RE TRYING TO MAKE AN OVERACTIVE IMAGINATION SOUND LIKE A SUPERPOWER.
LET'S DO PERIMENT. ANT YOU TAKE MY AND...
NO, REALLY. I THINK IT'S IMPORTANT FOR YOU TO DISTINGUISH THE FANTASY FROM THE REAL WORLD AROUND YOU.
I KNOW IT'S HARD TO ADMIT THAT YOU'RE JUST ANOTHER NORMAL KID...
...LIVING A NORMAL LIFE IN A WORLD THAT FEELS ANYTHING BUT NORMAL.
STILL, THERE'S POWER TO BE FOUND IN THAT KIND OF GROUNDING.
SEE? YOU'RE HOLDING ON RIGHT NOW, AND WHAT DO YOU SEE?
I GUESS... NOTHING?
NOTHING AT ALL.

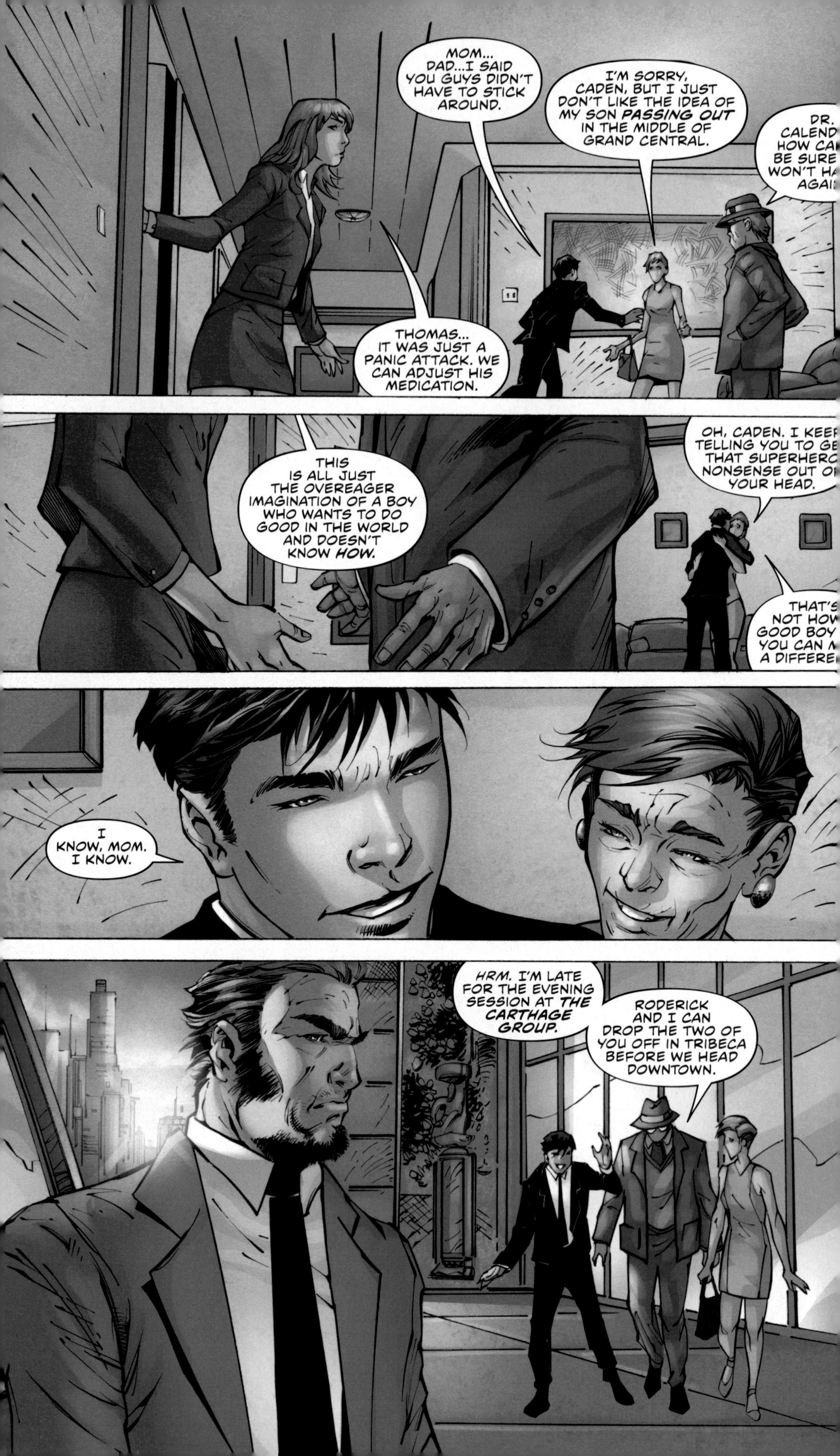
MOM... DAD...I SAID YOU GUYS DIDN'T HAVE TO STICK AROUND.
I'M SORRY, CADEN, BUT I JUST DON'T LIKE THE IDEA OF MY SON PASSING OUT IN THE MIDDLE OF GRAND CENTRAL.
THOMAS... IT WAS JUST A PANIC ATTACK. WE CAN ADJUST HIS MEDICATION.
THIS IS ALL JUST THE OVEREAGER IMAGINATION OF A BOY WHO WANTS TO DO GOOD IN THE WORLD AND DOESN'T KNOW HOW.
I KNOW, MOM. I KNOW.
HRM. I'M LATE FOR THE EVENING SESSION AT THE CARTHAGE GROUP.
RODERICK AND I CAN DROP THE TWO OF YOU OFF IN TRIBECA BEFORE WE HEAD DOWNTOWN.

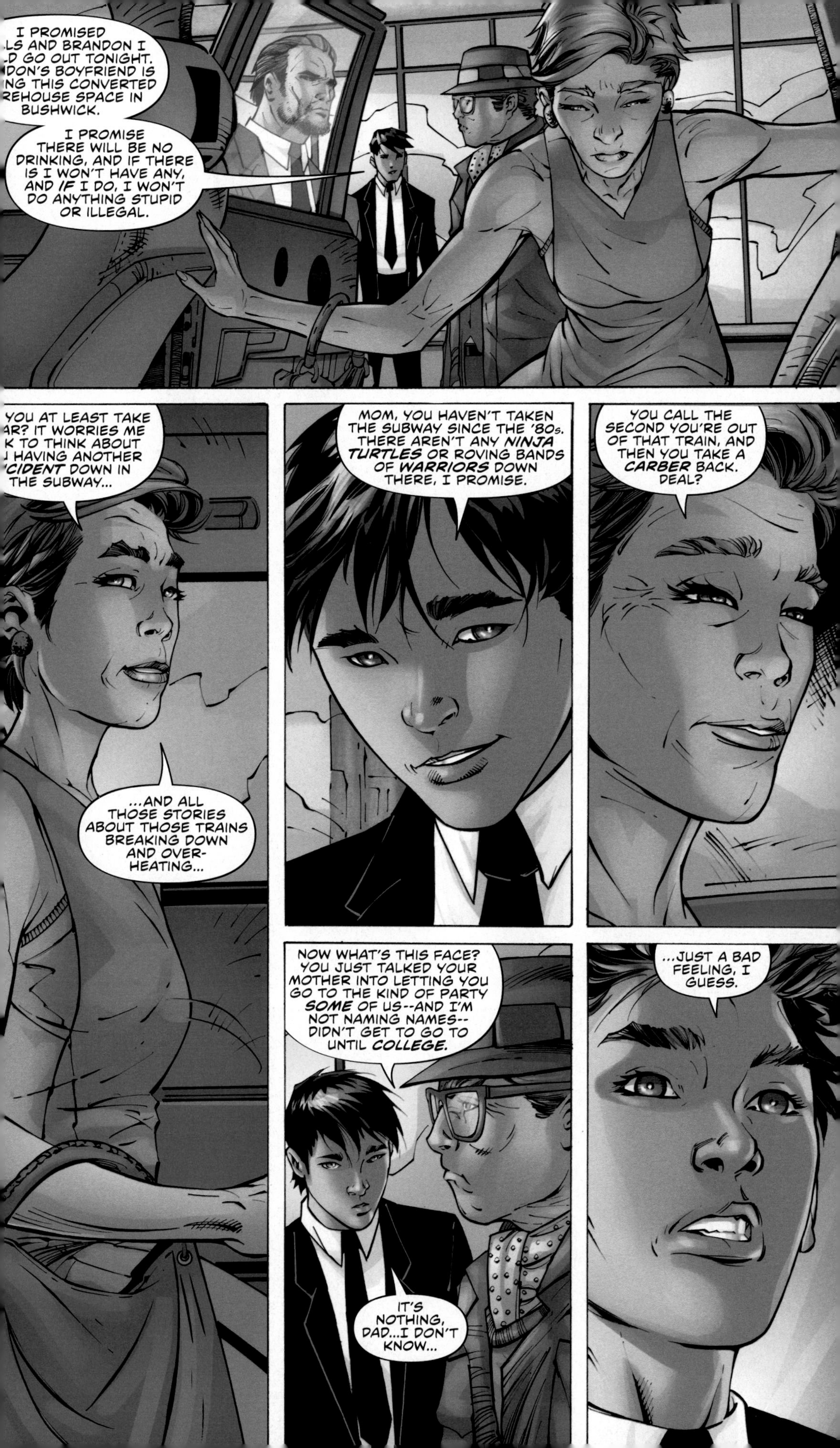
I PROMISED
LS AND BRANDON I
D GO OUT TONIGHT.
DON'S BOYFRIEND IS
NG THIS CONVERTED
REHOUSE SPACE IN
BUSHWICK.
I PROMISE THERE WILL BE NO DRINKING, AND IF THERE IS I WON'T HAVE ANY, AND *IF* I DO, I WON'T DO ANYTHING STUPID OR ILLEGAL.
YOU AT LEAST TAKE
AR? IT WORRIES ME
K TO THINK ABOUT
HAVING ANOTHER
CIDENT DOWN IN
THE SUBWAY...
...AND ALL THOSE STORIES ABOUT THOSE TRAINS BREAKING DOWN AND OVER-HEATING...
MOM, YOU HAVEN'T TAKEN THE SUBWAY SINCE THE '80s. THERE AREN'T ANY *NINJA TURTLES* OR ROVING BANDS OF *WARRIORS* DOWN THERE, I PROMISE.
YOU CALL THE SECOND YOU'RE OUT OF THAT TRAIN, AND THEN YOU TAKE A *CARBER* BACK. DEAL?
NOW WHAT'S THIS FACE? YOU JUST TALKED YOUR MOTHER INTO LETTING YOU GO TO THE KIND OF PARTY *SOME* OF US--AND I'M NOT NAMING NAMES--DIDN'T GET TO GO TO UNTIL *COLLEGE*.
IT'S NOTHING, DAD...I DON'T KNOW...
...JUST A BAD FEELING, I GUESS.

THE CAMPUS.
EST. 1732.
DOMAIN OF ACTION--
THE FIFTH HOUSE OF THE IMMORTALS.
ONE MILE BENEATH PHILADELPHIA...

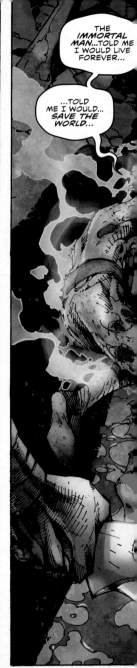

THE IMMORTAL MAN...TOLD ME I WOULD LIVE FOREVER...

...TOLD ME I WOULD... SAVE THE WORLD...

SHULK

HE LIED.

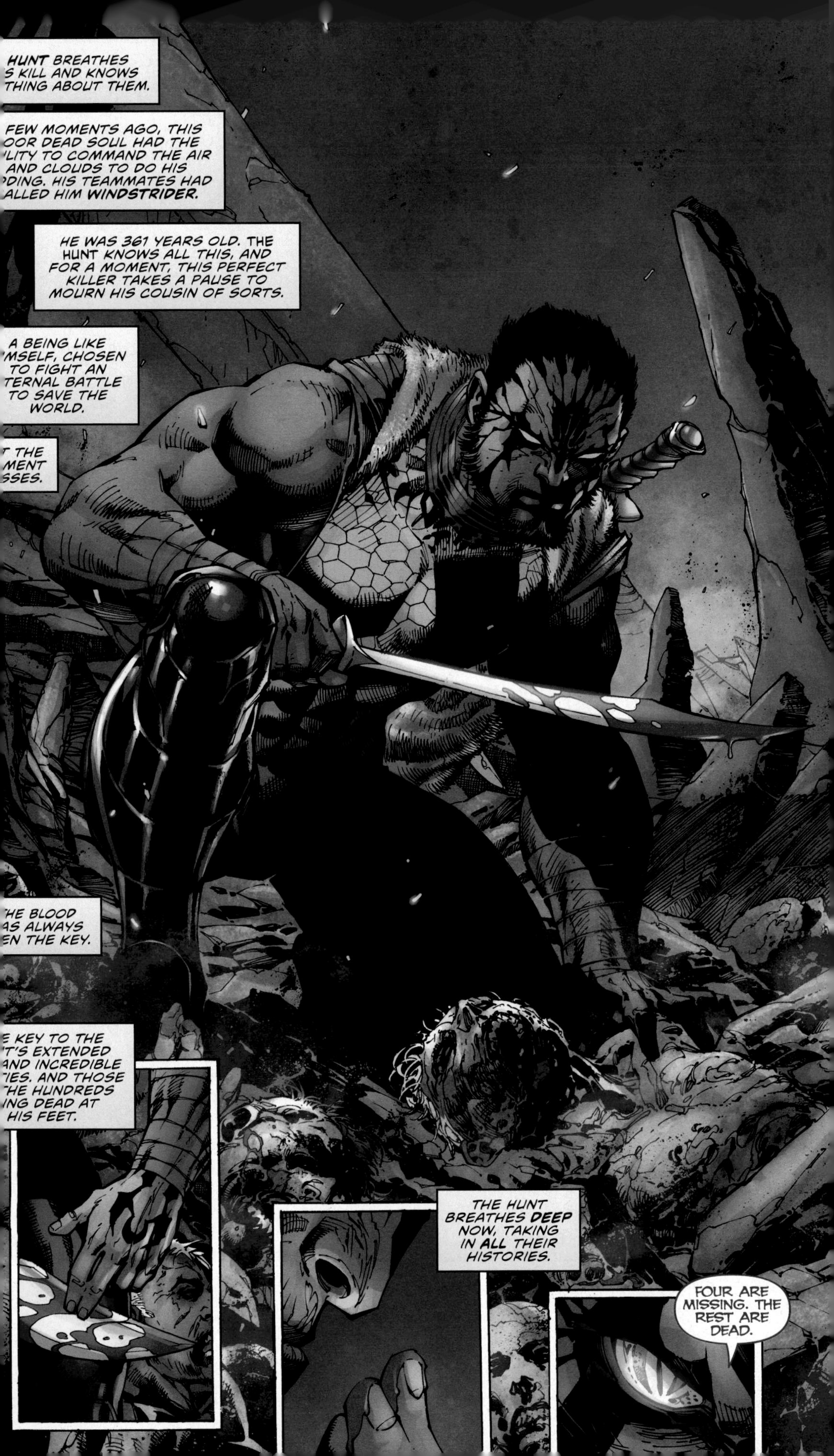

HUNT BREATHES S KILL AND KNOWS THING ABOUT THEM.
FEW MOMENTS AGO, THIS OOR DEAD SOUL HAD THE ILITY TO COMMAND THE AIR AND CLOUDS TO DO HIS DDING. HIS TEAMMATES HAD ALLED HIM WINDSTRIDER.
HE WAS 361 YEARS OLD. THE HUNT KNOWS ALL THIS, AND FOR A MOMENT, THIS PERFECT KILLER TAKES A PAUSE TO MOURN HIS COUSIN OF SORTS.
A BEING LIKE MSELF, CHOSEN TO FIGHT AN TERNAL BATTLE TO SAVE THE WORLD.
T THE MENT SSES.
HE BLOOD AS ALWAYS EN THE KEY.
E KEY TO THE T'S EXTENDED AND INCREDIBLE IES. AND THOSE THE HUNDREDS ING DEAD AT HIS FEET.
THE HUNT BREATHES DEEP NOW, TAKING IN ALL THEIR HISTORIES.
FOUR ARE MISSING. THE REST ARE DEAD.

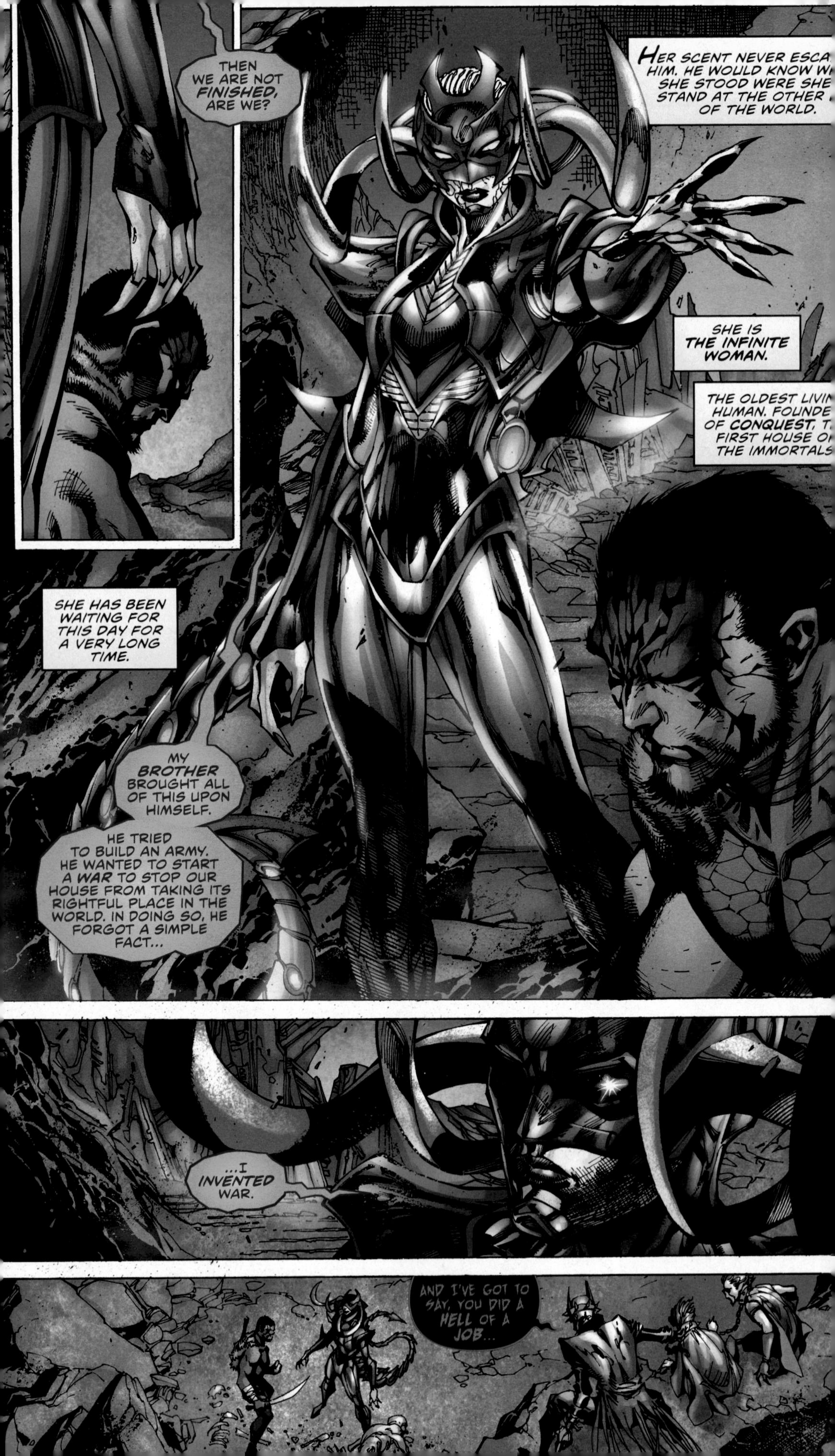

THEN WE ARE NOT FINISHED, ARE WE?
HER SCENT NEVER ESCA HIM. HE WOULD KNOW W SHE STOOD WERE SHE STAND AT THE OTHER OF THE WORLD.
SHE IS THE INFINITE WOMAN.
THE OLDEST LIVI HUMAN. FOUNDE OF CONQUEST, T FIRST HOUSE O THE IMMORTALS
SHE HAS BEEN WAITING FOR THIS DAY FOR A VERY LONG TIME.
MY BROTHER BROUGHT ALL OF THIS UPON HIMSELF.
HE TRIED TO BUILD AN ARMY. HE WANTED TO START A WAR TO STOP OUR HOUSE FROM TAKING ITS RIGHTFUL PLACE IN THE WORLD. IN DOING SO, HE FORGOT A SIMPLE FACT...
...I INVENTED WAR.
AND I'VE GOT TO SAY, YOU DID A HELL OF A JOB...

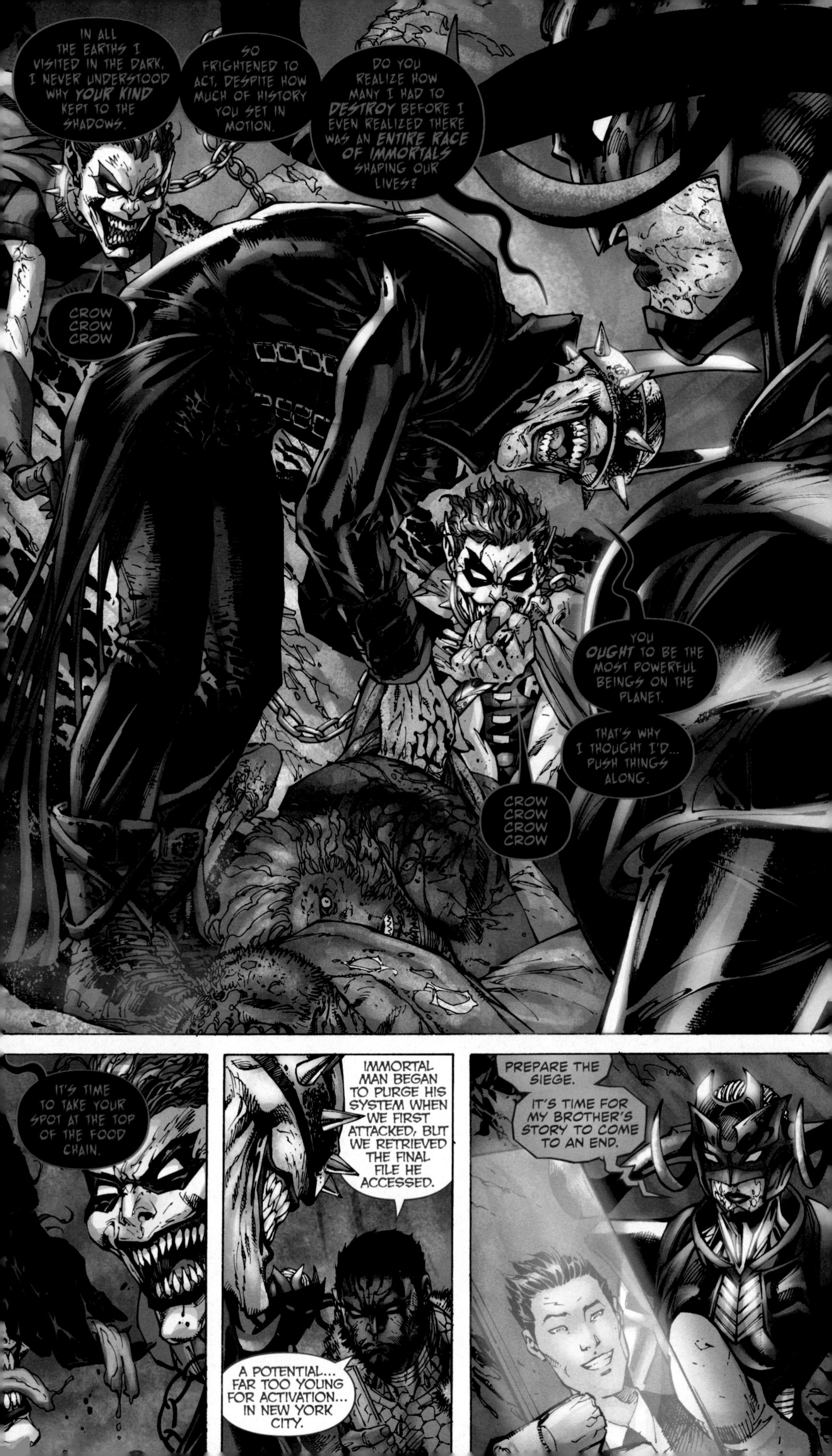
IN ALL THE EARTHS I VISITED IN THE DARK, I NEVER UNDERSTOOD WHY YOUR KIND KEPT TO THE SHADOWS.
SO FRIGHTENED TO ACT, DESPITE HOW MUCH OF HISTORY YOU SET IN MOTION.
DO YOU REALIZE HOW MANY I HAD TO DESTROY BEFORE I EVEN REALIZED THERE WAS AN ENTIRE RACE OF IMMORTALS SHAPING OUR LIVES?
CROW CROW CROW
YOU OUGHT TO BE THE MOST POWERFUL BEINGS ON THE PLANET.
THAT'S WHY I THOUGHT I'D... PUSH THINGS ALONG.
CROW CROW CROW CROW
IT'S TIME TO TAKE YOUR SPOT AT THE TOP OF THE FOOD CHAIN.
IMMORTAL MAN BEGAN TO PURGE HIS SYSTEM WHEN WE FIRST ATTACKED, BUT WE RETRIEVED THE FINAL FILE HE ACCESSED.
A POTENTIAL... FAR TOO YOUNG FOR ACTIVATION... IN NEW YORK CITY.
PREPARE THE SIEGE.
IT'S TIME FOR MY BROTHER'S STORY TO COME TO AN END.

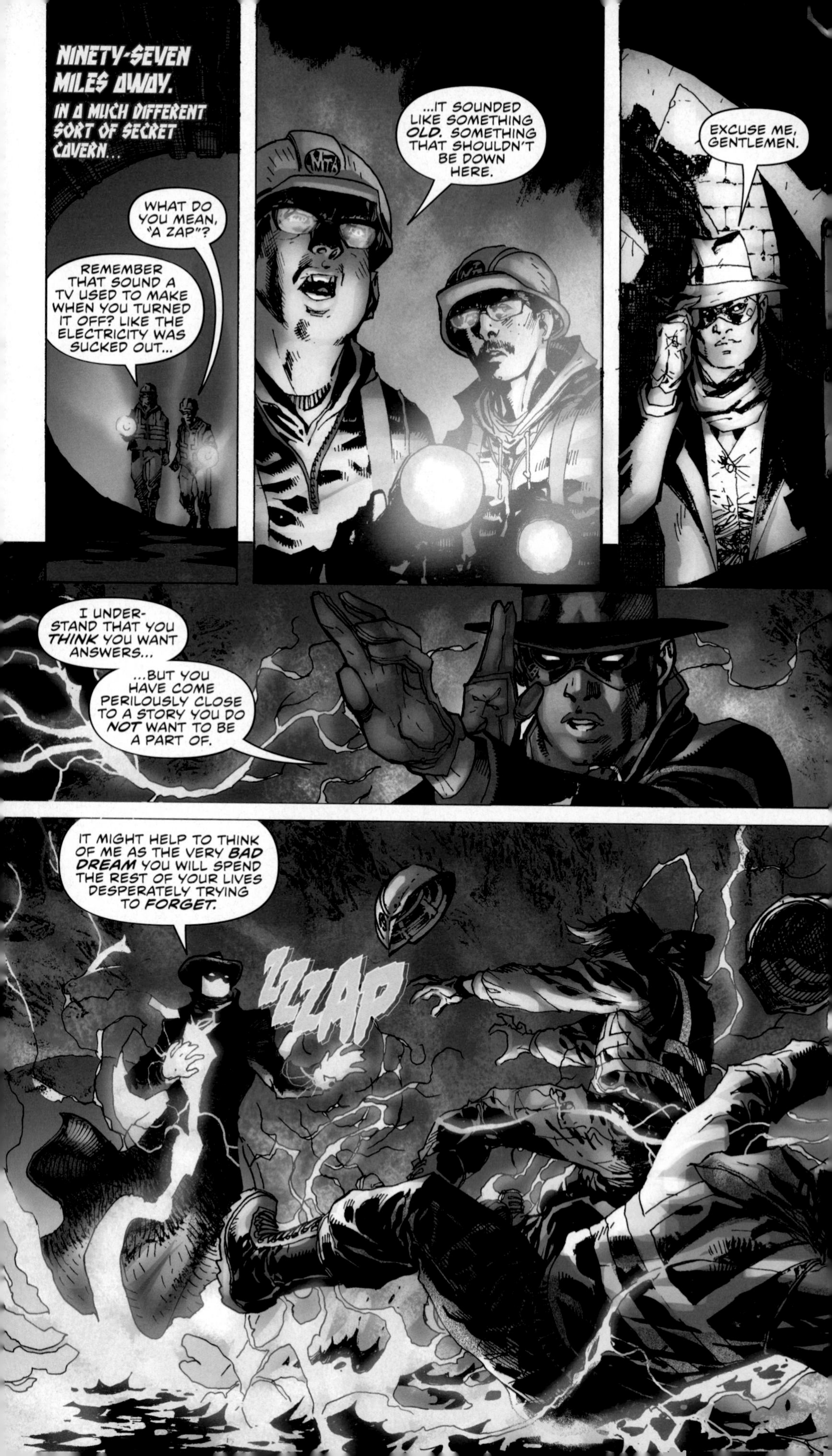
NINETY-SEVEN MILES AWAY.
IN A MUCH DIFFERENT SORT OF SECRET CAVERN...
WHAT DO YOU MEAN, "A ZAP"?
REMEMBER THAT SOUND A TV USED TO MAKE WHEN YOU TURNED IT OFF? LIKE THE ELECTRICITY WAS SUCKED OUT...
...IT SOUNDED LIKE SOMETHING OLD. SOMETHING THAT SHOULDN'T BE DOWN HERE.
EXCUSE ME, GENTLEMEN.
I UNDER-STAND THAT YOU THINK YOU WANT ANSWERS...
...BUT YOU HAVE COME PERILOUSLY CLOSE TO A STORY YOU DO NOT WANT TO BE A PART OF.
IT MIGHT HELP TO THINK OF ME AS THE VERY BAD DREAM YOU WILL SPEND THE REST OF YOUR LIVES DESPERATELY TRYING TO FORGET.
ZZZAP

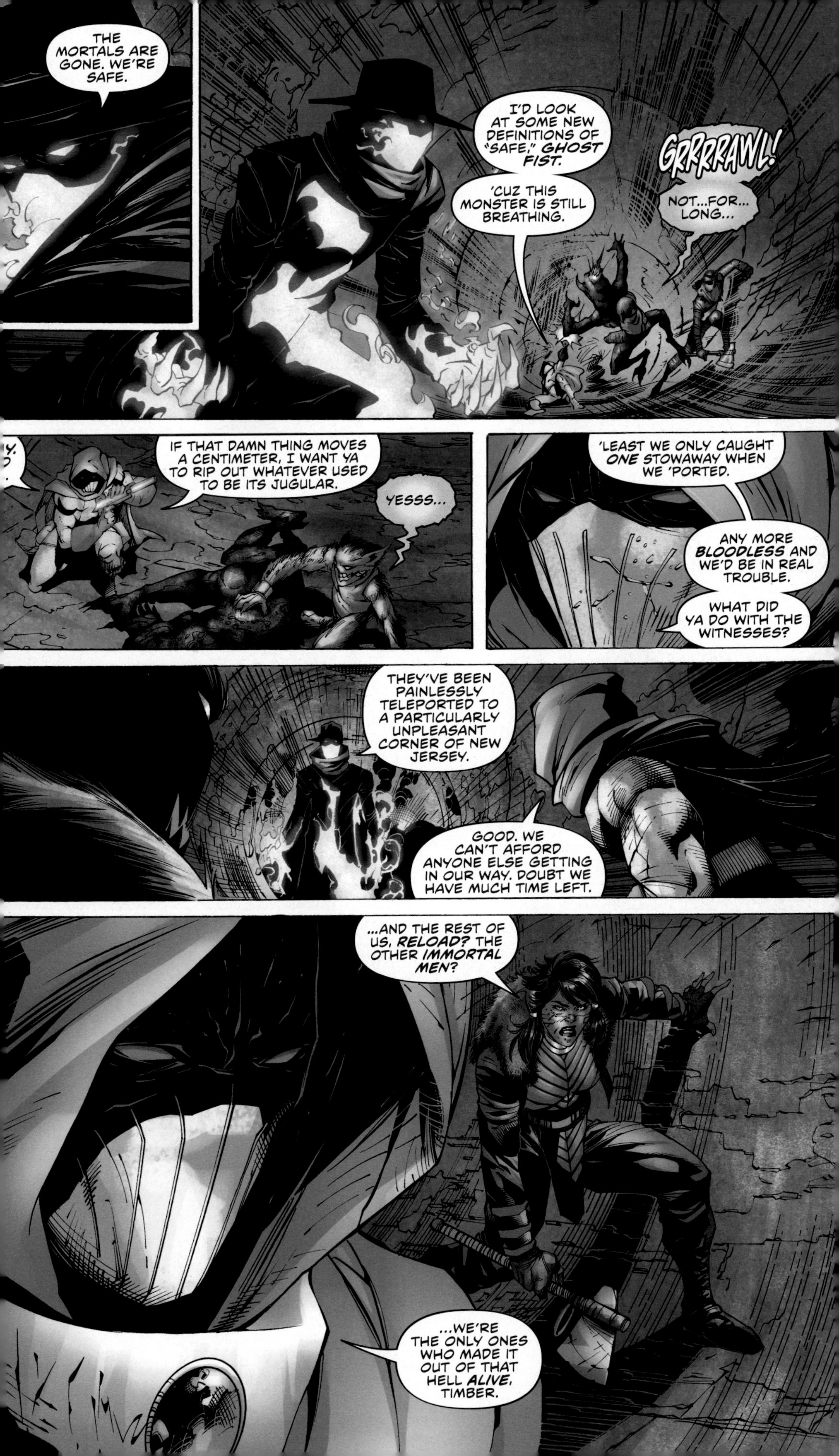
THE MORTALS ARE GONE. WE'RE SAFE.
I'D LOOK AT SOME NEW DEFINITIONS OF "SAFE," GHOST FIST.
'CUZ THIS MONSTER IS STILL BREATHING.
GRRRRAWL!
NOT...FOR... LONG...
IF THAT DAMN THING MOVES A CENTIMETER, I WANT YA TO RIP OUT WHATEVER USED TO BE ITS JUGULAR.
YESSS...
'LEAST WE ONLY CAUGHT ONE STOWAWAY WHEN WE 'PORTED.
ANY MORE BLOODLESS AND WE'D BE IN REAL TROUBLE.
WHAT DID YA DO WITH THE WITNESSES?
THEY'VE BEEN PAINLESSLY TELEPORTED TO A PARTICULARLY UNPLEASANT CORNER OF NEW JERSEY.
GOOD. WE CAN'T AFFORD ANYONE ELSE GETTING IN OUR WAY. DOUBT WE HAVE MUCH TIME LEFT.
...AND THE REST OF US, RELOAD? THE OTHER IMMORTAL MEN?
...WE'RE THE ONLY ONES WHO MADE IT OUT OF THAT HELL ALIVE, TIMBER.

THEN YOU *NEVER* SHOULD HAVE TAKEN US AWAY FROM THE BATTLEFIELD!

HUNDREDS DEAD! *HUNDREDS* OF OUR BROTHERS AND SISTERS! AND YOU DECIDED WE SHOULD *RETREAT?*

WE WERE *LOSING.* IMMORTAL MAN GAVE ME ORDERS. WHO I SHOULD GET TOGETHER IF THINGS WENT SOUTH. I FOLLOWED THEM TO THE *LETTER.*

YOU THINK I WOULDN'T RATHE HAVE FOUGHT TO TH END? YOU *KNOW* ME, TI YOU'VE KNOWN ME F THE BETTER PART O A *CENTURY.*

REMEMBER WHO WE ARE. WHY WE MADE THIS DEVIL'S BARGAIN. NONE OF US MATTER, IN THE FACE OF FOREVER. WHAT MATTERS IS THE *DREAM.*

WHY NEW YORK...? YOU KNOW I HAVE... *HISTORY* HERE.

THAT'S WHERE THE *KID* IS.

THE KID THE BOSS MAN NEEDS US TO GET OUR HANDS ON.

OUR...BROTHERS AND SISTERS...

...DESERVE MORE FROM US. THEY DESERVE OUR TIME...OUR PRAYERS.

BUT WE ARE THE *HOUSE OF ACTION.*

WHO IS THIS CHILD?

THE KID'S NAME IS *CADEN PARK.*

AND THE BOSS SAYS HE'S GOING TO *SAVE THE WORLD.*

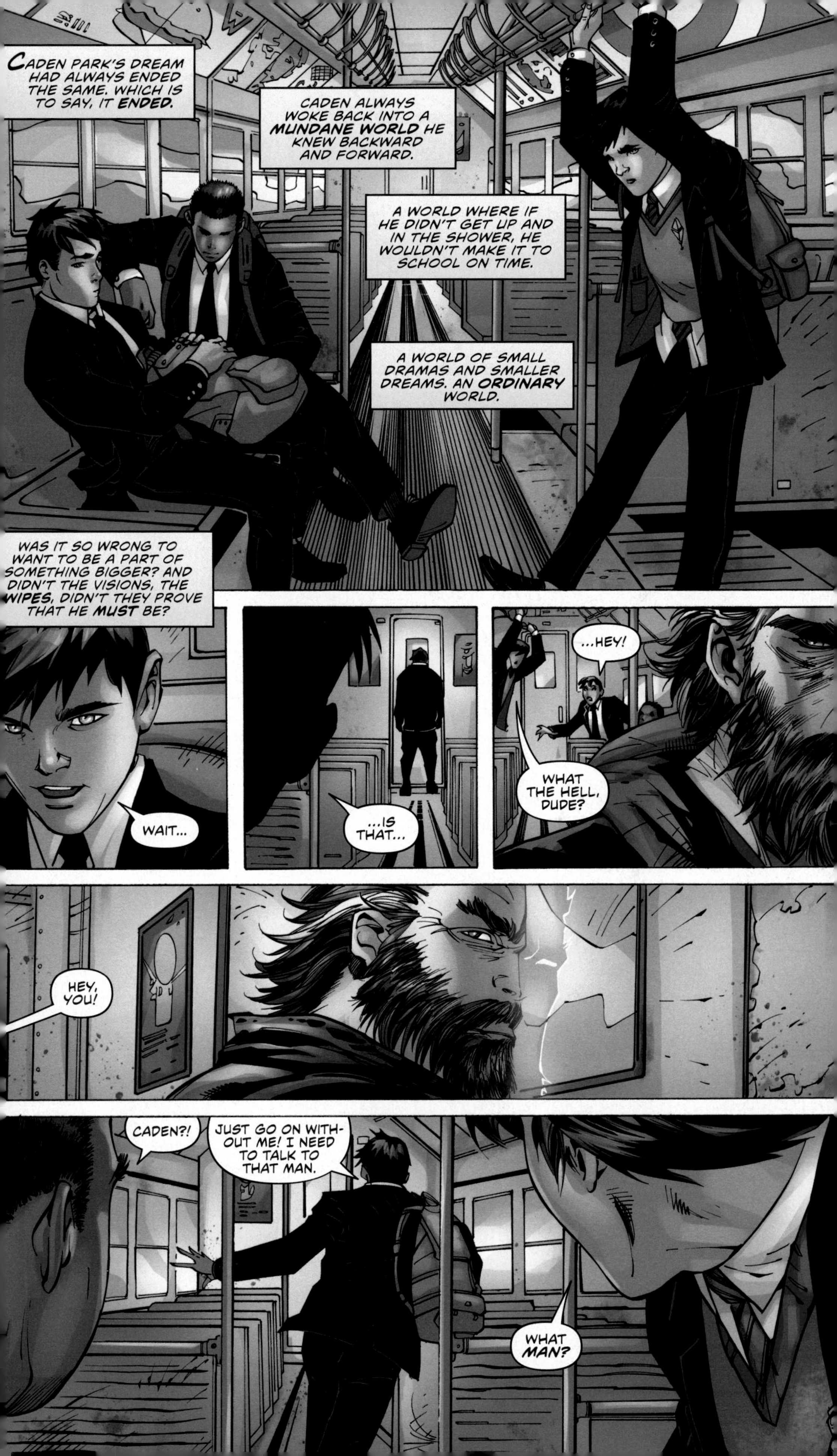
CADEN PARK'S DREAM HAD ALWAYS ENDED THE SAME. WHICH IS TO SAY, IT ENDED.
CADEN ALWAYS WOKE BACK INTO A MUNDANE WORLD HE KNEW BACKWARD AND FORWARD.
A WORLD WHERE IF HE DIDN'T GET UP AND IN THE SHOWER, HE WOULDN'T MAKE IT TO SCHOOL ON TIME.
A WORLD OF SMALL DRAMAS AND SMALLER DREAMS. AN ORDINARY WORLD.
WAS IT SO WRONG TO WANT TO BE A PART OF SOMETHING BIGGER? AND DIDN'T THE VISIONS, THE WIPES, DIDN'T THEY PROVE THAT HE MUST BE?
WAIT...
...IS THAT...
...HEY!
WHAT THE HELL, DUDE?
HEY, YOU!
CADEN?!
JUST GO ON WITH-OUT ME! I NEED TO TALK TO THAT MAN.
WHAT MAN?

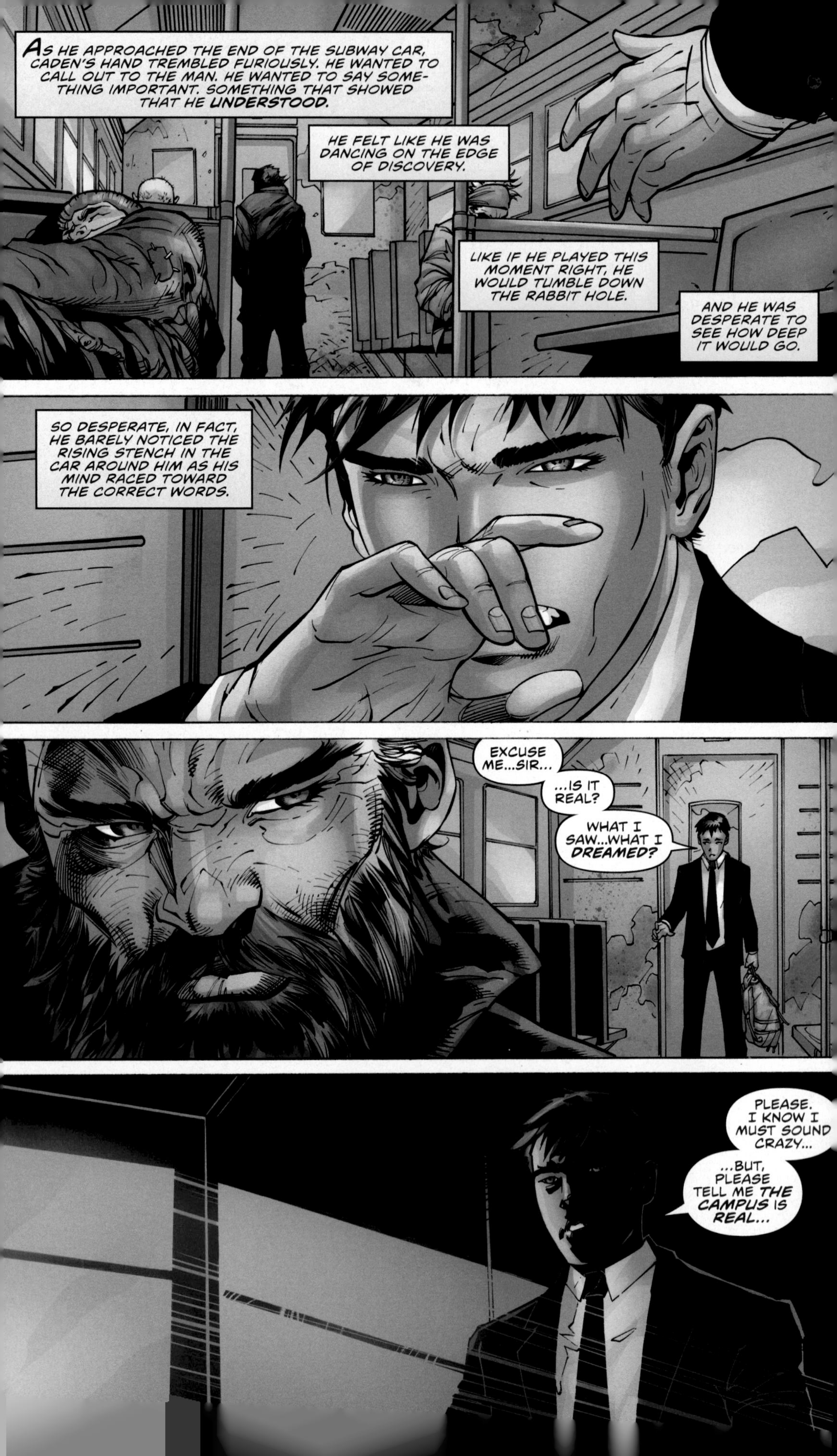
AS HE APPROACHED THE END OF THE SUBWAY CAR, CADEN'S HAND TREMBLED FURIOUSLY. HE WANTED TO CALL OUT TO THE MAN. HE WANTED TO SAY SOMETHING IMPORTANT. SOMETHING THAT SHOWED THAT HE UNDERSTOOD.
HE FELT LIKE HE WAS DANCING ON THE EDGE OF DISCOVERY.
LIKE IF HE PLAYED THIS MOMENT RIGHT, HE WOULD TUMBLE DOWN THE RABBIT HOLE.
AND HE WAS DESPERATE TO SEE HOW DEEP IT WOULD GO.
SO DESPERATE, IN FACT, HE BARELY NOTICED THE RISING STENCH IN THE CAR AROUND HIM AS HIS MIND RACED TOWARD THE CORRECT WORDS.
EXCUSE ME...SIR...
...IS IT REAL?
WHAT I SAW...WHAT I DREAMED?
PLEASE. I KNOW I MUST SOUND CRAZY...
...BUT, PLEASE TELL ME THE CAMPUS IS REAL...

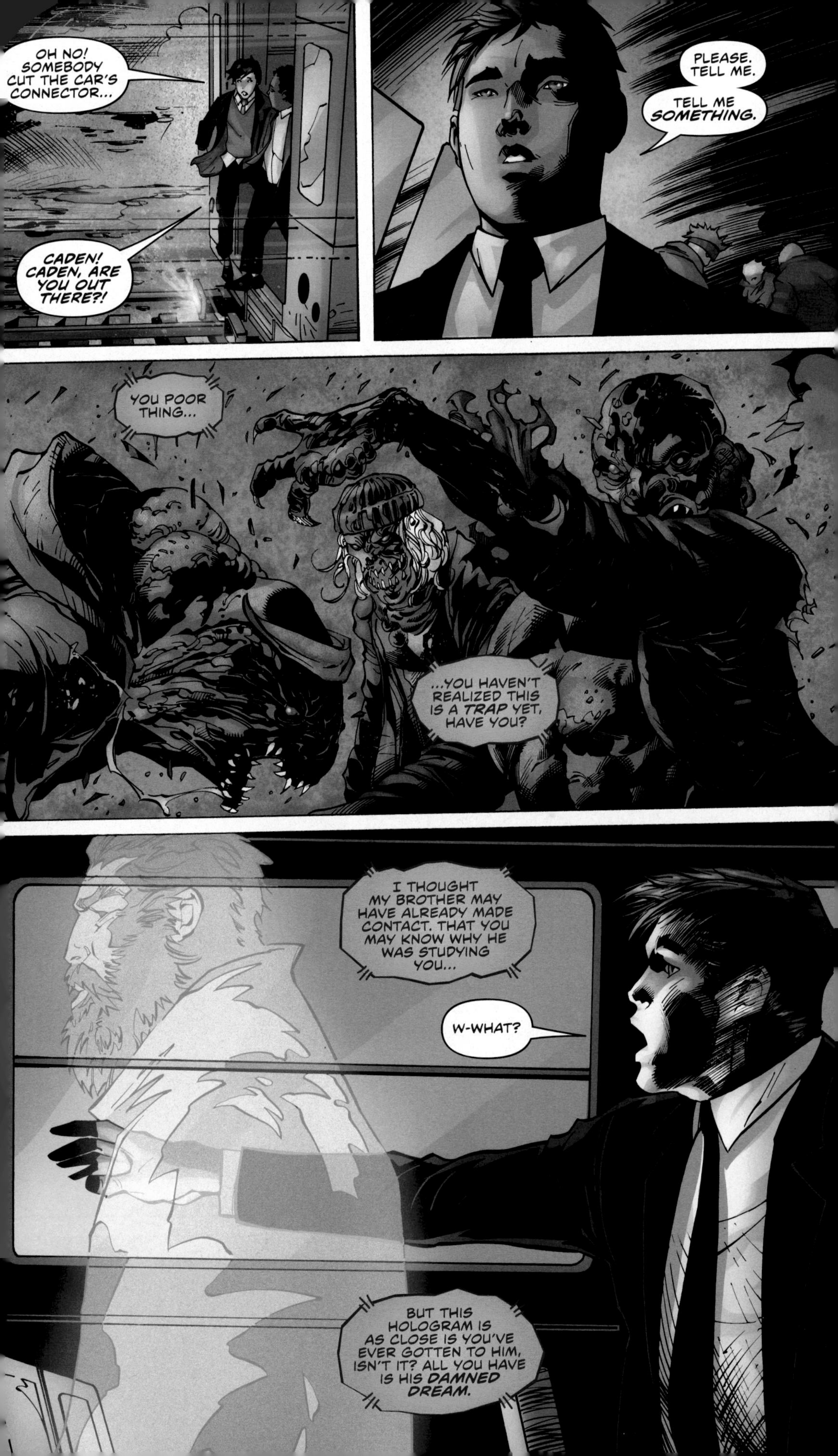
OH NO! SOMEBODY CUT THE CAR'S CONNECTOR...
CADEN! CADEN, ARE YOU OUT THERE?!
PLEASE. TELL ME.
TELL ME SOMETHING.
YOU POOR THING...
...YOU HAVEN'T REALIZED THIS IS A TRAP YET, HAVE YOU?
I THOUGHT MY BROTHER MAY HAVE ALREADY MADE CONTACT. THAT YOU MAY KNOW WHY HE WAS STUDYING YOU...
W-WHAT?
BUT THIS HOLOGRAM IS AS CLOSE IS YOU'VE EVER GOTTEN TO HIM, ISN'T IT? ALL YOU HAVE IS HIS DAMNED DREAM.

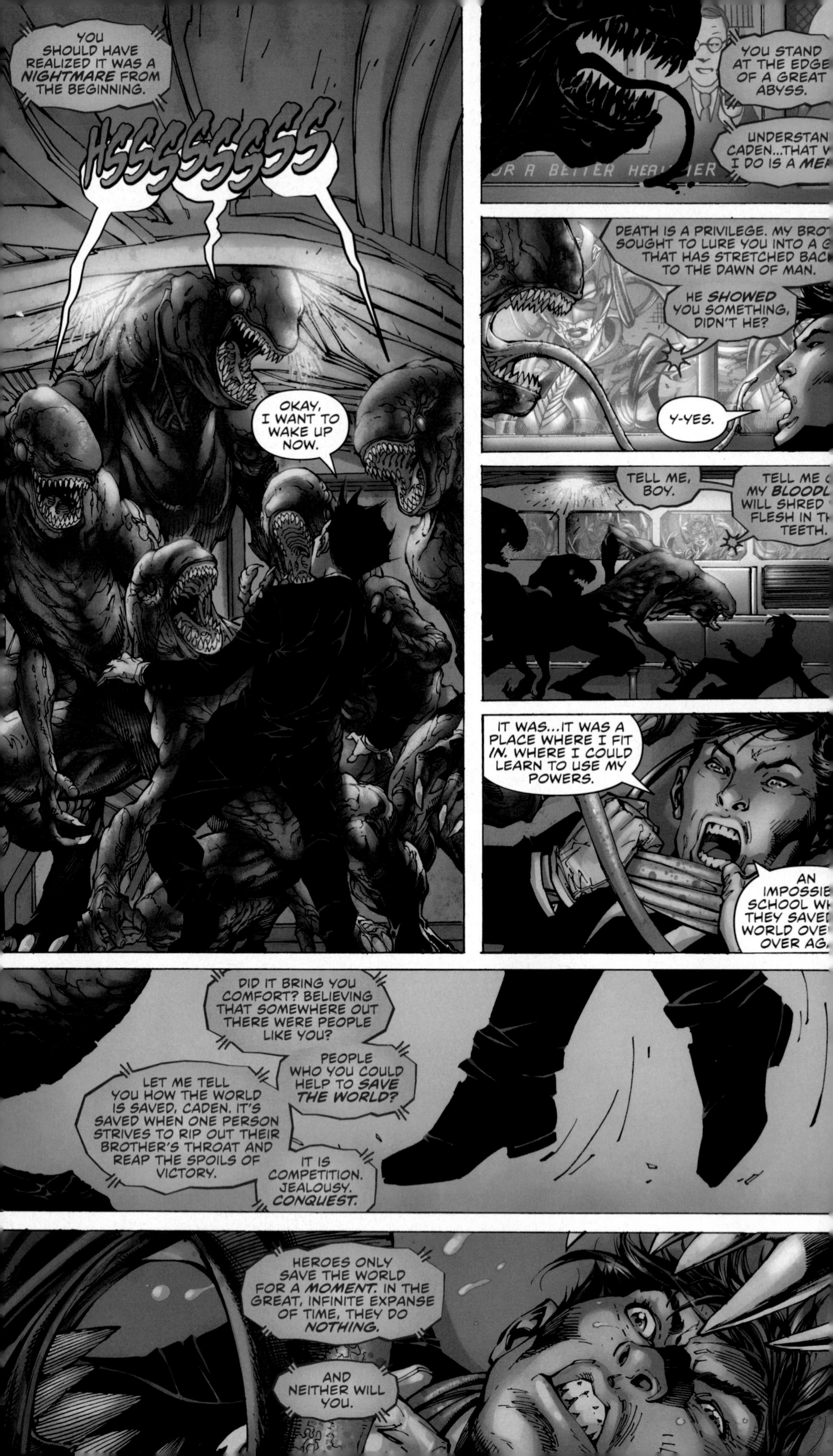
YOU SHOULD HAVE REALIZED IT WAS A NIGHTMARE FROM THE BEGINNING.
HSSSSSSSSS
OKAY, I WANT TO WAKE UP NOW.
YOU STAND AT THE EDGE OF A GREAT ABYSS.
UNDERSTAN CADEN...THAT W I DO IS A MER
OR A BETTER HEALTHIER
DEATH IS A PRIVILEGE. MY BROT SOUGHT TO LURE YOU INTO A G THAT HAS STRETCHED BAC TO THE DAWN OF MAN.
HE SHOWED YOU SOMETHING, DIDN'T HE?
Y-YES.
TELL ME, BOY.
TELL ME MY BLOODL WILL SHRED FLESH IN TH TEETH.
IT WAS...IT WAS A PLACE WHERE I FIT IN. WHERE I COULD LEARN TO USE MY POWERS.
AN IMPOSSIE SCHOOL WH THEY SAVED WORLD OVE OVER AG
DID IT BRING YOU COMFORT? BELIEVING THAT SOMEWHERE OUT THERE WERE PEOPLE LIKE YOU?
PEOPLE WHO YOU COULD HELP TO SAVE THE WORLD?
LET ME TELL YOU HOW THE WORLD IS SAVED, CADEN. IT'S SAVED WHEN ONE PERSON STRIVES TO RIP OUT THEIR BROTHER'S THROAT AND REAP THE SPOILS OF VICTORY.
IT IS COMPETITION. JEALOUSY. CONQUEST.
HEROES ONLY SAVE THE WORLD FOR A MOMENT. IN THE GREAT, INFINITE EXPANSE OF TIME, THEY DO NOTHING.
AND NEITHER WILL YOU.

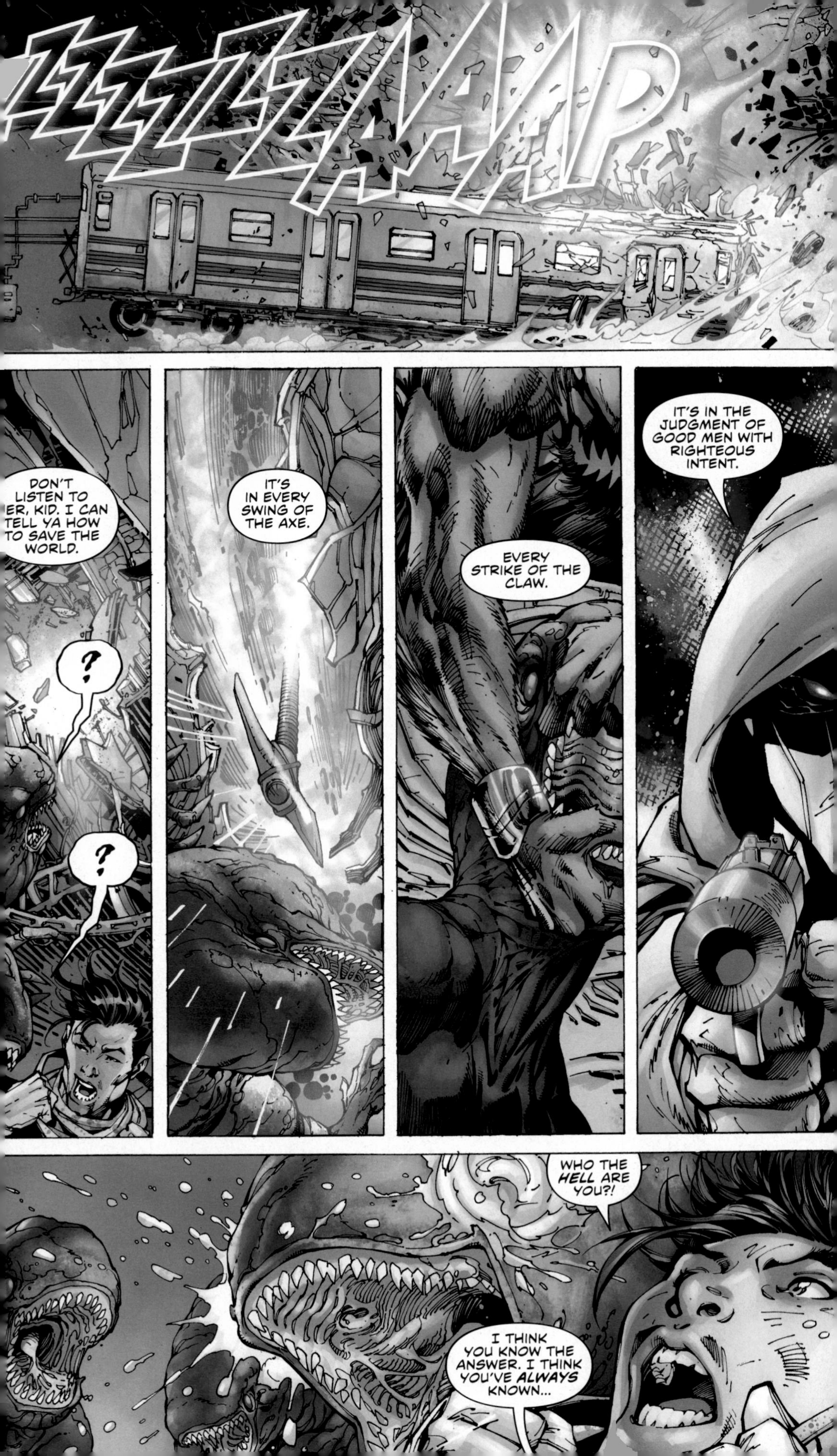
ZZZZZZAAAP
DON'T LISTEN TO ER, KID. I CAN TELL YA HOW TO SAVE THE WORLD.
?
?
IT'S IN EVERY SWING OF THE AXE.
EVERY STRIKE OF THE CLAW.
IT'S IN THE JUDGMENT OF GOOD MEN WITH RIGHTEOUS INTENT.
WHO THE *HELL* ARE YOU?!
I THINK YOU KNOW THE ANSWER. I THINK YOU'VE *ALWAYS* KNOWN...

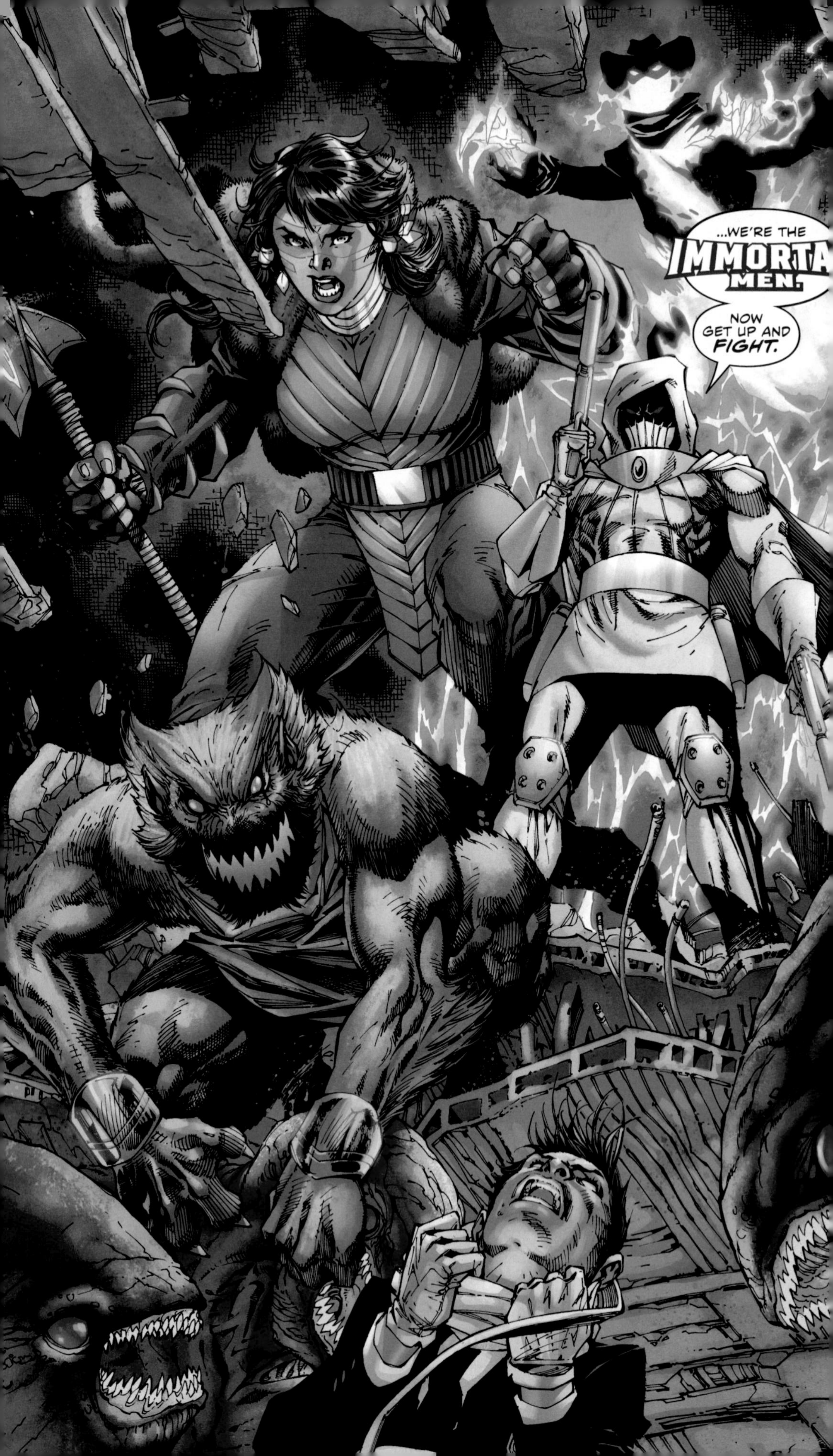
...WE'RE THE IMMORTAL MEN.
NOW GET UP AND FIGHT.

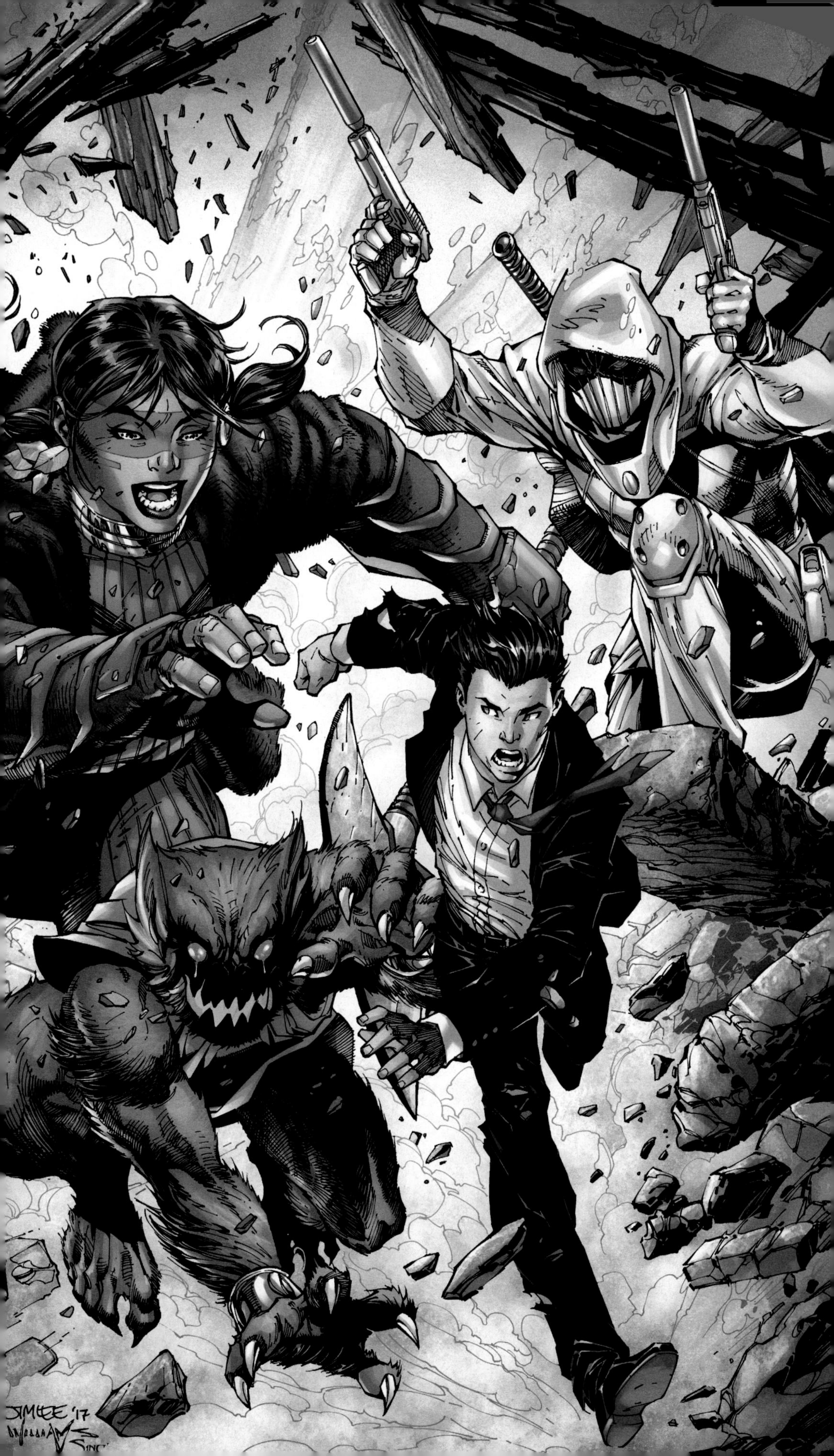

THE
IMMORTAL MEN
#2

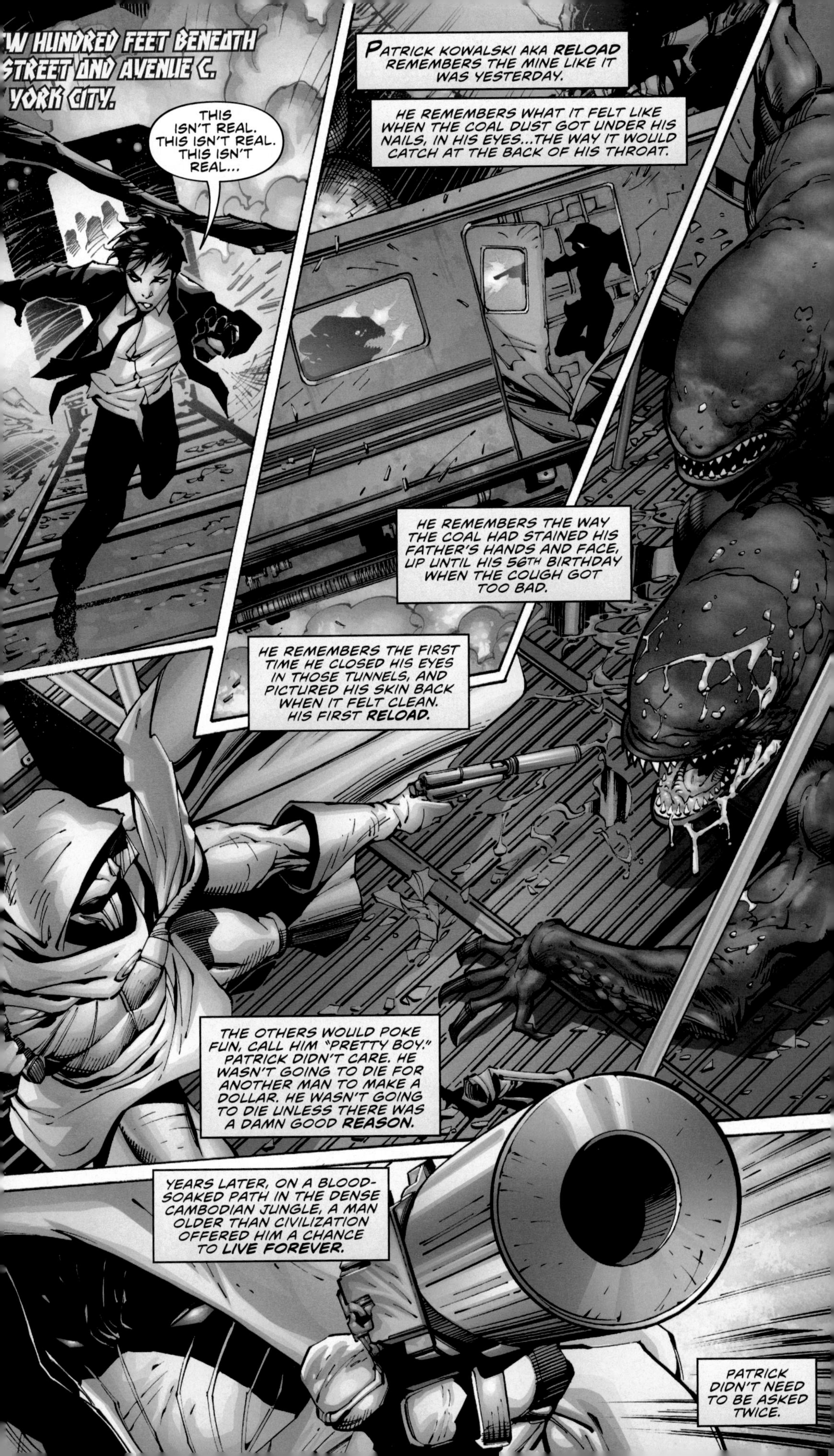
W HUNDRED FEET BENEATH STREET AND AVENUE C. YORK CITY.
THIS ISN'T REAL. THIS ISN'T REAL. THIS ISN'T REAL...
PATRICK KOWALSKI AKA RELOAD REMEMBERS THE MINE LIKE IT WAS YESTERDAY.
HE REMEMBERS WHAT IT FELT LIKE WHEN THE COAL DUST GOT UNDER HIS NAILS, IN HIS EYES...THE WAY IT WOULD CATCH AT THE BACK OF HIS THROAT.
HE REMEMBERS THE WAY THE COAL HAD STAINED HIS FATHER'S HANDS AND FACE, UP UNTIL HIS 56TH BIRTHDAY WHEN THE COUGH GOT TOO BAD.
HE REMEMBERS THE FIRST TIME HE CLOSED HIS EYES IN THOSE TUNNELS, AND PICTURED HIS SKIN BACK WHEN IT FELT CLEAN. HIS FIRST RELOAD.
THE OTHERS WOULD POKE FUN, CALL HIM "PRETTY BOY." PATRICK DIDN'T CARE. HE WASN'T GOING TO DIE FOR ANOTHER MAN TO MAKE A DOLLAR. HE WASN'T GOING TO DIE UNLESS THERE WAS A DAMN GOOD REASON.
YEARS LATER, ON A BLOOD-SOAKED PATH IN THE DENSE CAMBODIAN JUNGLE, A MAN OLDER THAN CIVILIZATION OFFERED HIM A CHANCE TO LIVE FOREVER.
PATRICK DIDN'T NEED TO BE ASKED TWICE.

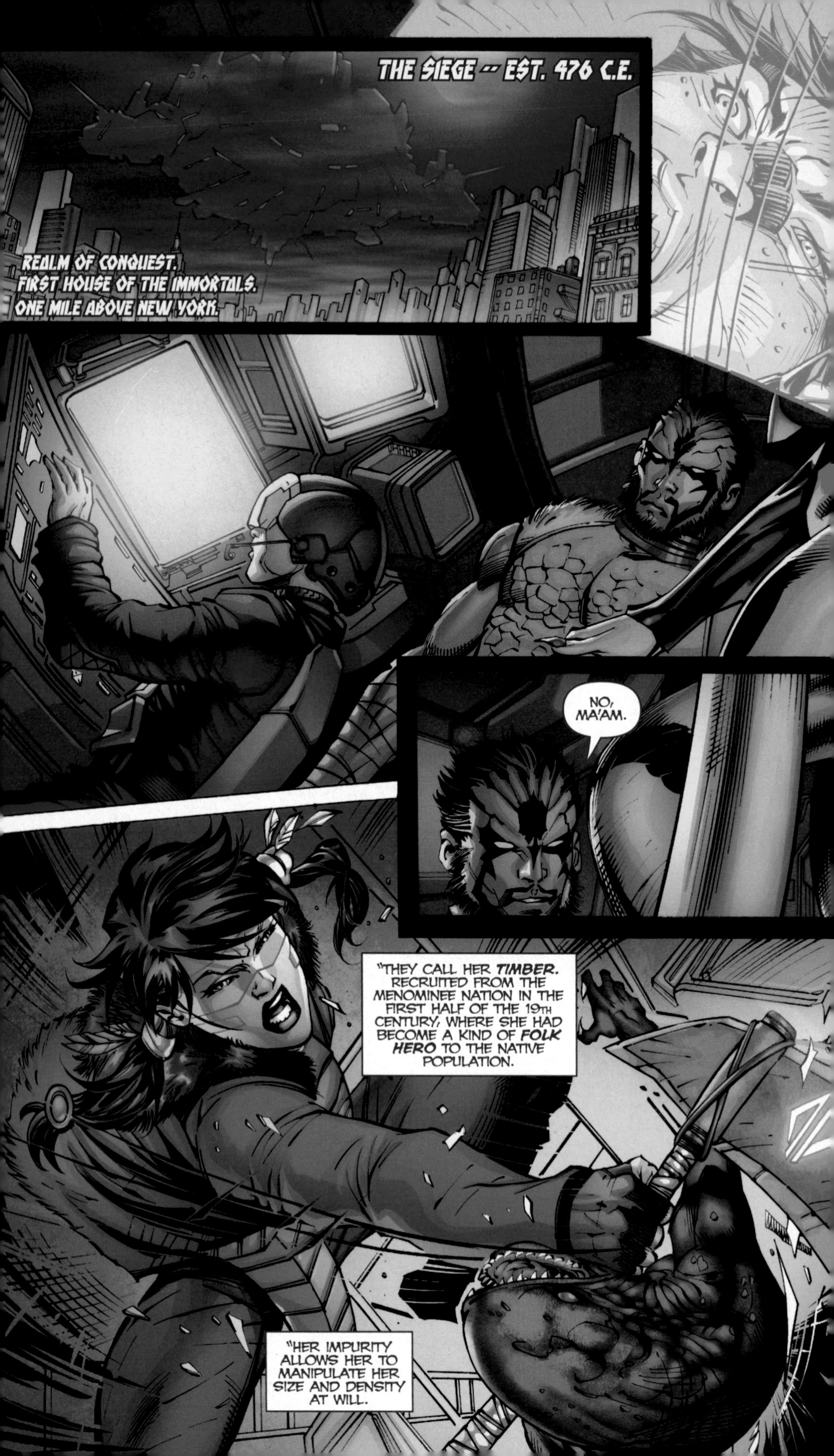
THE SIEGE -- EST. 476 C.E.
REALM OF CONQUEST. FIRST HOUSE OF THE IMMORTALS. ONE MILE ABOVE NEW YORK.
NO, MA'AM.
"THEY CALL HER TIMBER. RECRUITED FROM THE MENOMINEE NATION IN THE FIRST HALF OF THE 19TH CENTURY, WHERE SHE HAD BECOME A KIND OF FOLK HERO TO THE NATIVE POPULATION.
"HER IMPURITY ALLOWS HER TO MANIPULATE HER SIZE AND DENSITY AT WILL.

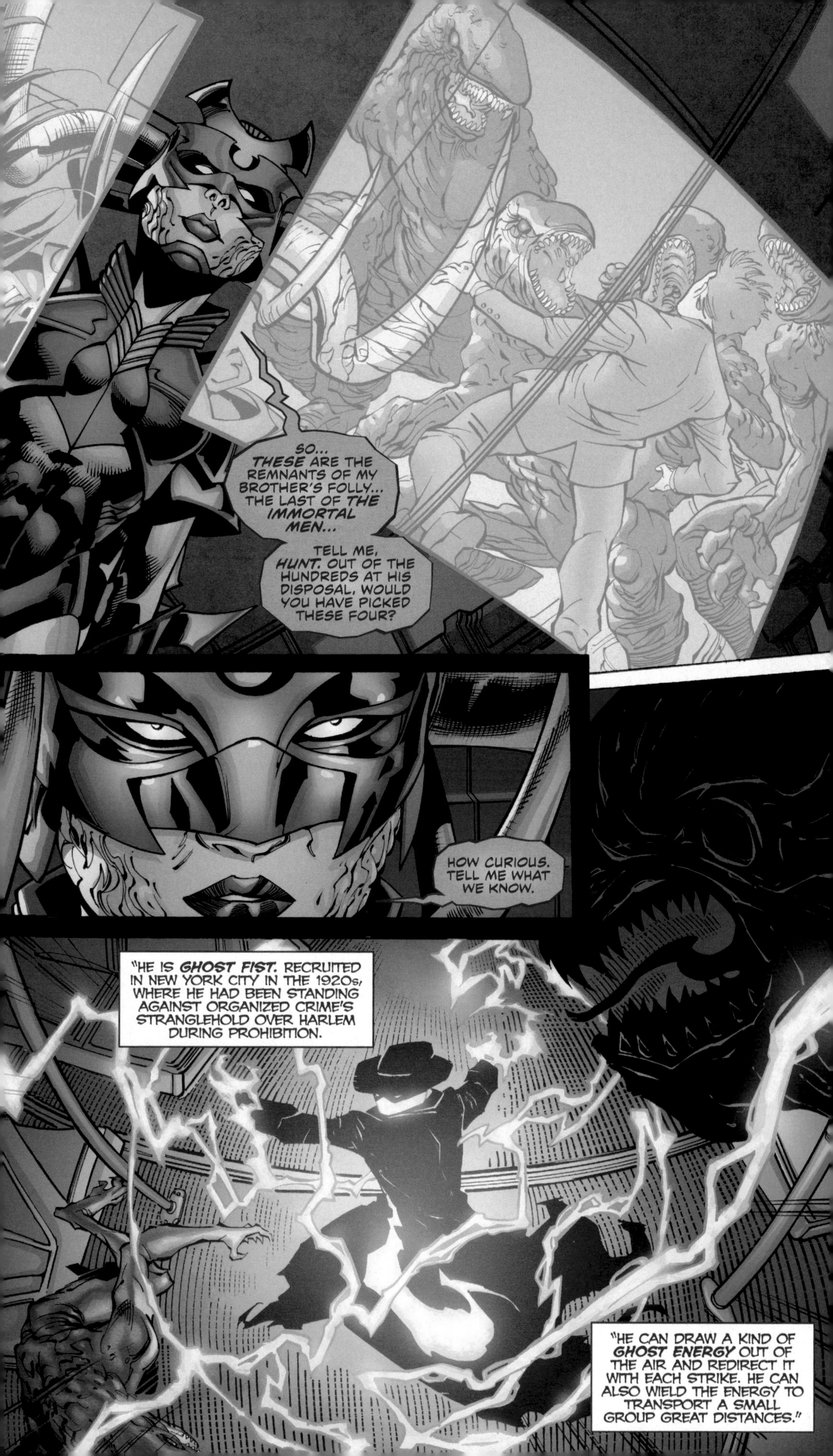
SO... THESE ARE THE REMNANTS OF MY BROTHER'S FOLLY... THE LAST OF THE IMMORTAL MEN...
TELL ME, HUNT. OUT OF THE HUNDREDS AT HIS DISPOSAL, WOULD YOU HAVE PICKED THESE FOUR?
HOW CURIOUS. TELL ME WHAT WE KNOW.
"HE IS GHOST FIST. RECRUITED IN NEW YORK CITY IN THE 1920s, WHERE HE HAD BEEN STANDING AGAINST ORGANIZED CRIME'S STRANGLEHOLD OVER HARLEM DURING PROHIBITION.
"HE CAN DRAW A KIND OF GHOST ENERGY OUT OF THE AIR AND REDIRECT IT WITH EACH STRIKE. HE CAN ALSO WIELD THE ENERGY TO TRANSPORT A SMALL GROUP GREAT DISTANCES."

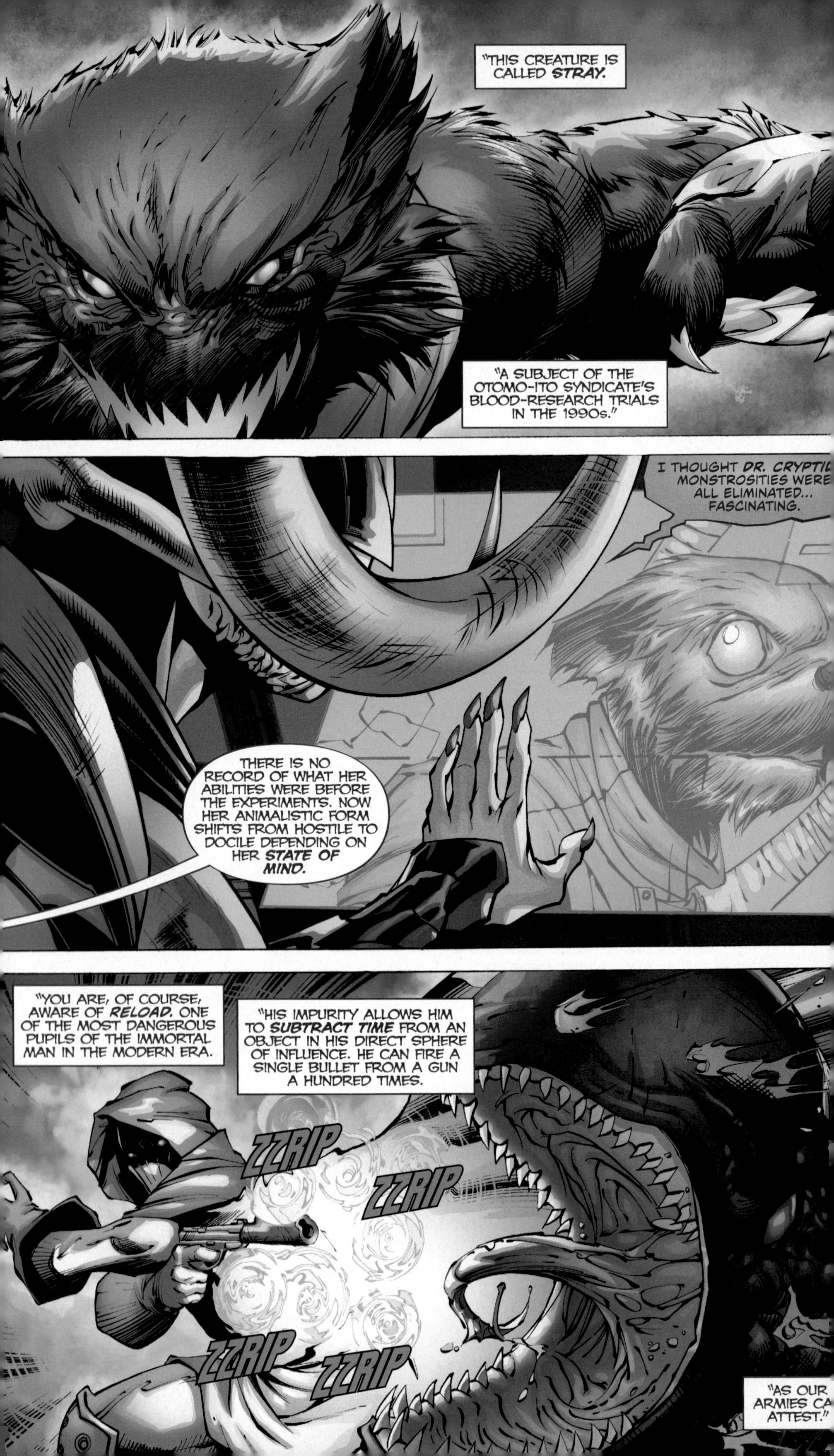
"THIS CREATURE IS CALLED STRAY.
"A SUBJECT OF THE OTOMO-ITO SYNDICATE'S BLOOD-RESEARCH TRIALS IN THE 1990s."
I THOUGHT DR. CRYPTIC MONSTROSITIES WERE ALL ELIMINATED... FASCINATING.
THERE IS NO RECORD OF WHAT HER ABILITIES WERE BEFORE THE EXPERIMENTS. NOW HER ANIMALISTIC FORM SHIFTS FROM HOSTILE TO DOCILE DEPENDING ON HER STATE OF MIND.
"YOU ARE, OF COURSE, AWARE OF RELOAD. ONE OF THE MOST DANGEROUS PUPILS OF THE IMMORTAL MAN IN THE MODERN ERA.
"HIS IMPURITY ALLOWS HIM TO SUBTRACT TIME FROM AN OBJECT IN HIS DIRECT SPHERE OF INFLUENCE. HE CAN FIRE A SINGLE BULLET FROM A GUN A HUNDRED TIMES.
ZZRIP
ZZRIP
ZZRIP
ZZRIP
"AS OUR ARMIES CA ATTEST."

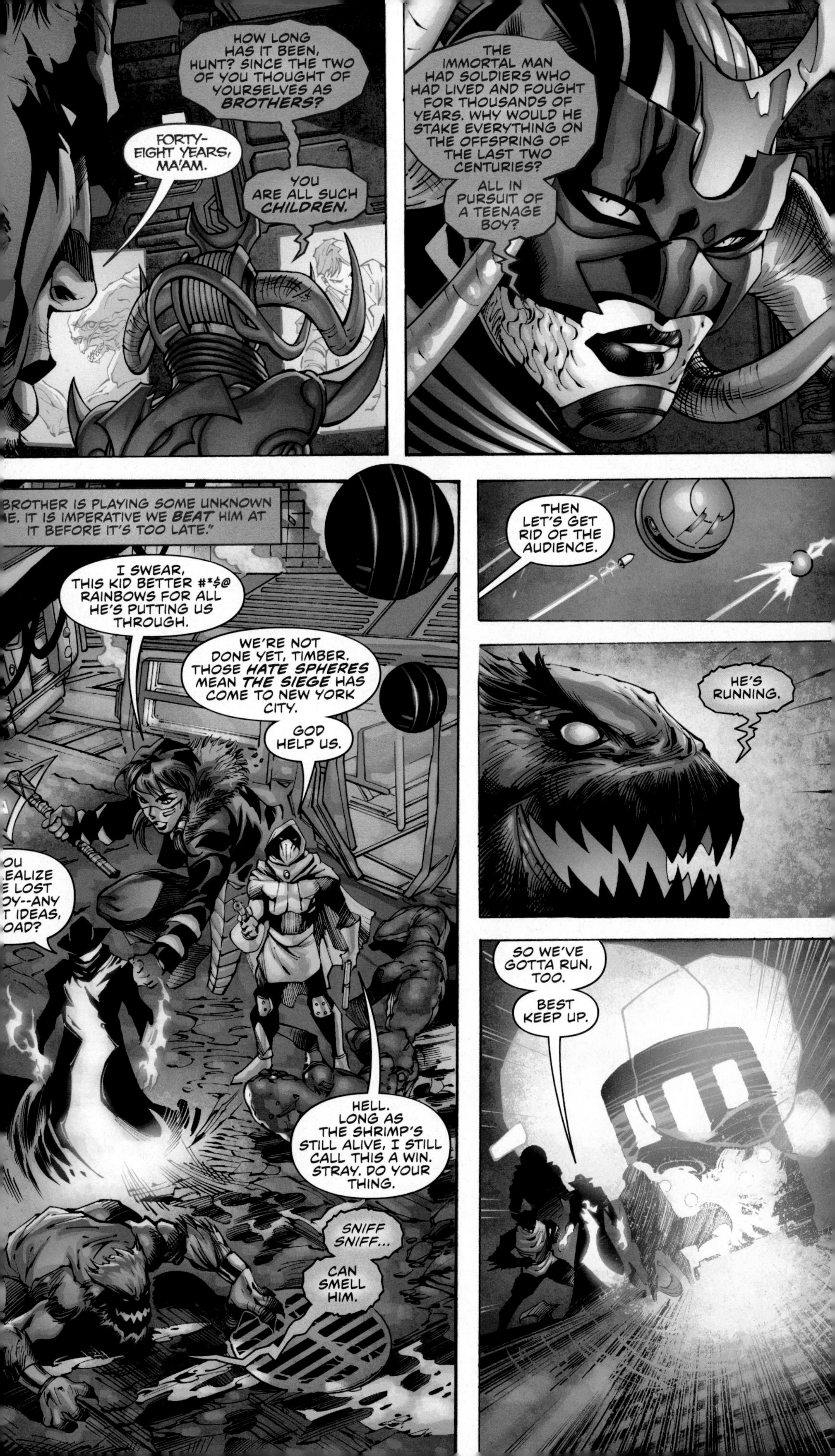

HOW LONG HAS IT BEEN, HUNT? SINCE THE TWO OF YOU THOUGHT OF YOURSELVES AS BROTHERS?
FORTY-EIGHT YEARS, MA'AM.
YOU ARE ALL SUCH CHILDREN.
THE IMMORTAL MAN HAD SOLDIERS WHO HAD LIVED AND FOUGHT FOR THOUSANDS OF YEARS. WHY WOULD HE STAKE EVERYTHING ON THE OFFSPRING OF THE LAST TWO CENTURIES?
ALL IN PURSUIT OF A TEENAGE BOY?
BROTHER IS PLAYING SOME UNKNOWN E. IT IS IMPERATIVE WE BEAT HIM AT IT BEFORE IT'S TOO LATE."
I SWEAR, THIS KID BETTER #*$@ RAINBOWS FOR ALL HE'S PUTTING US THROUGH.
WE'RE NOT DONE YET, TIMBER. THOSE HATE SPHERES MEAN THE SIEGE HAS COME TO NEW YORK CITY.
GOD HELP US.
OU EALIZE E LOST OY--ANY T IDEAS, OAD?
HELL. LONG AS THE SHRIMP'S STILL ALIVE, I STILL CALL THIS A WIN. STRAY. DO YOUR THING.
SNIFF SNIFF...
CAN SMELL HIM.
THEN LET'S GET RID OF THE AUDIENCE.
HE'S RUNNING.
SO WE'VE GOTTA RUN, TOO.
BEST KEEP UP.

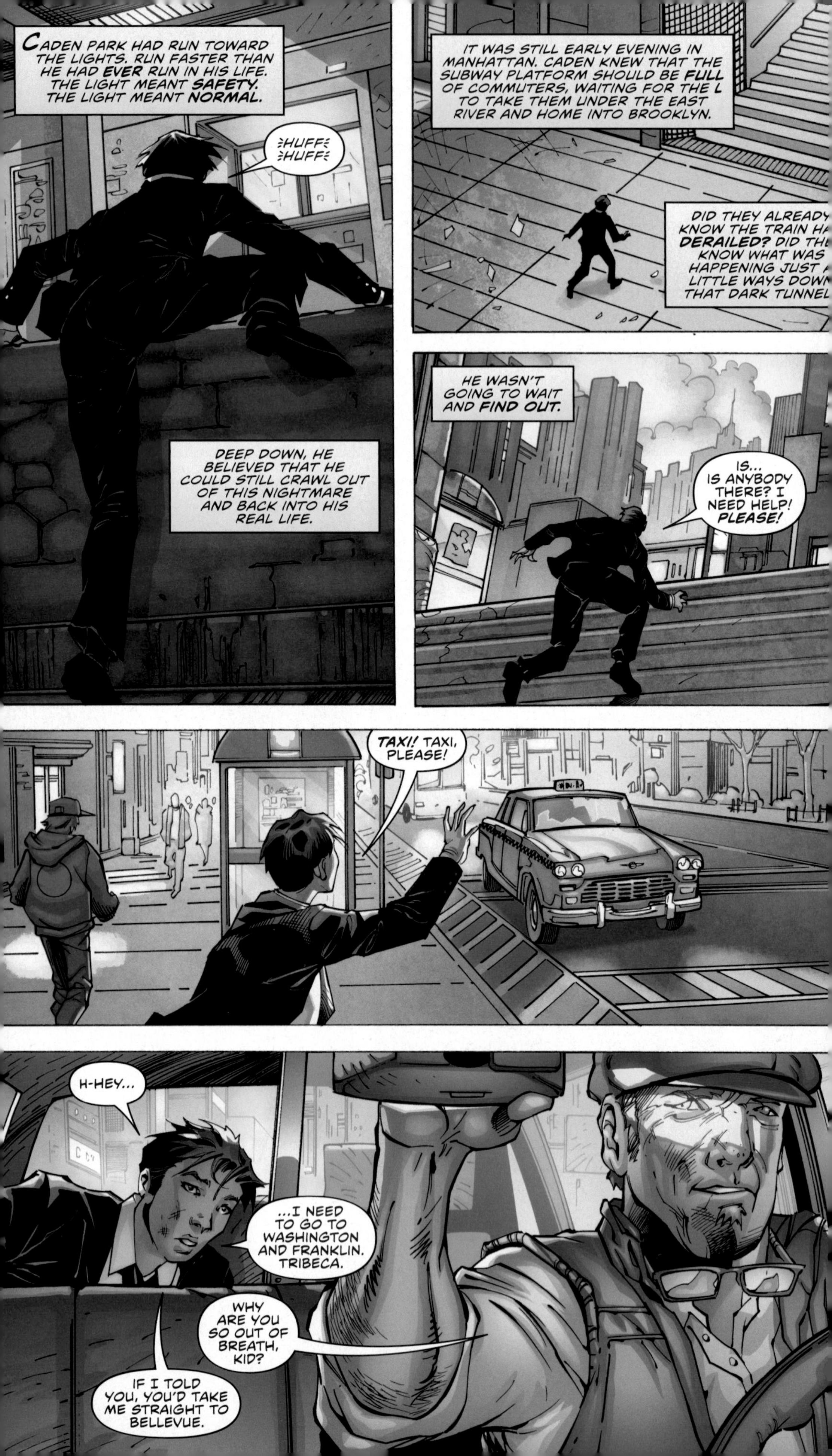
CADEN PARK HAD RUN TOWARD THE LIGHTS. RUN FASTER THAN HE HAD EVER RUN IN HIS LIFE. THE LIGHT MEANT SAFETY. THE LIGHT MEANT NORMAL.
HUFF HUFF
DEEP DOWN, HE BELIEVED THAT HE COULD STILL CRAWL OUT OF THIS NIGHTMARE AND BACK INTO HIS REAL LIFE.
IT WAS STILL EARLY EVENING IN MANHATTAN. CADEN KNEW THAT THE SUBWAY PLATFORM SHOULD BE FULL OF COMMUTERS, WAITING FOR THE L TO TAKE THEM UNDER THE EAST RIVER AND HOME INTO BROOKLYN.
DID THEY ALREADY KNOW THE TRAIN HA DERAILED? DID TH KNOW WHAT WAS HAPPENING JUST A LITTLE WAYS DOWN THAT DARK TUNNEL
HE WASN'T GOING TO WAIT AND FIND OUT.
IS... IS ANYBODY THERE? I NEED HELP! PLEASE!
TAXI! TAXI, PLEASE!
H-HEY...
...I NEED TO GO TO WASHINGTON AND FRANKLIN. TRIBECA.
WHY ARE YOU SO OUT OF BREATH, KID?
IF I TOLD YOU, YOU'D TAKE ME STRAIGHT TO BELLEVUE.

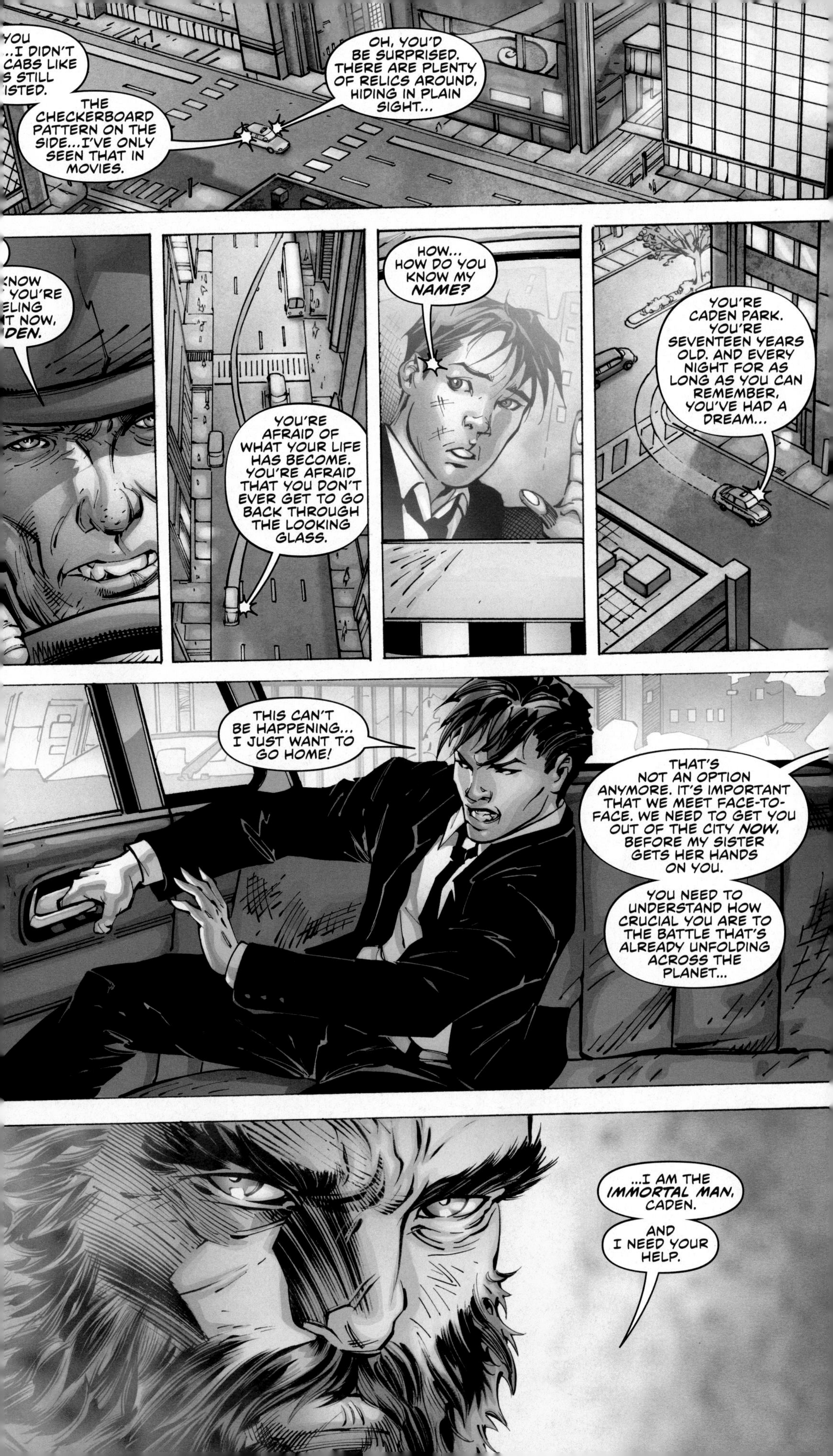
YOU ...I DIDN'T CABS LIKE S STILL ISTED.
THE CHECKERBOARD PATTERN ON THE SIDE...I'VE ONLY SEEN THAT IN MOVIES.
OH, YOU'D BE SURPRISED. THERE ARE PLENTY OF RELICS AROUND, HIDING IN PLAIN SIGHT...
KNOW YOU'RE ELING T NOW, DEN.
YOU'RE AFRAID OF WHAT YOUR LIFE HAS BECOME. YOU'RE AFRAID THAT YOU DON'T EVER GET TO GO BACK THROUGH THE LOOKING GLASS.
HOW... HOW DO YOU KNOW MY *NAME?*
YOU'RE CADEN PARK. YOU'RE SEVENTEEN YEARS OLD. AND EVERY NIGHT FOR AS LONG AS YOU CAN REMEMBER, YOU'VE HAD A DREAM...
THIS CAN'T BE HAPPENING... I JUST WANT TO GO HOME!
THAT'S NOT AN OPTION ANYMORE. IT'S IMPORTANT THAT WE MEET FACE-TO-FACE. WE NEED TO GET YOU OUT OF THE CITY *NOW,* BEFORE MY SISTER GETS HER HANDS ON YOU.
YOU NEED TO UNDERSTAND HOW CRUCIAL YOU ARE TO THE BATTLE THAT'S ALREADY UNFOLDING ACROSS THE PLANET...
...I AM THE *IMMORTAL MAN,* CADEN.
AND I NEED YOUR HELP.

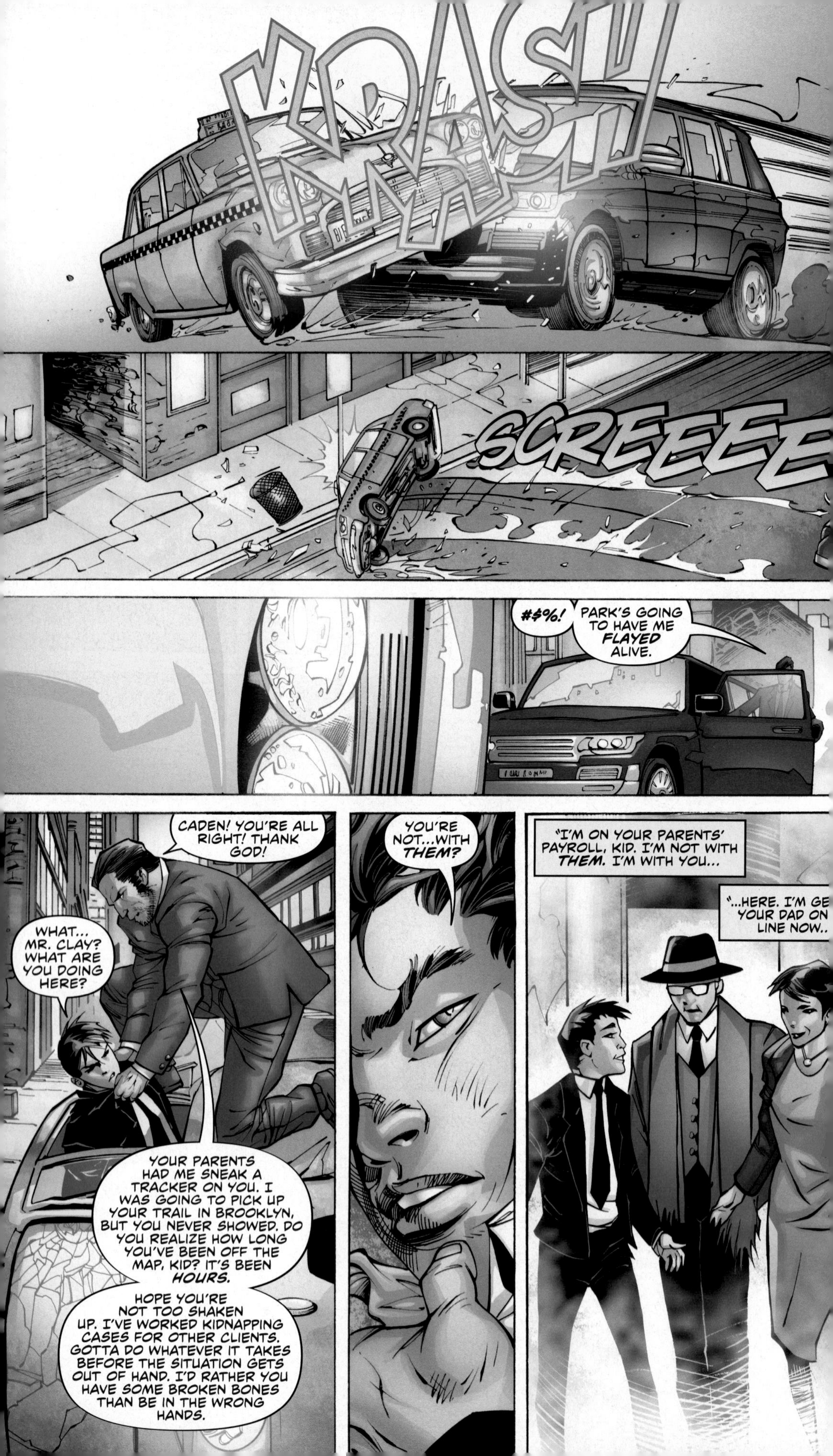
KRASH
SCREEEE
#$%!
PARK'S GOING TO HAVE ME FLAYED ALIVE.
CADEN! YOU'RE ALL RIGHT! THANK GOD!
WHAT... MR. CLAY? WHAT ARE YOU DOING HERE?
YOUR PARENTS HAD ME SNEAK A TRACKER ON YOU. I WAS GOING TO PICK UP YOUR TRAIL IN BROOKLYN, BUT YOU NEVER SHOWED. DO YOU REALIZE HOW LONG YOU'VE BEEN OFF THE MAP, KID? IT'S BEEN HOURS.
HOPE YOU'RE NOT TOO SHAKEN UP. I'VE WORKED KIDNAPPING CASES FOR OTHER CLIENTS. GOTTA DO WHATEVER IT TAKES BEFORE THE SITUATION GETS OUT OF HAND. I'D RATHER YOU HAVE SOME BROKEN BONES THAN BE IN THE WRONG HANDS.
YOU'RE NOT...WITH THEM?
"I'M ON YOUR PARENTS' PAYROLL, KID. I'M NOT WITH THEM. I'M WITH YOU...
"...HERE. I'M GE YOUR DAD ON LINE NOW..

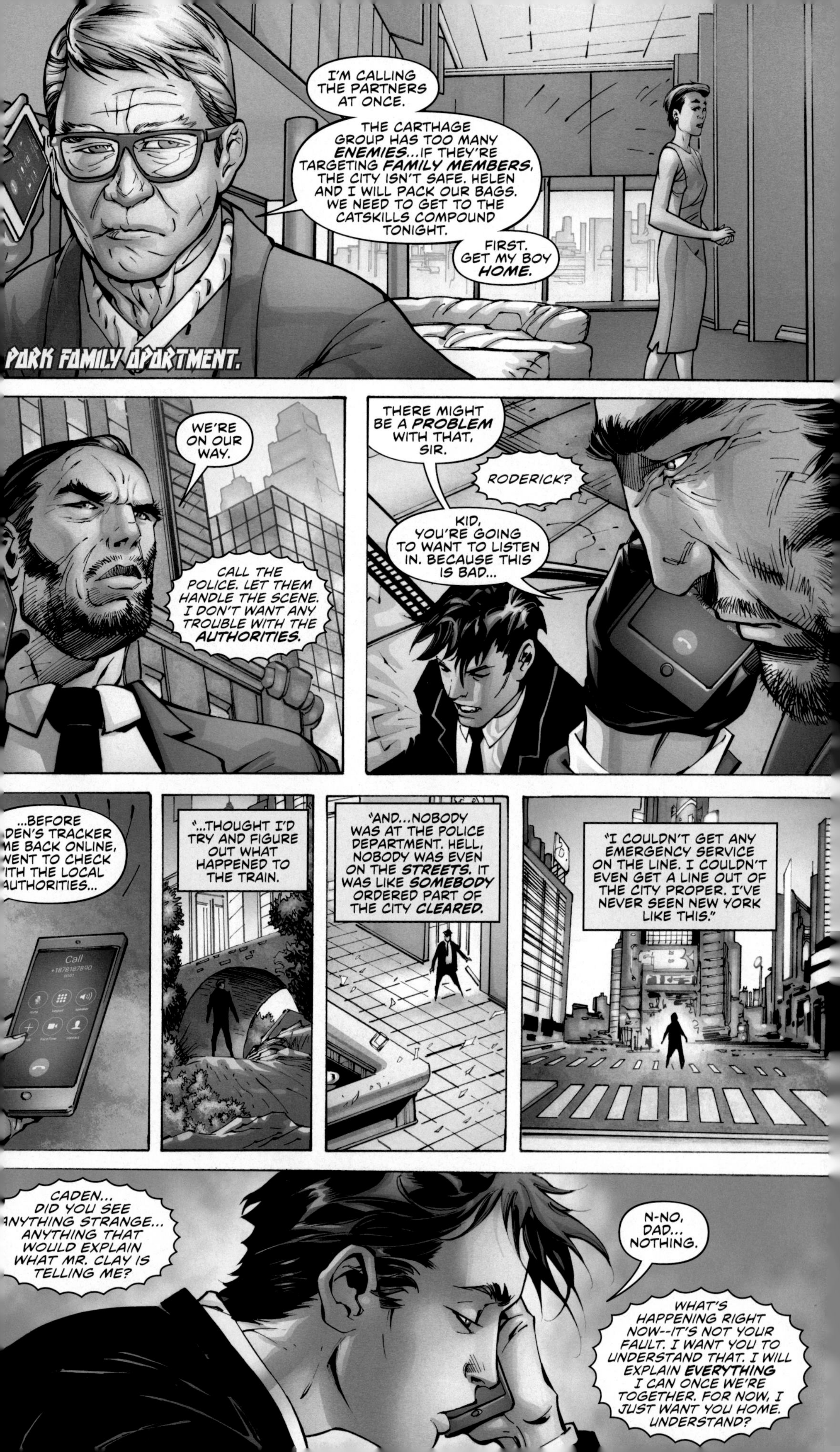
PARK FAMILY APARTMENT.
I'M CALLING THE PARTNERS AT ONCE.
THE CARTHAGE GROUP HAS TOO MANY ENEMIES...IF THEY'RE TARGETING FAMILY MEMBERS, THE CITY ISN'T SAFE. HELEN AND I WILL PACK OUR BAGS. WE NEED TO GET TO THE CATSKILLS COMPOUND TONIGHT.
FIRST. GET MY BOY HOME.
WE'RE ON OUR WAY.
CALL THE POLICE. LET THEM HANDLE THE SCENE. I DON'T WANT ANY TROUBLE WITH THE AUTHORITIES.
THERE MIGHT BE A PROBLEM WITH THAT, SIR.
RODERICK?
KID, YOU'RE GOING TO WANT TO LISTEN IN. BECAUSE THIS IS BAD...
...BEFORE DEN'S TRACKER ME BACK ONLINE, WENT TO CHECK ITH THE LOCAL AUTHORITIES...
Call
"...THOUGHT I'D TRY AND FIGURE OUT WHAT HAPPENED TO THE TRAIN.
"AND...NOBODY WAS AT THE POLICE DEPARTMENT. HELL, NOBODY WAS EVEN ON THE STREETS. IT WAS LIKE SOMEBODY ORDERED PART OF THE CITY CLEARED.
"I COULDN'T GET ANY EMERGENCY SERVICE ON THE LINE. I COULDN'T EVEN GET A LINE OUT OF THE CITY PROPER. I'VE NEVER SEEN NEW YORK LIKE THIS."
CADEN... DID YOU SEE ANYTHING STRANGE... ANYTHING THAT WOULD EXPLAIN WHAT MR. CLAY IS TELLING ME?
N-NO, DAD... NOTHING.
WHAT'S HAPPENING RIGHT NOW--IT'S NOT YOUR FAULT. I WANT YOU TO UNDERSTAND THAT. I WILL EXPLAIN EVERYTHING I CAN ONCE WE'RE TOGETHER. FOR NOW, I JUST WANT YOU HOME. UNDERSTAND?

TRIBECA

ALL RIGHT, KID. I KNOW I'M JUST *THE HELP*, BUT YOU NEED TO DO WHATEVER YOU CAN TO GET YOUR PARENTS OUT OF THERE AS FAST AS POSSIBLE.

I DON'T LIKE HOW #%# QUIET THESE STREETS ARE. DO YOU UNDER-STAND ME?

SIR, YES, SIR.

THAT BETTER N BE *SASS* HEARING

WAIT... HOLD O DAMN SEC

...OH GOD...

KID, WHAT THE HELL HAVE YOU GOTTEN YOURSELF INTO?

OKAY. NEW PLAN.

YOU RUN LIKE HELL FROM THESE MONSTERS, AND I'M GOING TO TRY NOT TO DIE.

MR. CLAY?!

RUN!

MR. CAVANAUGH! DON'T GO OUTSIDE, OKAY? HEAD INTO THE BACK ROOM AND LOCK THE DOOR!

SOMETHING REALLY WEIRD IS GOING ON.

D ON, RODERICK. LEAVE U.S. AND TAKE THE CUSHY ATE-SECTOR GIG. YOU'LL ER HAVE TO DEAL WITH ER-POWERED FREAKS AND MONSTERS AGAIN."

YEAH #$#@ RIGHT.

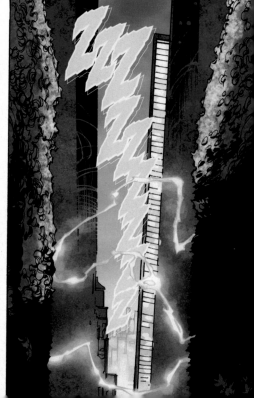

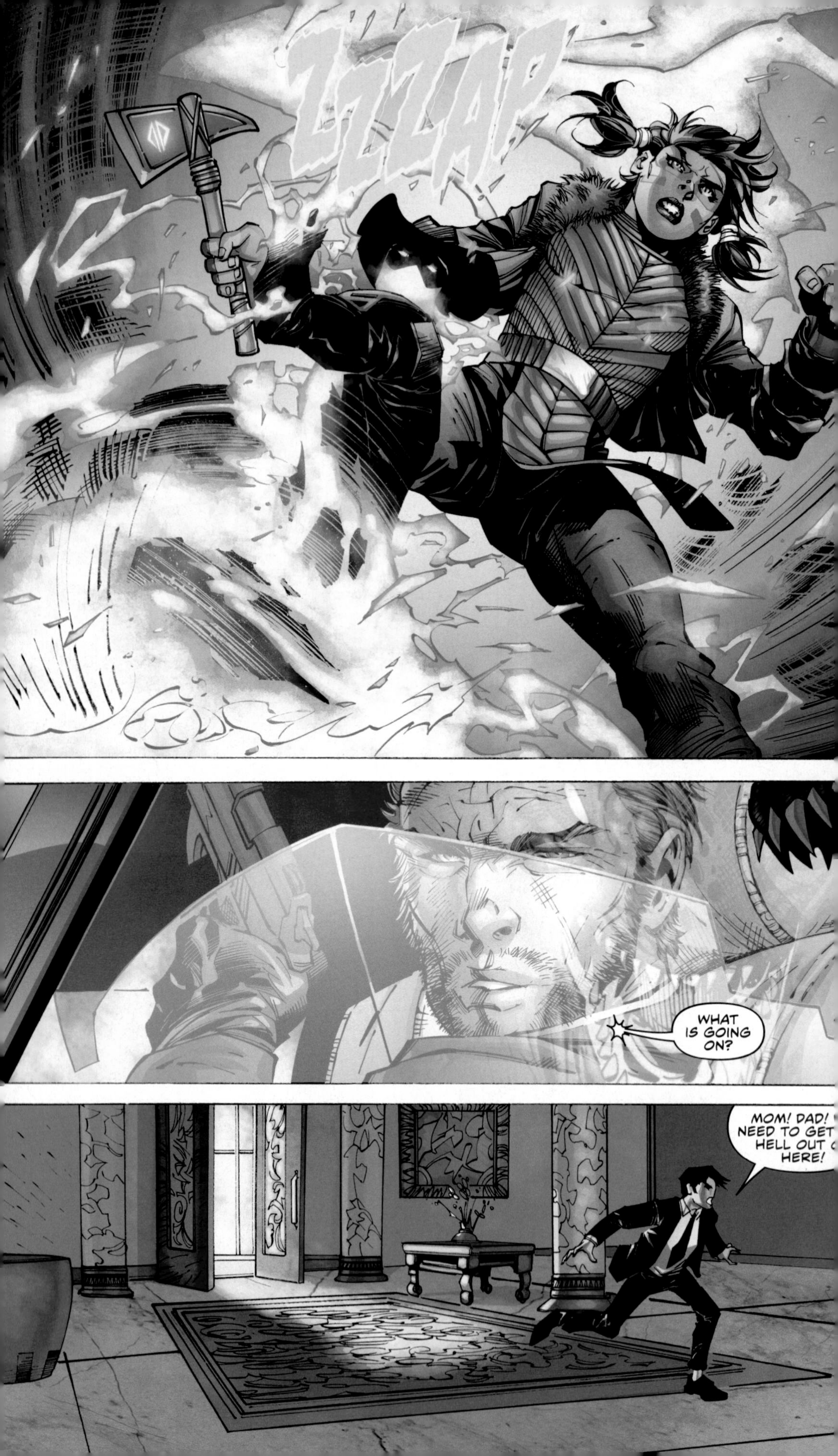
ZZZAP
WHAT IS GOING ON?
MOM! DAD! NEED TO GET HELL OUT HERE!

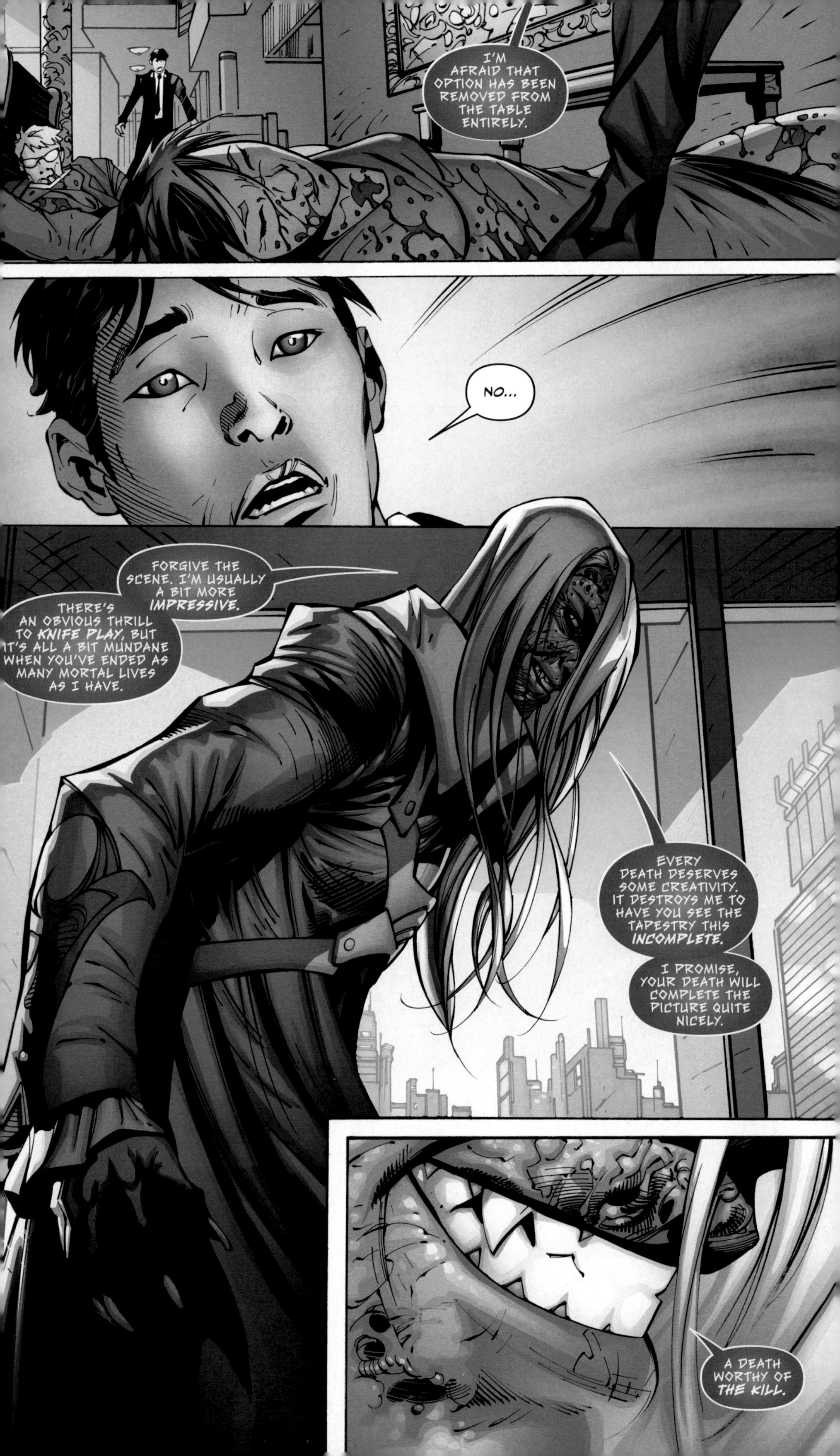
I'M AFRAID THAT OPTION HAS BEEN REMOVED FROM THE TABLE ENTIRELY.
NO...
FORGIVE THE SCENE. I'M USUALLY A BIT MORE *IMPRESSIVE.*
THERE'S AN OBVIOUS THRILL TO *KNIFE PLAY,* BUT IT'S ALL A BIT MUNDANE WHEN YOU'VE ENDED AS MANY MORTAL LIVES AS I HAVE.
EVERY DEATH DESERVES SOME CREATIVITY. IT DESTROYS ME TO HAVE YOU SEE THE TAPESTRY THIS *INCOMPLETE.*
I PROMISE, YOUR DEATH WILL COMPLETE THE PICTURE QUITE NICELY.
A DEATH WORTHY OF *THE KILL.*

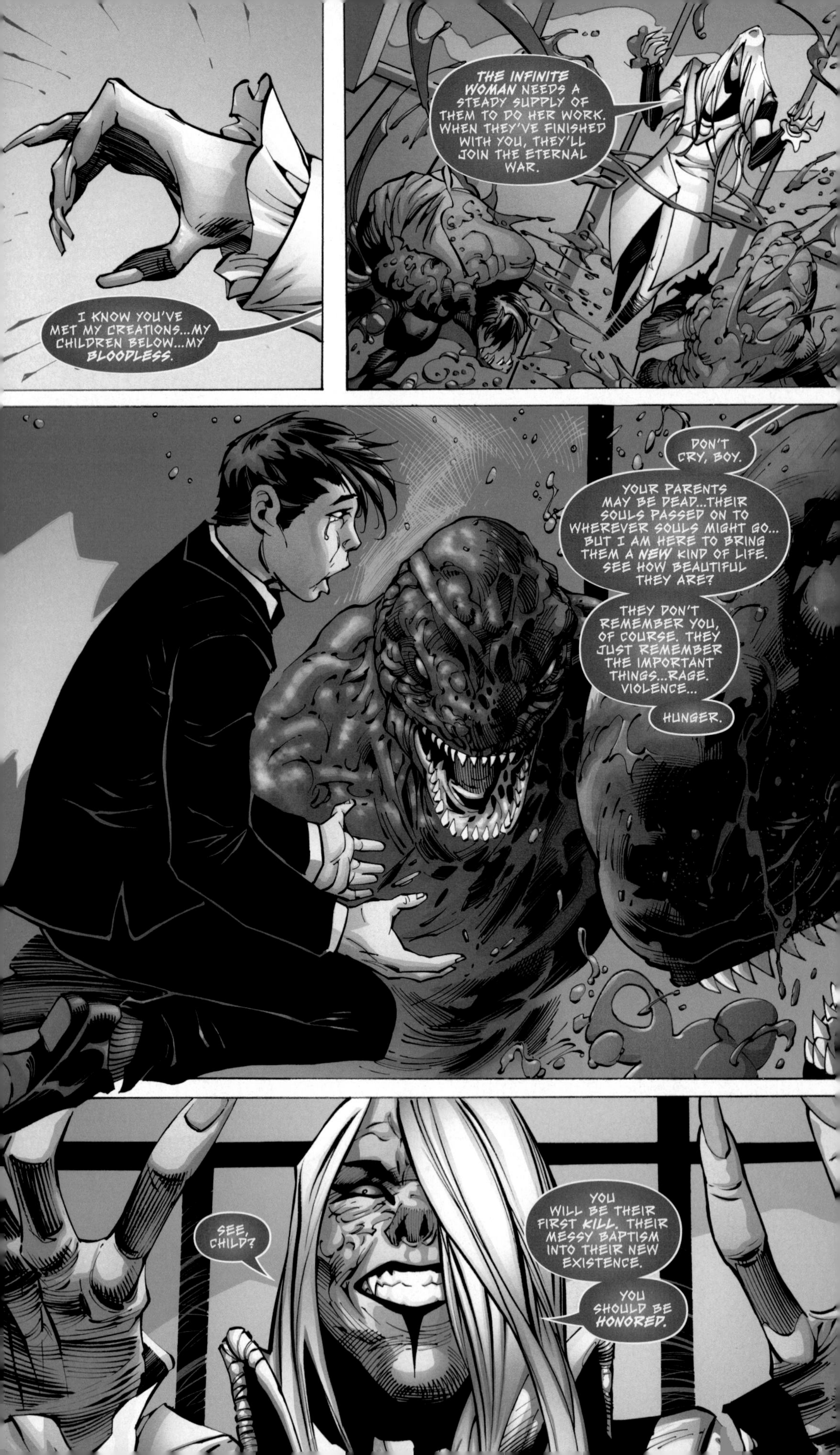
I KNOW YOU'VE MET MY CREATIONS...MY CHILDREN BELOW...MY BLOODLESS.
THE INFINITE WOMAN NEEDS A STEADY SUPPLY OF THEM TO DO HER WORK. WHEN THEY'VE FINISHED WITH YOU, THEY'LL JOIN THE ETERNAL WAR.
DON'T CRY, BOY.
YOUR PARENTS MAY BE DEAD...THEIR SOULS PASSED ON TO WHEREVER SOULS MIGHT GO... BUT I AM HERE TO BRING THEM A NEW KIND OF LIFE. SEE HOW BEAUTIFUL THEY ARE?
THEY DON'T REMEMBER YOU, OF COURSE. THEY JUST REMEMBER THE IMPORTANT THINGS...RAGE. VIOLENCE...
HUNGER.
SEE, CHILD?
YOU WILL BE THEIR FIRST KILL. THEIR MESSY BAPTISM INTO THEIR NEW EXISTENCE.
YOU SHOULD BE HONORED.

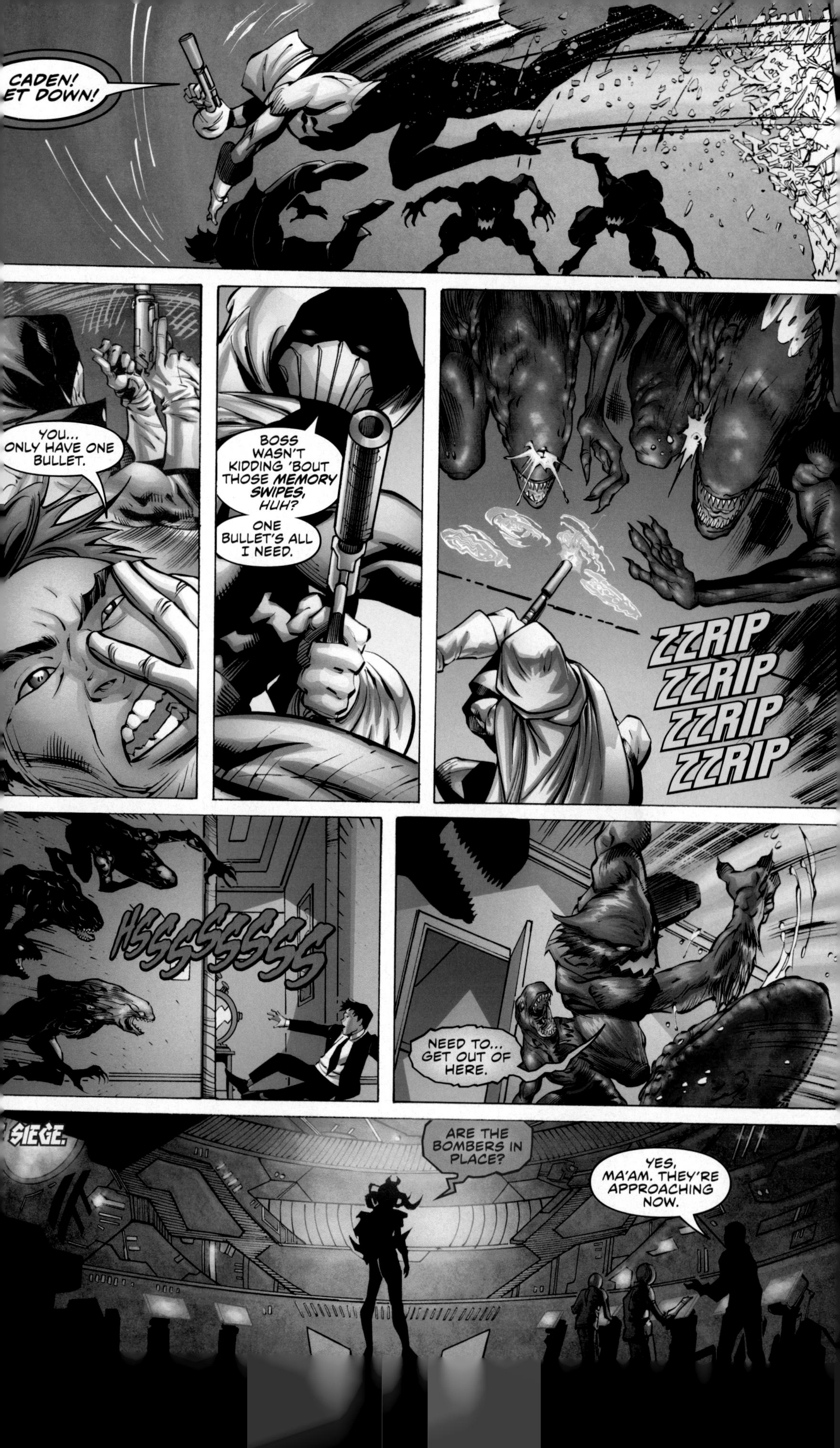
CADEN!
ET DOWN!
YOU... ONLY HAVE ONE BULLET.
BOSS WASN'T KIDDING 'BOUT THOSE MEMORY SWIPES, HUH?
ONE BULLET'S ALL I NEED.
ZZRIP ZZRIP ZZRIP ZZRIP
HSSSSSSSS
NEED TO... GET OUT OF HERE.
SIEGE.
ARE THE BOMBERS IN PLACE?
YES, MA'AM. THEY'RE APPROACHING NOW.

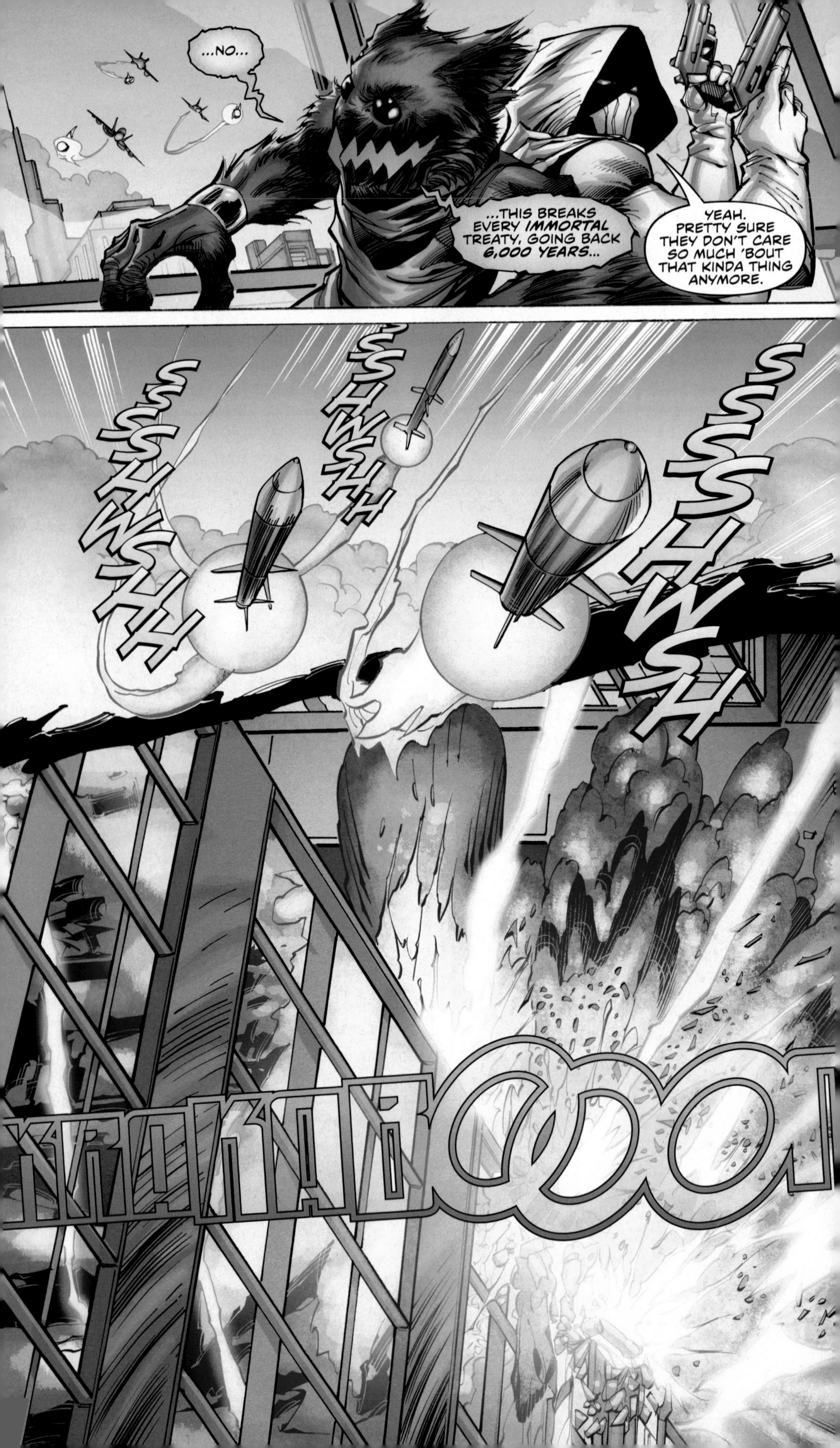
...NO...
...THIS BREAKS EVERY *IMMORTAL* TREATY, GOING BACK 6,000 YEARS...
YEAH. PRETTY SURE THEY DON'T CARE SO MUCH 'BOUT THAT KINDA THING ANYMORE.
SSSHWSHH
SSHWSHH
SSSHWSH

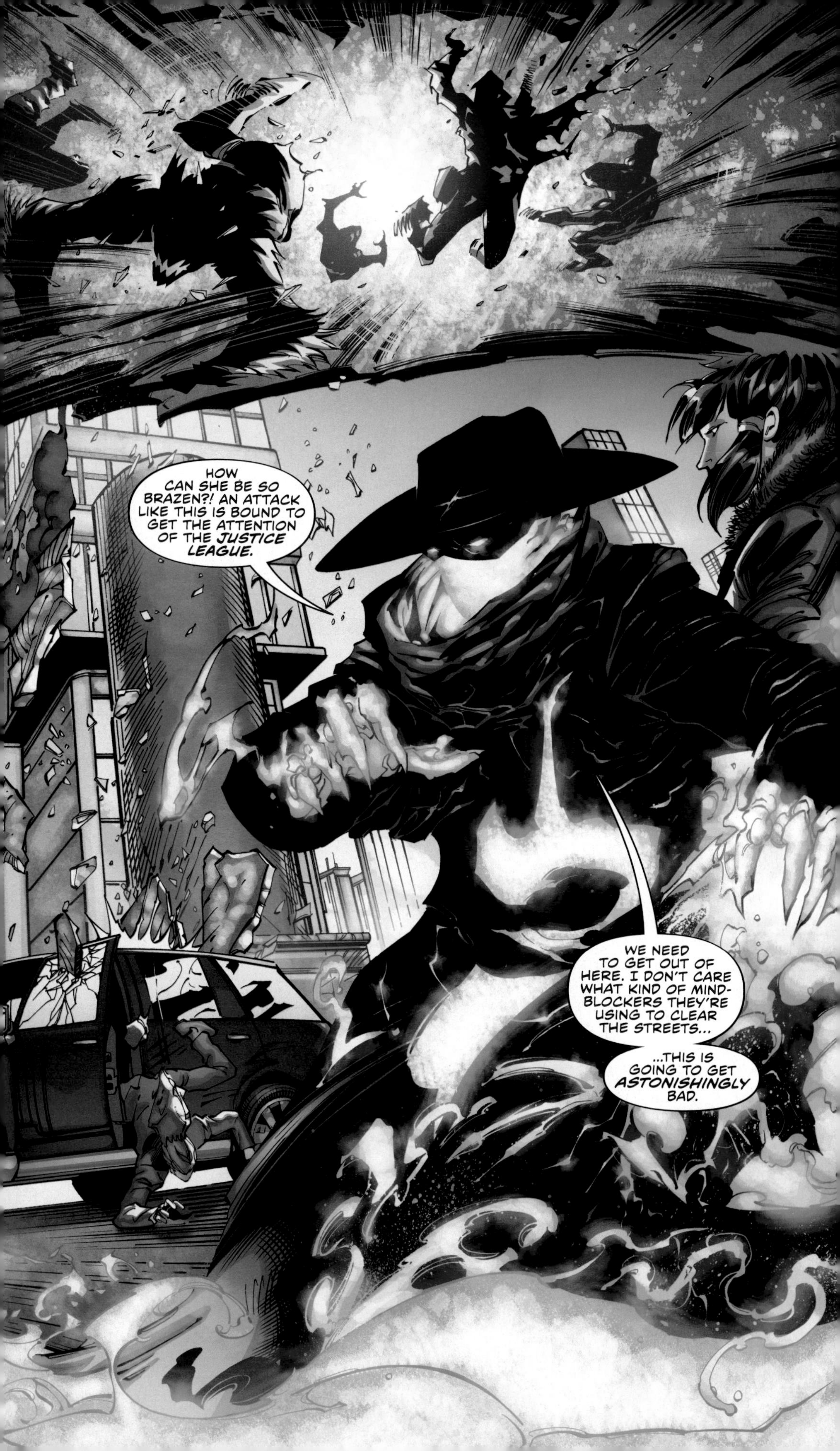
HOW CAN SHE BE SO BRAZEN?! AN ATTACK LIKE THIS IS BOUND TO GET THE ATTENTION OF THE *JUSTICE LEAGUE.*
WE NEED TO GET OUT OF HERE. I DON'T CARE WHAT KIND OF MIND-BLOCKERS THEY'RE USING TO CLEAR THE STREETS...
...THIS IS GOING TO GET *ASTONISHINGLY* BAD.

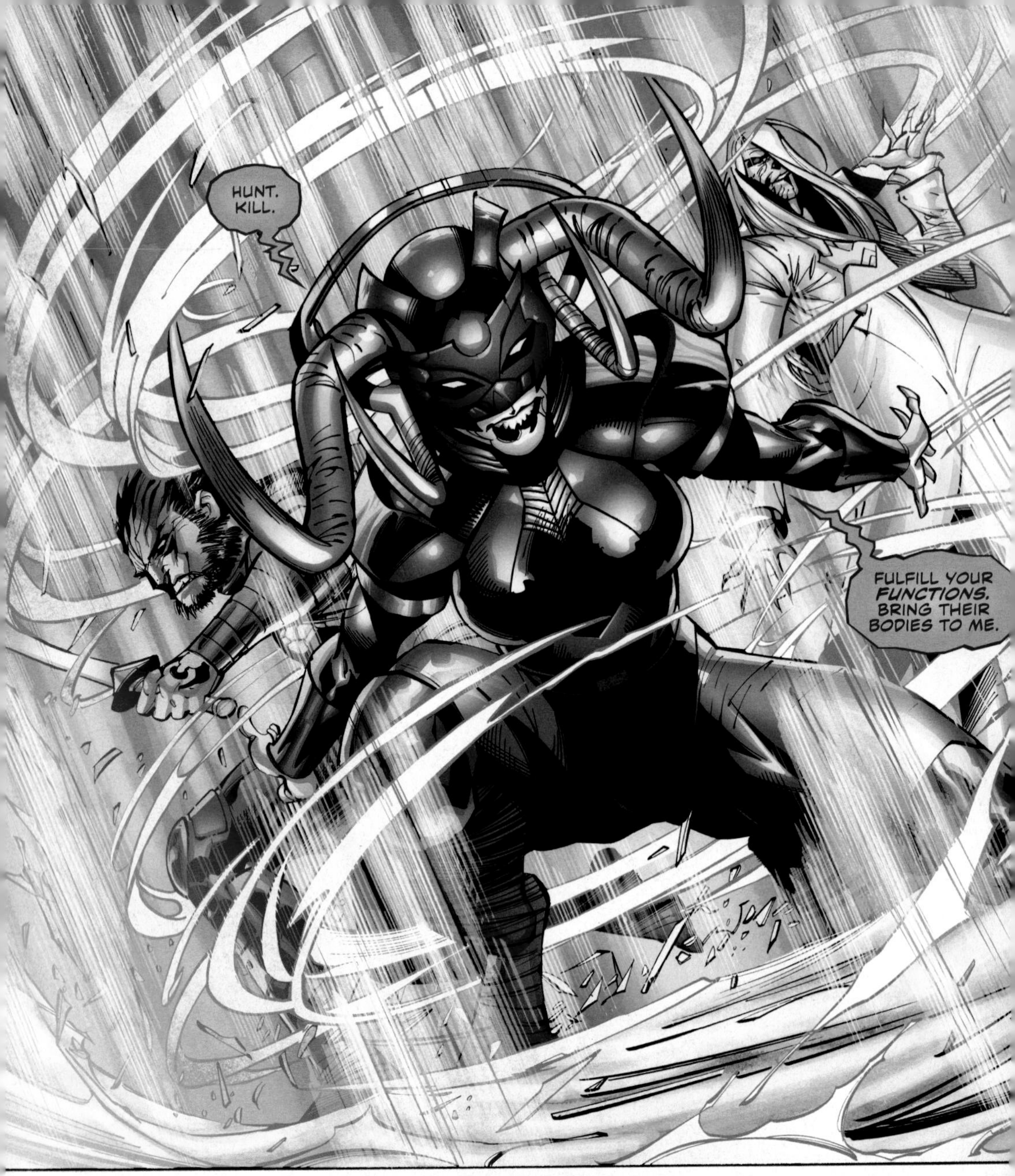
HUNT. KILL.
FULFILL YOUR *FUNCTIONS*. BRING THEIR BODIES TO ME.

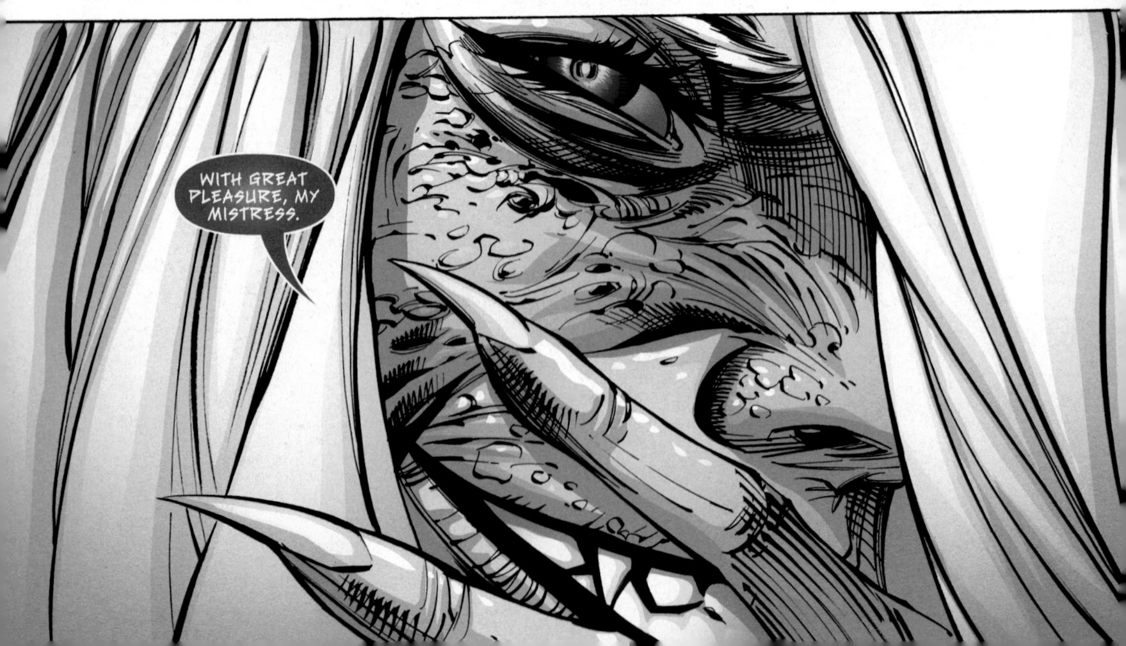
WITH GREAT PLEASURE, MY MISTRESS.

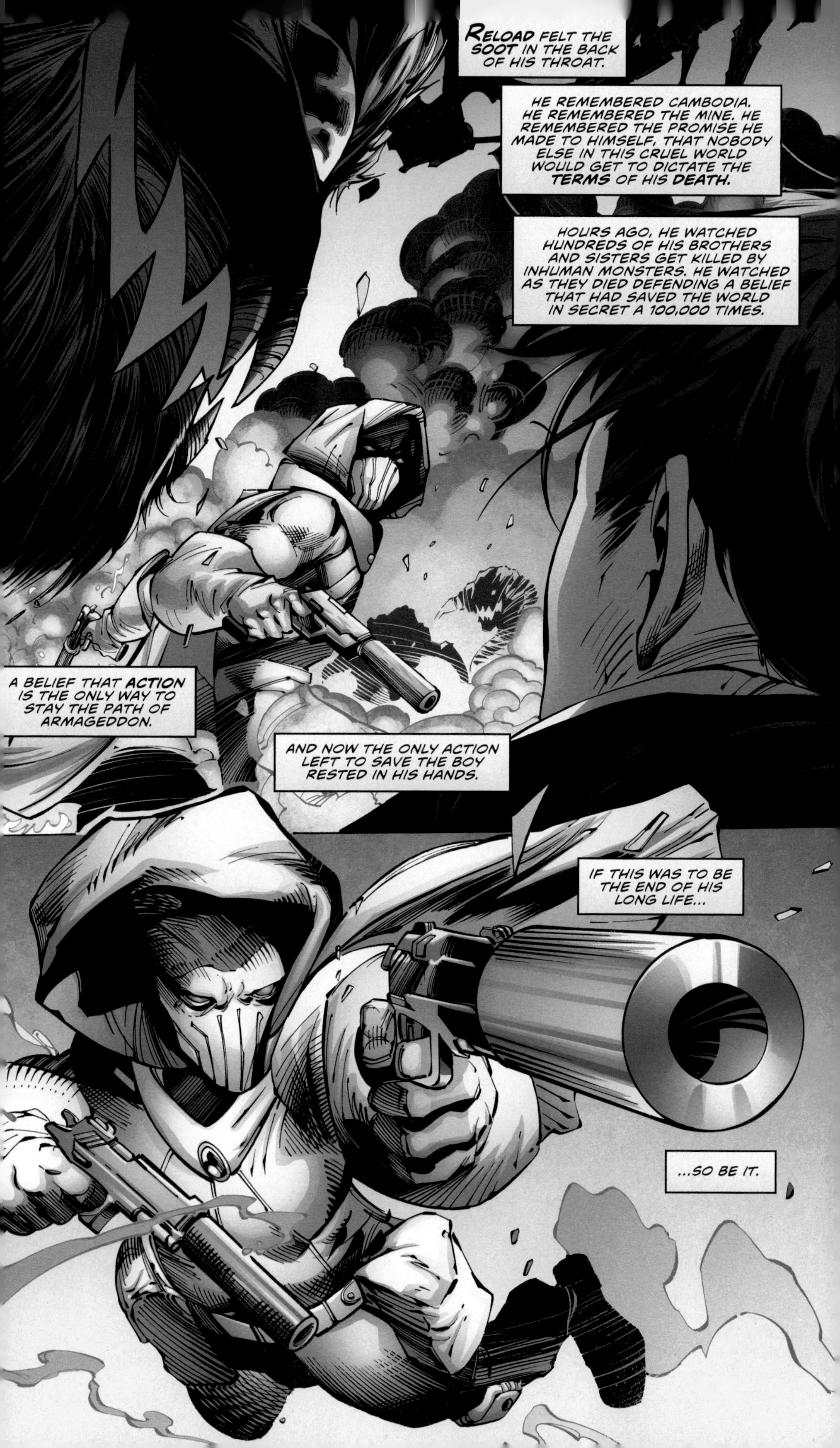
RELOAD FELT THE SOOT IN THE BACK OF HIS THROAT.
HE REMEMBERED CAMBODIA. HE REMEMBERED THE MINE. HE REMEMBERED THE PROMISE HE MADE TO HIMSELF, THAT NOBODY ELSE IN THIS CRUEL WORLD WOULD GET TO DICTATE THE TERMS OF HIS DEATH.
HOURS AGO, HE WATCHED HUNDREDS OF HIS BROTHERS AND SISTERS GET KILLED BY INHUMAN MONSTERS. HE WATCHED AS THEY DIED DEFENDING A BELIEF THAT HAD SAVED THE WORLD IN SECRET A 100,000 TIMES.
A BELIEF THAT ACTION IS THE ONLY WAY TO STAY THE PATH OF ARMAGEDDON.
AND NOW THE ONLY ACTION LEFT TO SAVE THE BOY RESTED IN HIS HANDS.
IF THIS WAS TO BE THE END OF HIS LONG LIFE...
...SO BE IT.

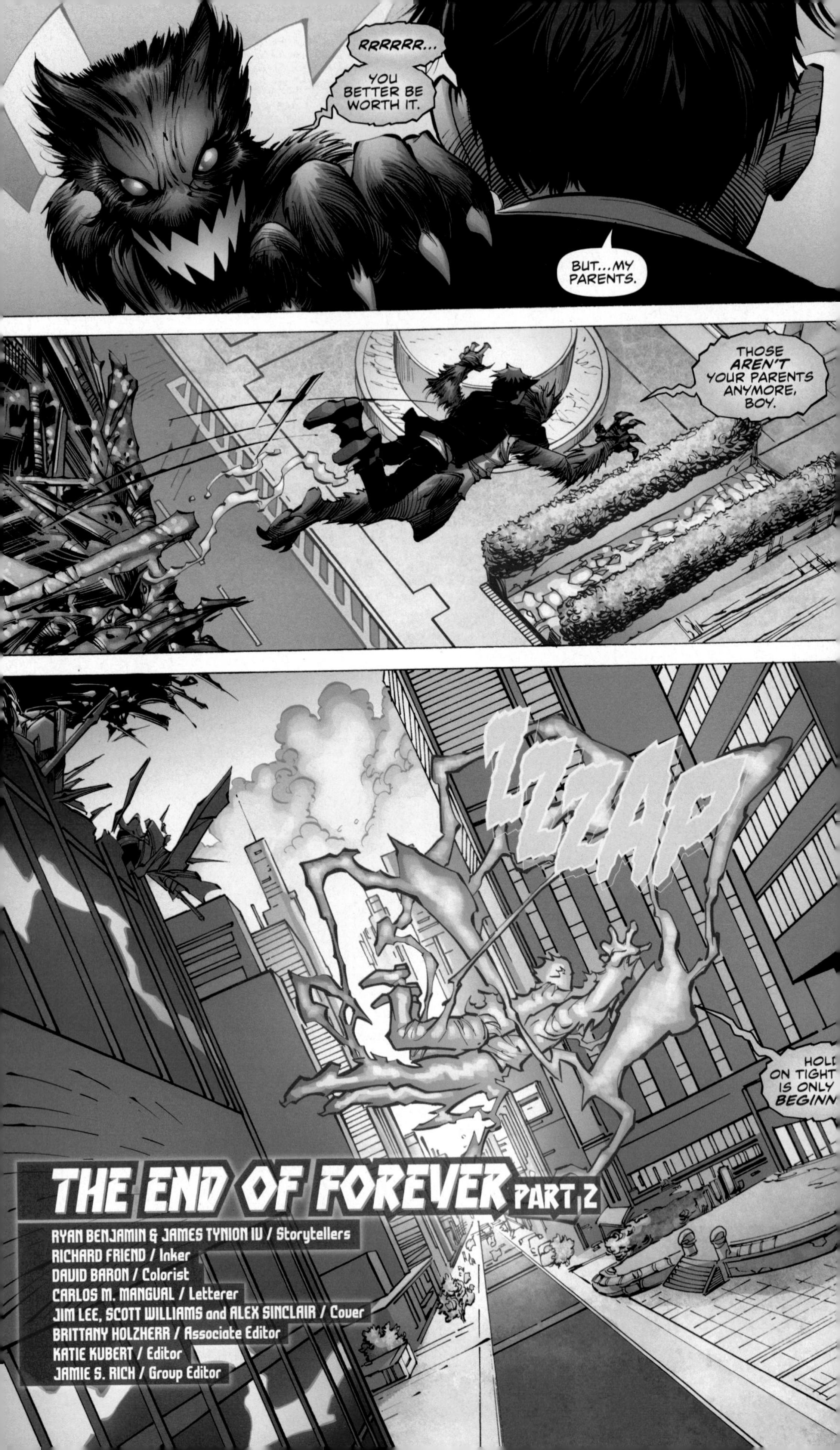
RRRRRR...
YOU BETTER BE WORTH IT.
BUT...MY PARENTS.
THOSE AREN'T YOUR PARENTS ANYMORE, BOY.
ZZZAP
HOLD ON TIGHT IS ONLY BEGINN
THE END OF FOREVER PART 2
RYAN BENJAMIN & JAMES TYNION IV / Storytellers
RICHARD FRIEND / Inker
DAVID BARON / Colorist
CARLOS M. MANGUAL / Letterer
JIM LEE, SCOTT WILLIAMS and ALEX SINCLAIR / Cover
BRITTANY HOLZHERR / Associate Editor
KATIE KUBERT / Editor
JAMIE S. RICH / Group Editor

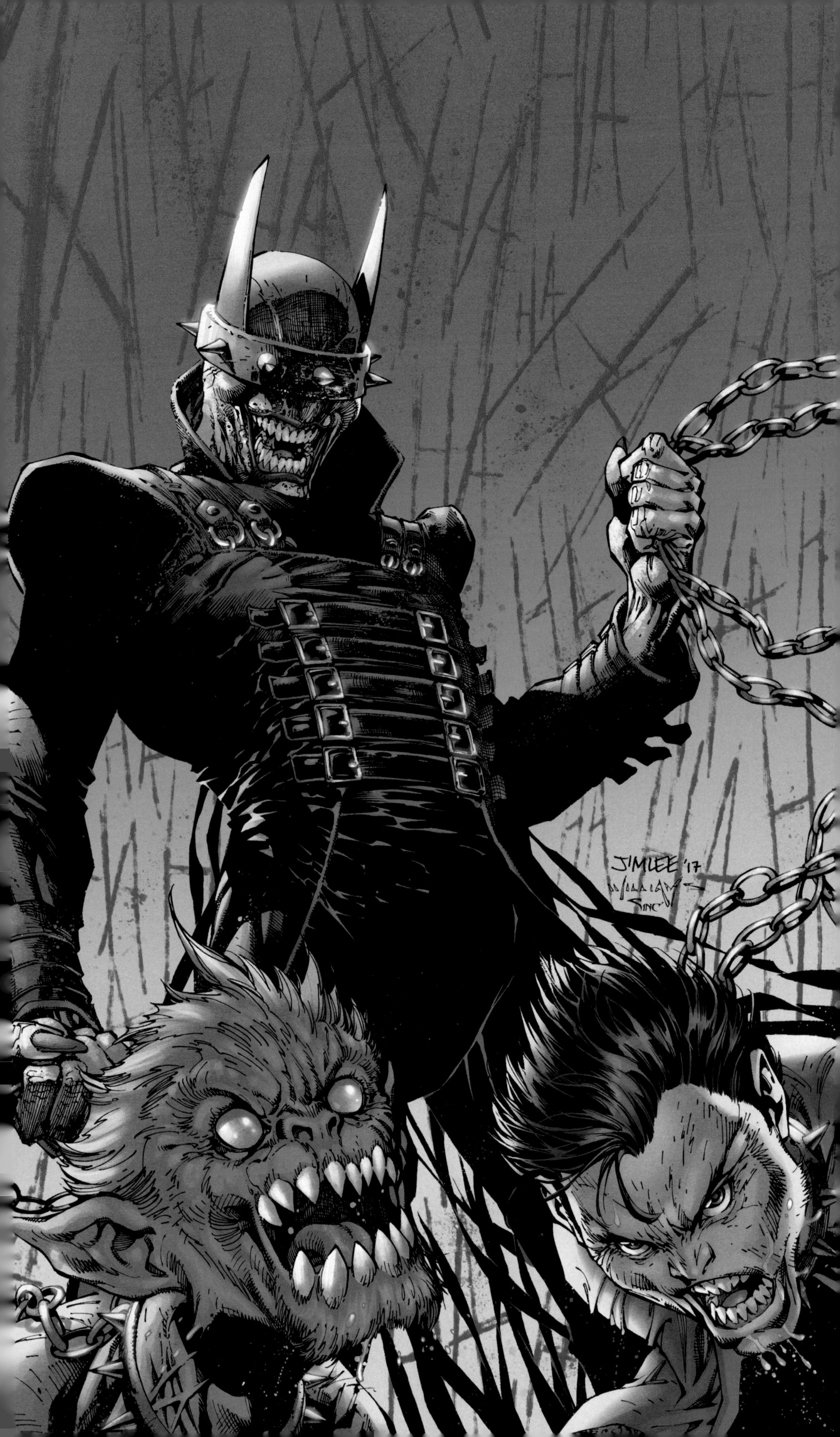
JIMLEE '17

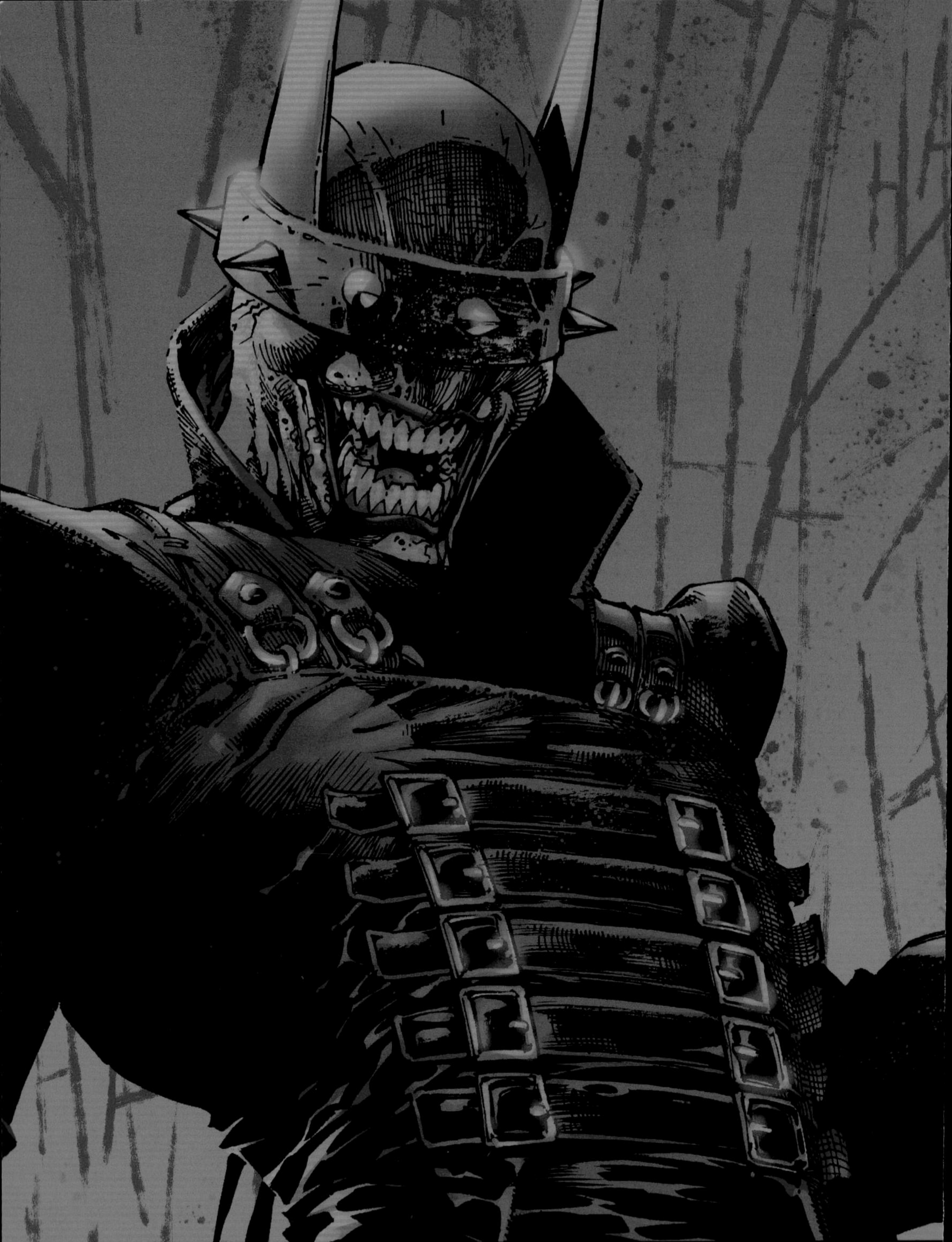

THE IMMORTAL MEN
#3

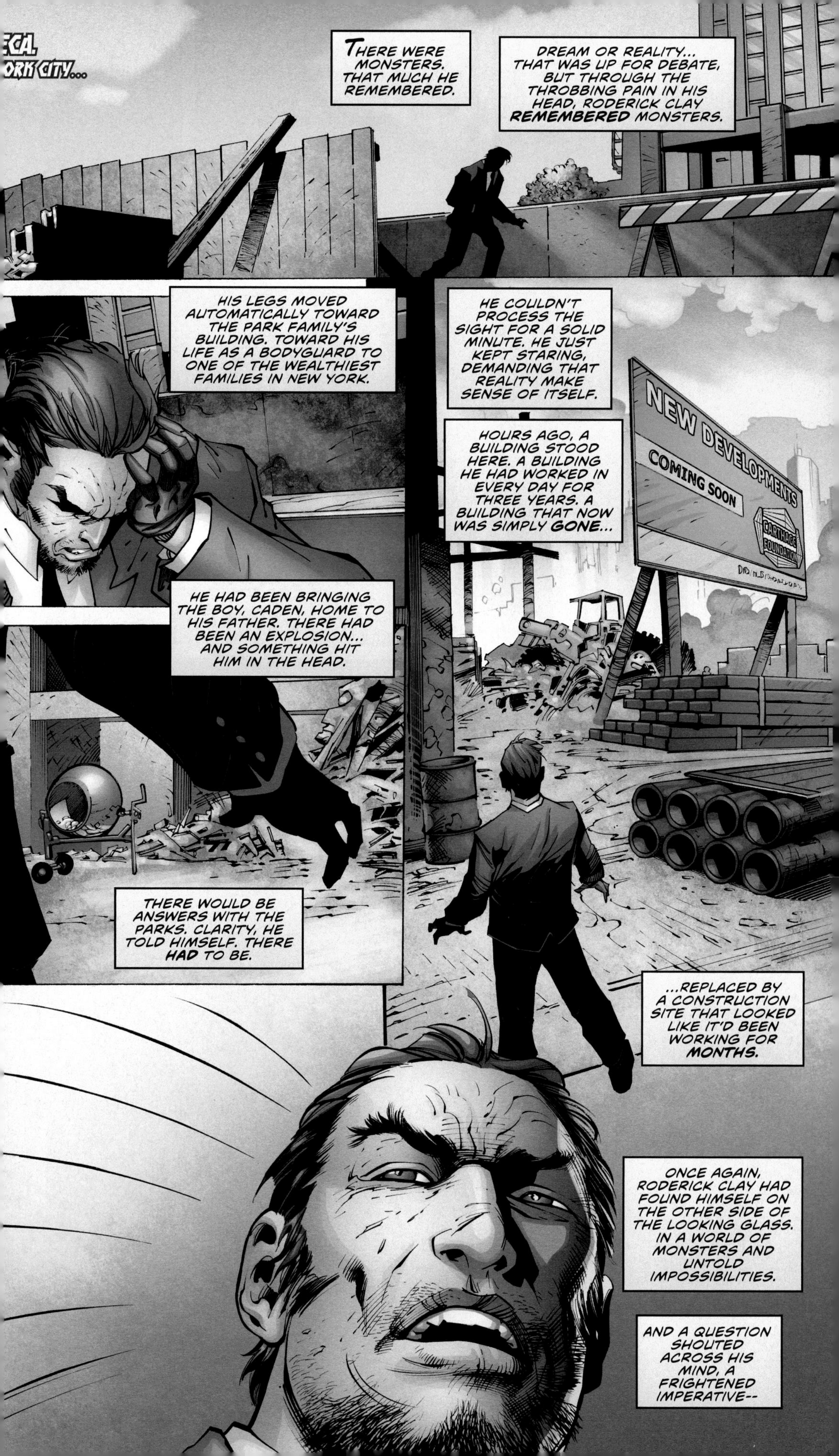
ECA.
ORK CITY...
THERE WERE MONSTERS. THAT MUCH HE REMEMBERED.
DREAM OR REALITY... THAT WAS UP FOR DEBATE, BUT THROUGH THE THROBBING PAIN IN HIS HEAD, RODERICK CLAY REMEMBERED MONSTERS.
HIS LEGS MOVED AUTOMATICALLY TOWARD THE PARK FAMILY'S BUILDING. TOWARD HIS LIFE AS A BODYGUARD TO ONE OF THE WEALTHIEST FAMILIES IN NEW YORK.
HE HAD BEEN BRINGING THE BOY, CADEN, HOME TO HIS FATHER. THERE HAD BEEN AN EXPLOSION... AND SOMETHING HIT HIM IN THE HEAD.
THERE WOULD BE ANSWERS WITH THE PARKS. CLARITY, HE TOLD HIMSELF. THERE HAD TO BE.
HE COULDN'T PROCESS THE SIGHT FOR A SOLID MINUTE. HE JUST KEPT STARING, DEMANDING THAT REALITY MAKE SENSE OF ITSELF.
NEW DEVELOPMENTS
COMING SOON
CARTHAGE FOUNDATION
HOURS AGO, A BUILDING STOOD HERE. A BUILDING HE HAD WORKED IN EVERY DAY FOR THREE YEARS. A BUILDING THAT NOW WAS SIMPLY GONE...
...REPLACED BY A CONSTRUCTION SITE THAT LOOKED LIKE IT'D BEEN WORKING FOR MONTHS.
ONCE AGAIN, RODERICK CLAY HAD FOUND HIMSELF ON THE OTHER SIDE OF THE LOOKING GLASS. IN A WORLD OF MONSTERS AND UNTOLD IMPOSSIBILITIES.
AND A QUESTION SHOUTED ACROSS HIS MIND, A FRIGHTENED IMPERATIVE--

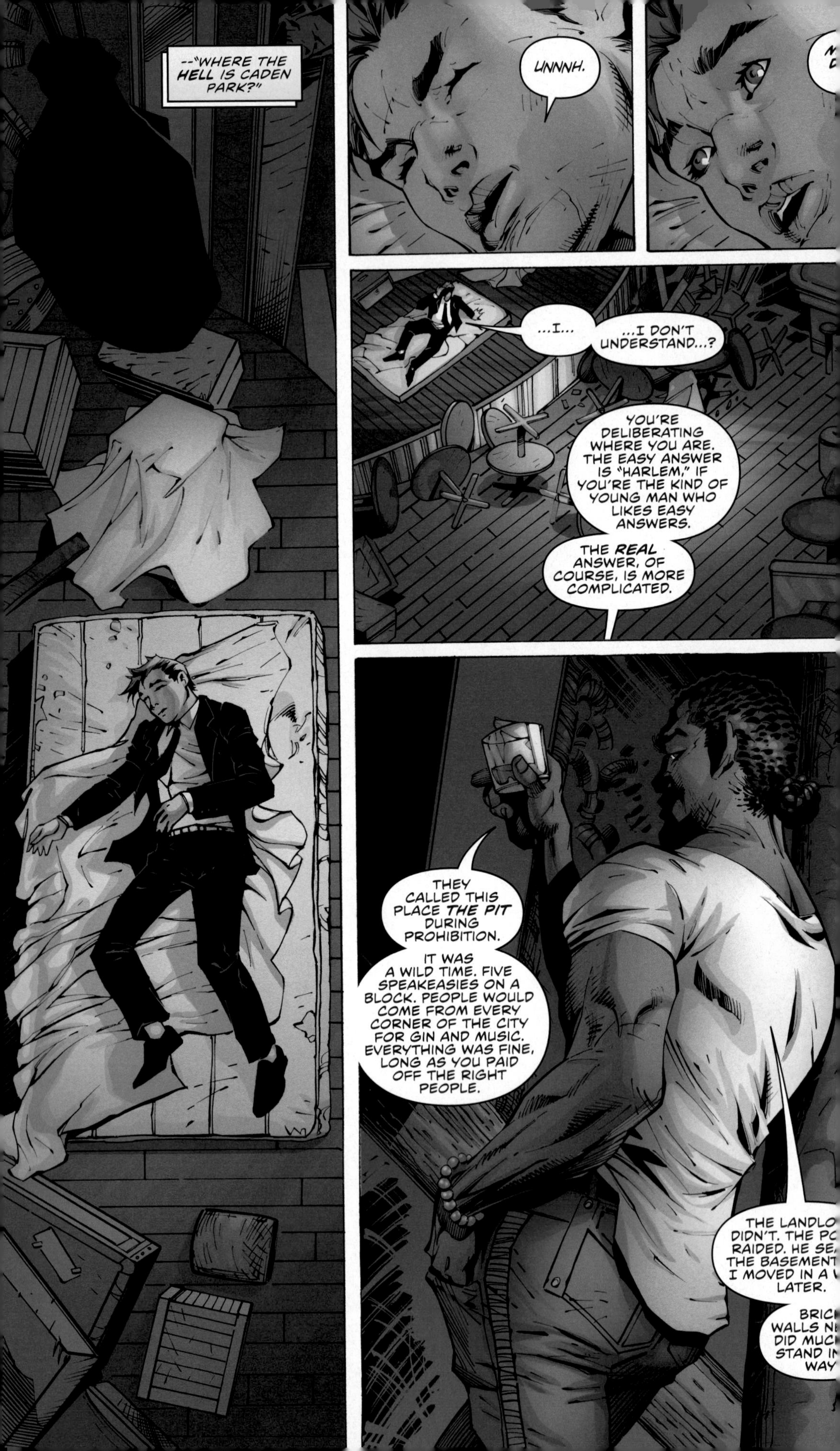
--"WHERE THE HELL IS CADEN PARK?"
UNNNH.
...I...
...I DON'T UNDERSTAND...?
YOU'RE DELIBERATING WHERE YOU ARE. THE EASY ANSWER IS "HARLEM," IF YOU'RE THE KIND OF YOUNG MAN WHO LIKES EASY ANSWERS.
THE REAL ANSWER, OF COURSE, IS MORE COMPLICATED.
THEY CALLED THIS PLACE THE PIT DURING PROHIBITION.
IT WAS A WILD TIME. FIVE SPEAKEASIES ON A BLOCK. PEOPLE WOULD COME FROM EVERY CORNER OF THE CITY FOR GIN AND MUSIC. EVERYTHING WAS FINE, LONG AS YOU PAID OFF THE RIGHT PEOPLE.
THE LANDLO DIDN'T. THE PO RAIDED. HE SE THE BASEMENT I MOVED IN A LATER.
BRIC WALLS N DID MUC STAND I WAY

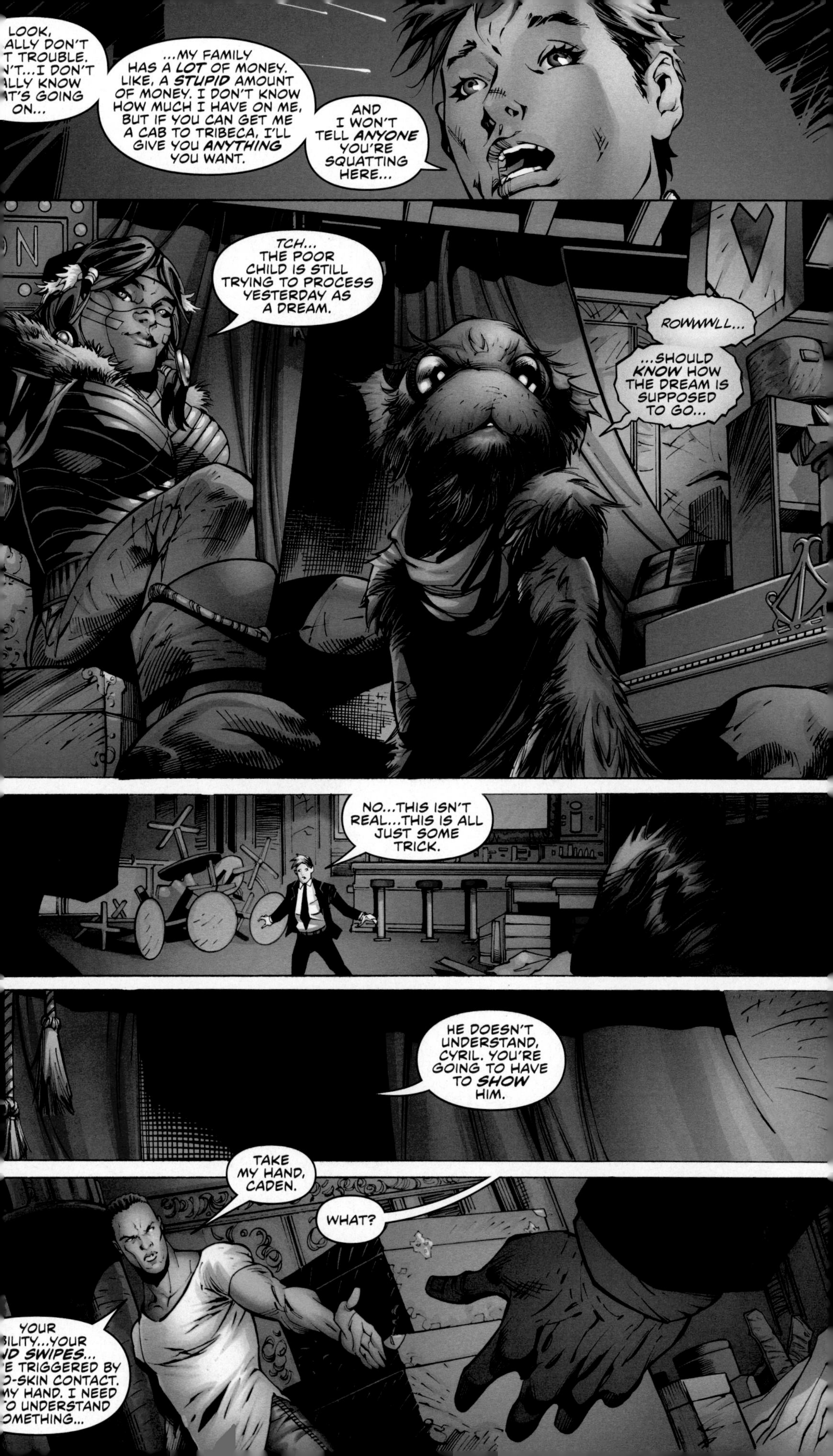
LOOK, ALLY DON'T T TROUBLE. N'T...I DON'T ALLY KNOW AT'S GOING ON...
...MY FAMILY HAS A LOT OF MONEY. LIKE, A STUPID AMOUNT OF MONEY. I DON'T KNOW HOW MUCH I HAVE ON ME, BUT IF YOU CAN GET ME A CAB TO TRIBECA, I'LL GIVE YOU ANYTHING YOU WANT.
AND I WON'T TELL ANYONE YOU'RE SQUATTING HERE...
TCH... THE POOR CHILD IS STILL TRYING TO PROCESS YESTERDAY AS A DREAM.
ROWWWLL...
...SHOULD KNOW HOW THE DREAM IS SUPPOSED TO GO...
NO...THIS ISN'T REAL...THIS IS ALL JUST SOME TRICK.
HE DOESN'T UNDERSTAND, CYRIL. YOU'RE GOING TO HAVE TO SHOW HIM.
TAKE MY HAND, CADEN.
WHAT?
YOUR BILITY...YOUR ND SWIPES... E TRIGGERED BY O-SKIN CONTACT. MY HAND. I NEED O UNDERSTAND OMETHING...

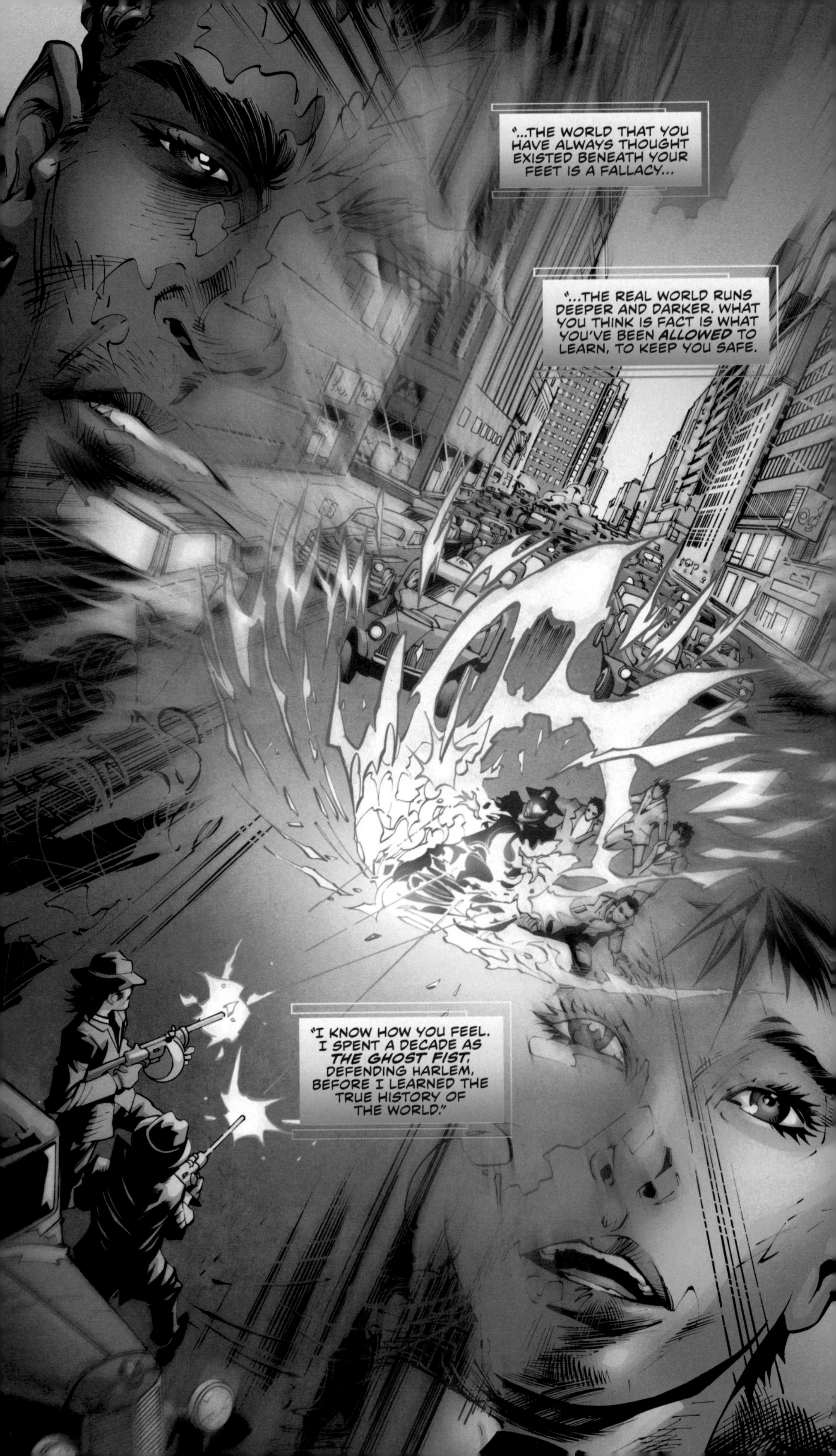
"...THE WORLD THAT YOU HAVE ALWAYS THOUGHT EXISTED BENEATH YOUR FEET IS A FALLACY...
"...THE REAL WORLD RUNS DEEPER AND DARKER. WHAT YOU THINK IS FACT IS WHAT YOU'VE BEEN *ALLOWED* TO LEARN, TO KEEP YOU SAFE.
"I KNOW HOW YOU FEEL. I SPENT A DECADE AS *THE GHOST FIST,* DEFENDING HARLEM, BEFORE I LEARNED THE TRUE HISTORY OF THE WORLD."

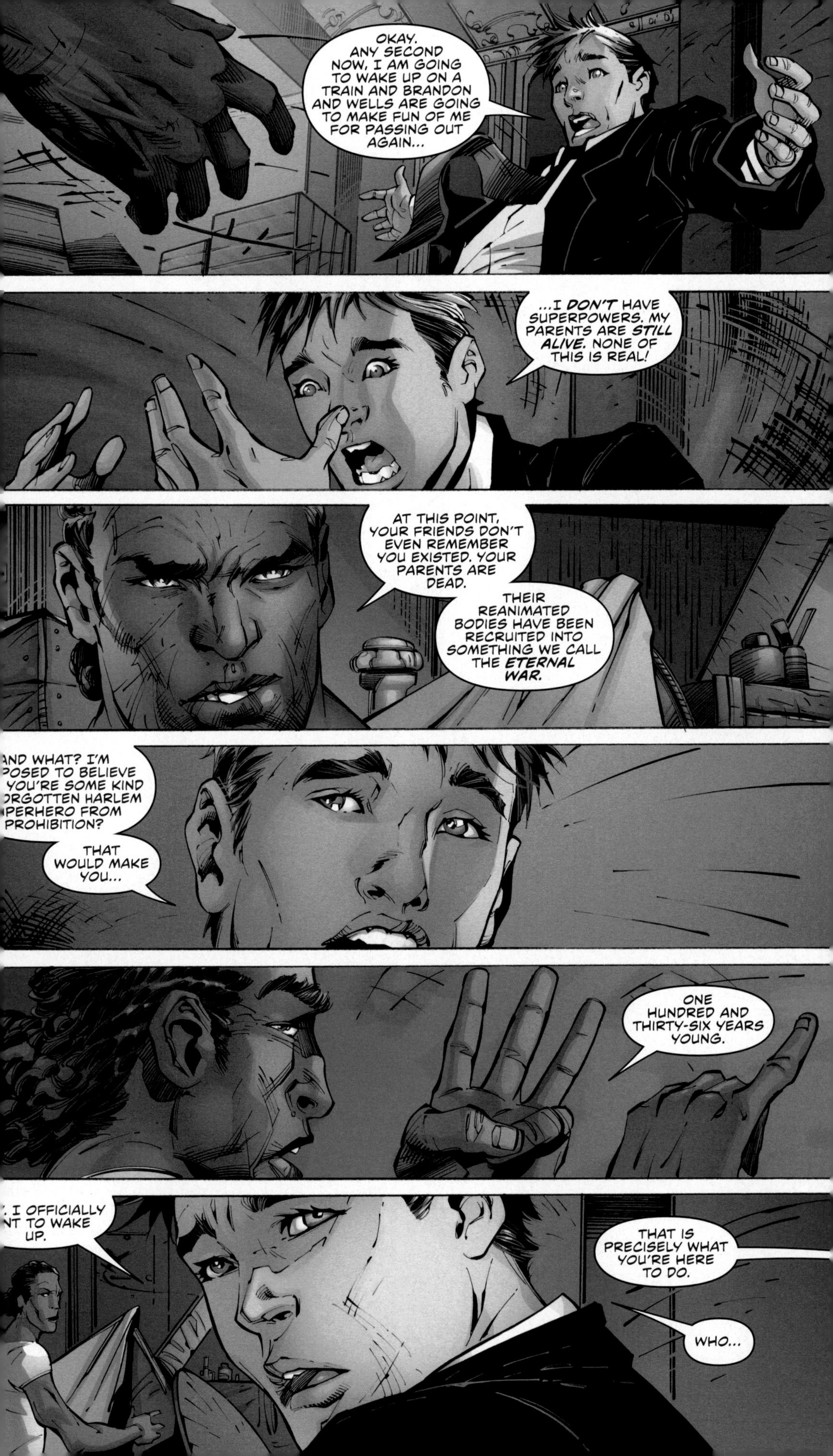
OKAY. ANY SECOND NOW, I AM GOING TO WAKE UP ON A TRAIN AND BRANDON AND WELLS ARE GOING TO MAKE FUN OF ME FOR PASSING OUT AGAIN...
...I DON'T HAVE SUPERPOWERS. MY PARENTS ARE STILL ALIVE. NONE OF THIS IS REAL!
AT THIS POINT, YOUR FRIENDS DON'T EVEN REMEMBER YOU EXISTED. YOUR PARENTS ARE DEAD.
THEIR REANIMATED BODIES HAVE BEEN RECRUITED INTO SOMETHING WE CALL THE ETERNAL WAR.
AND WHAT? I'M POSED TO BELIEVE YOU'RE SOME KIND ORGOTTEN HARLEM PERHERO FROM PROHIBITION?
THAT WOULD MAKE YOU...
ONE HUNDRED AND THIRTY-SIX YEARS YOUNG.
I OFFICIALLY NT TO WAKE UP.
THAT IS PRECISELY WHAT YOU'RE HERE TO DO.
WHO...

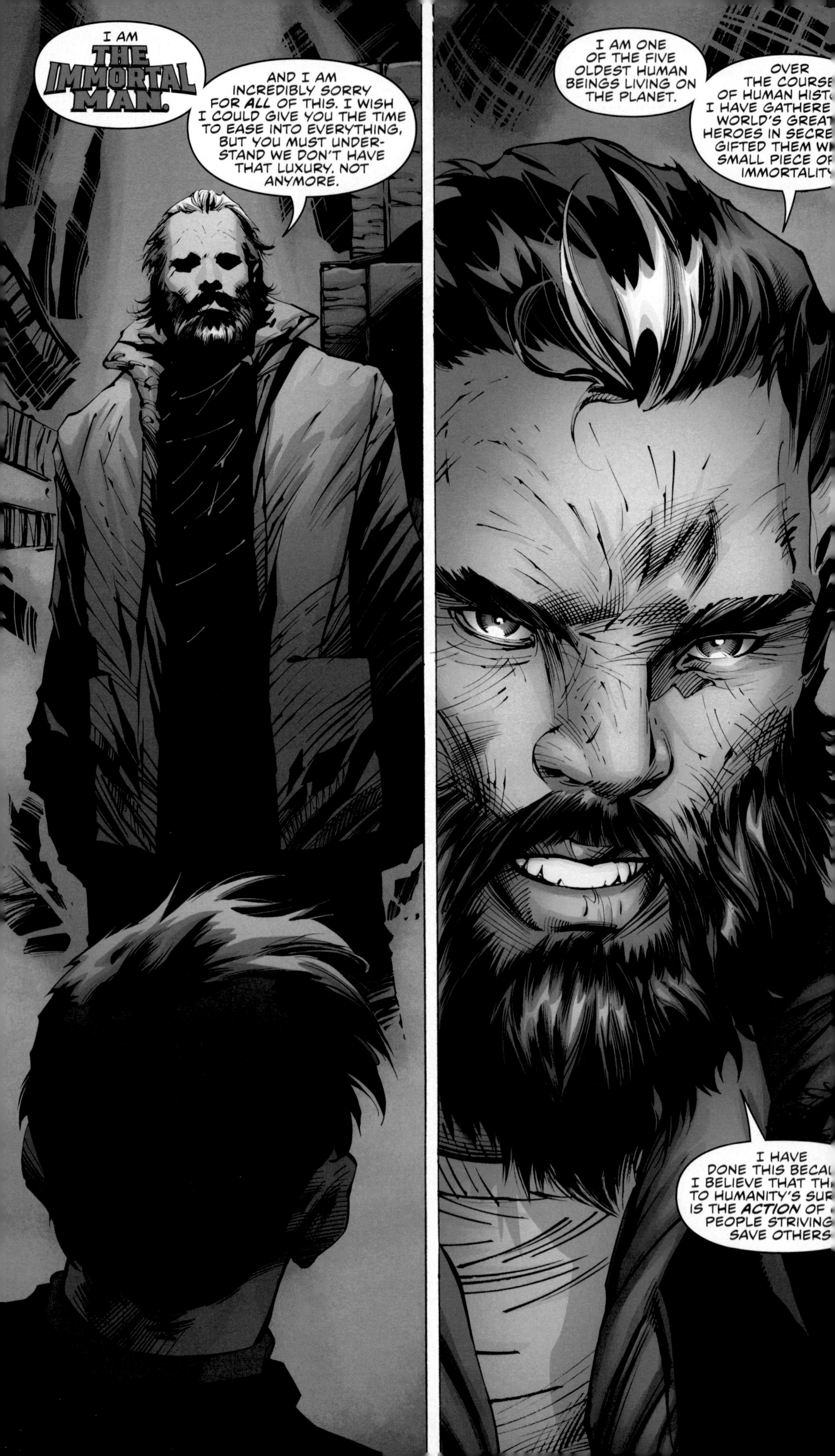

I AM THE IMMORTAL MAN.
AND I AM INCREDIBLY SORRY FOR ALL OF THIS. I WISH I COULD GIVE YOU THE TIME TO EASE INTO EVERYTHING, BUT YOU MUST UNDERSTAND WE DON'T HAVE THAT LUXURY. NOT ANYMORE.
I AM ONE OF THE FIVE OLDEST HUMAN BEINGS LIVING ON THE PLANET.
OVER THE COURSE OF HUMAN HIST I HAVE GATHERE WORLD'S GREAT HEROES IN SECRE GIFTED THEM W SMALL PIECE OF IMMORTALITY
I HAVE DONE THIS BECA I BELIEVE THAT TH TO HUMANITY'S SU IS THE ACTION OF PEOPLE STRIVING SAVE OTHERS

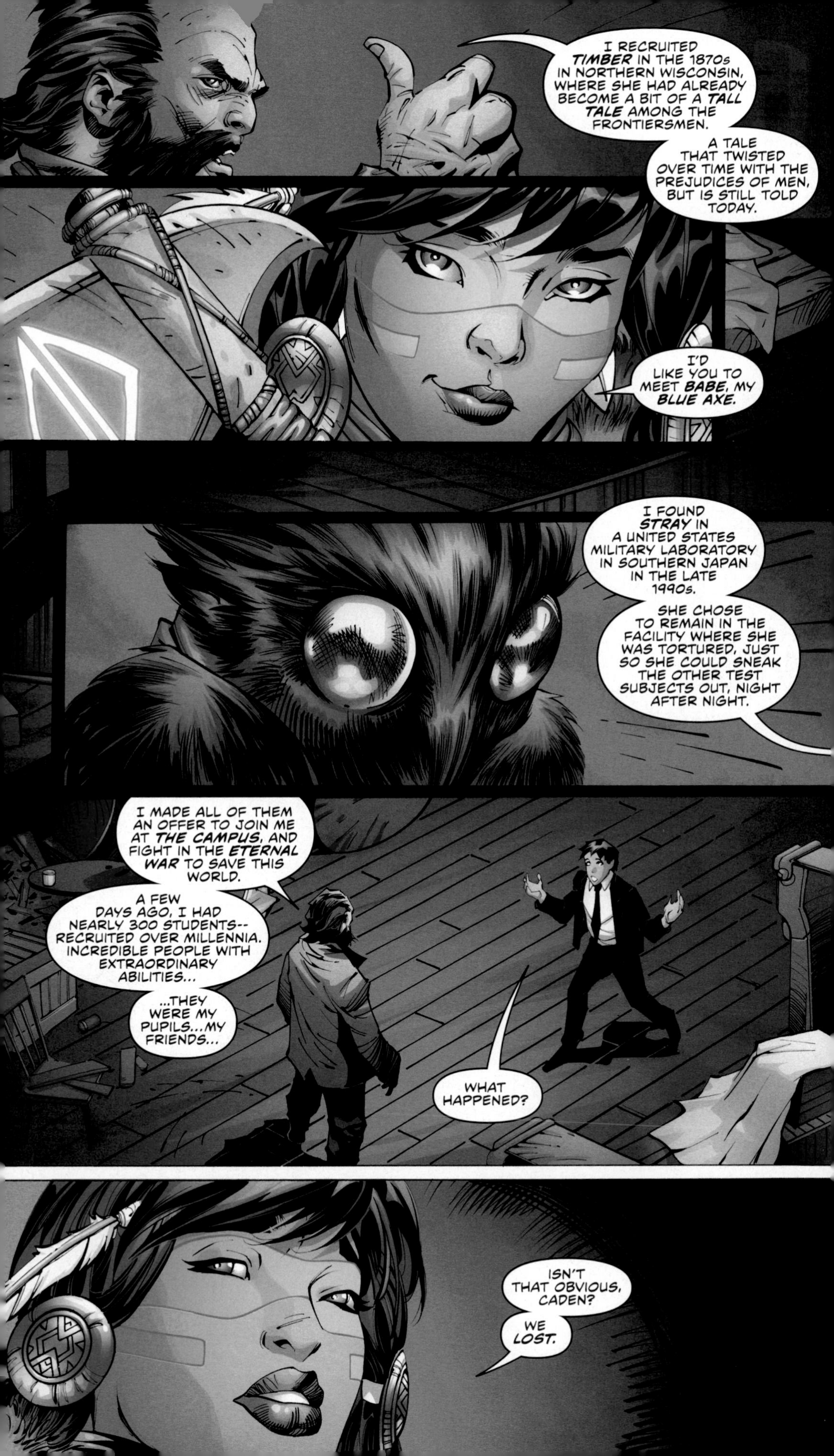

I RECRUITED TIMBER IN THE 1870s IN NORTHERN WISCONSIN, WHERE SHE HAD ALREADY BECOME A BIT OF A TALL TALE AMONG THE FRONTIERSMEN.
A TALE THAT TWISTED OVER TIME WITH THE PREJUDICES OF MEN, BUT IS STILL TOLD TODAY.
I'D LIKE YOU TO MEET BABE, MY BLUE AXE.
I FOUND STRAY IN A UNITED STATES MILITARY LABORATORY IN SOUTHERN JAPAN IN THE LATE 1990s.
SHE CHOSE TO REMAIN IN THE FACILITY WHERE SHE WAS TORTURED, JUST SO SHE COULD SNEAK THE OTHER TEST SUBJECTS OUT, NIGHT AFTER NIGHT.
I MADE ALL OF THEM AN OFFER TO JOIN ME AT THE CAMPUS, AND FIGHT IN THE ETERNAL WAR TO SAVE THIS WORLD.
A FEW DAYS AGO, I HAD NEARLY 300 STUDENTS-- RECRUITED OVER MILLENNIA. INCREDIBLE PEOPLE WITH EXTRAORDINARY ABILITIES...
...THEY WERE MY PUPILS...MY FRIENDS...
WHAT HAPPENED?
ISN'T THAT OBVIOUS, CADEN?
WE LOST.

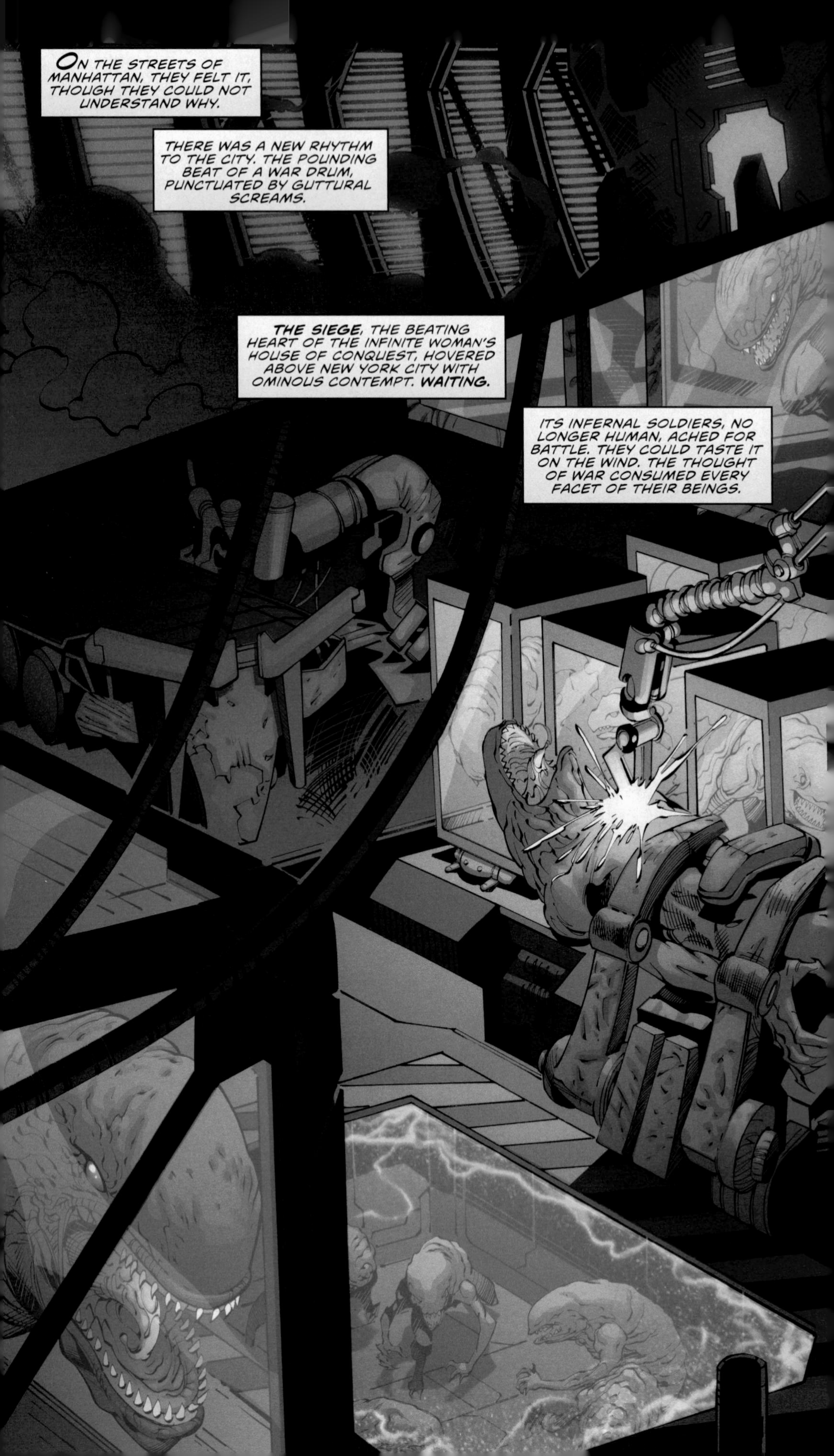
ON THE STREETS OF MANHATTAN, THEY FELT IT, THOUGH THEY COULD NOT UNDERSTAND WHY.
THERE WAS A NEW RHYTHM TO THE CITY. THE POUNDING BEAT OF A WAR DRUM, PUNCTUATED BY GUTTURAL SCREAMS.
THE SIEGE, THE BEATING HEART OF THE INFINITE WOMAN'S HOUSE OF CONQUEST, HOVERED ABOVE NEW YORK CITY WITH OMINOUS CONTEMPT. WAITING.
ITS INFERNAL SOLDIERS, NO LONGER HUMAN, ACHED FOR BATTLE. THEY COULD TASTE IT ON THE WIND. THE THOUGHT OF WAR CONSUMED EVERY FACET OF THEIR BEINGS.

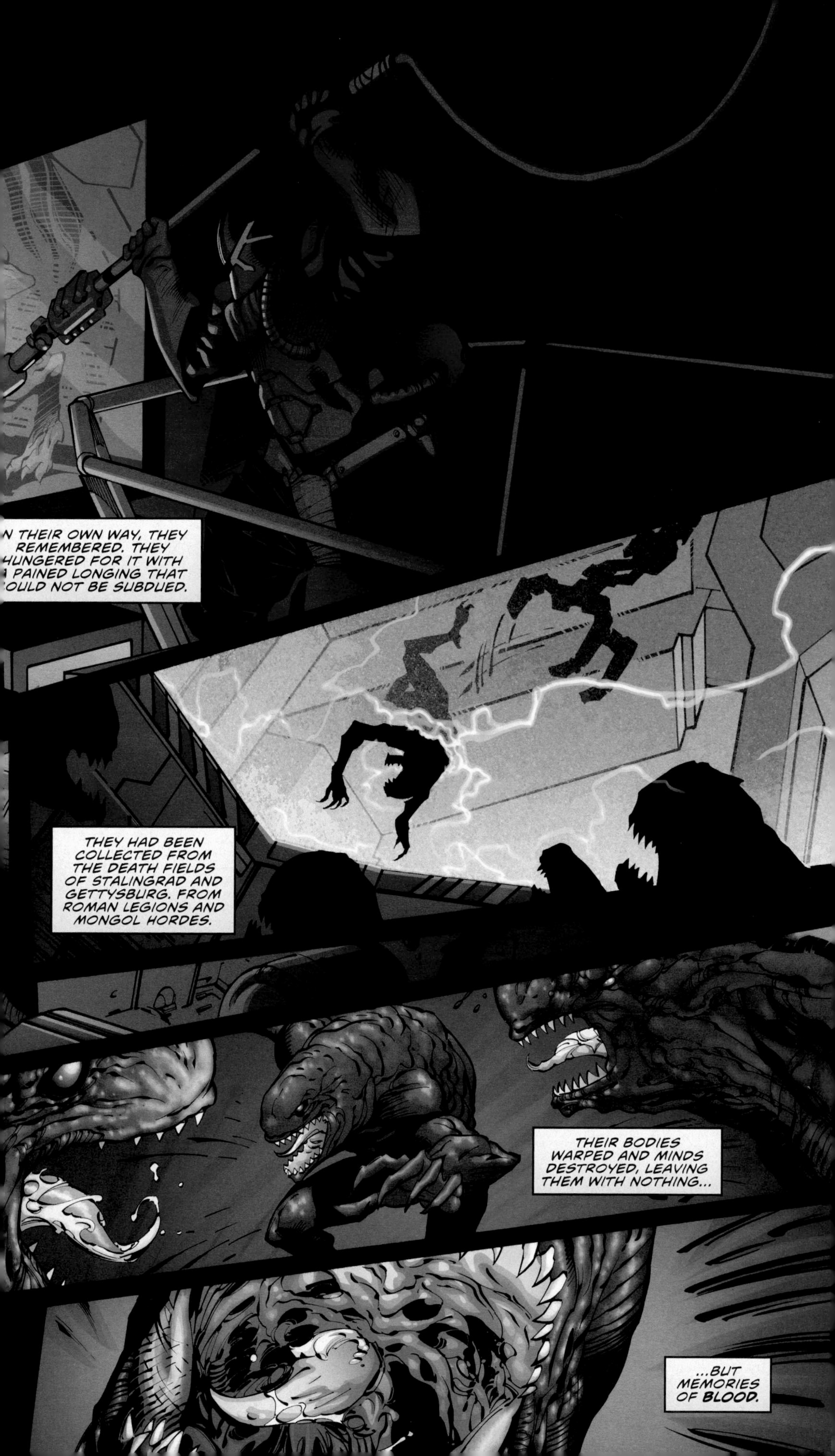
N THEIR OWN WAY, THEY REMEMBERED. THEY HUNGERED FOR IT WITH A PAINED LONGING THAT COULD NOT BE SUBDUED.
THEY HAD BEEN COLLECTED FROM THE DEATH FIELDS OF STALINGRAD AND GETTYSBURG. FROM ROMAN LEGIONS AND MONGOL HORDES.
THEIR BODIES WARPED AND MINDS DESTROYED, LEAVING THEM WITH NOTHING...
...BUT MEMORIES OF BLOOD.

THE BLOOD HAD BROUGHT *HIM.* THE SCOURGE OF THE DARK MULTIVERSE. THE CLOWN KING OF HORROR.

THE BATMAN WHO LAUGHS.

YOU HAVE WHAT YOU NEED, THEN?

YOU'VE SEPARATED THE BLOOD FROM YOUR BROTHER'S IMMORTAL MEN FOR THE FORGING...

...YOU UNDERSTAND WHAT YOU HAVE TO DO *NEXT,* INFINITE WOMAN.

EVERY WORLD IN THE DARK MULTIVERSE THAT INCLUDED YOUR KIND, THE IMMORTALS... THEY BANDED BEHIND THE HOUSE OF ACTION WHEN THEIR ENDS CAME.

YOUR SIBLINGS' PHILOSOPHIES OF HOW TO SAVE THE WORLD, ALL THEIR PRECIOUS "HOUSES," THEY AMOUNTED TO *NOTHING* IN THE END.

THEY ALL DIED *WITH* THEIR WORLDS, SCREAMING.

I UNDERSTAND WHAT LITTLE YOU HAVE TOLD ME.

I SHOULD KN... I KILLED T... MYSELF.

HEH.

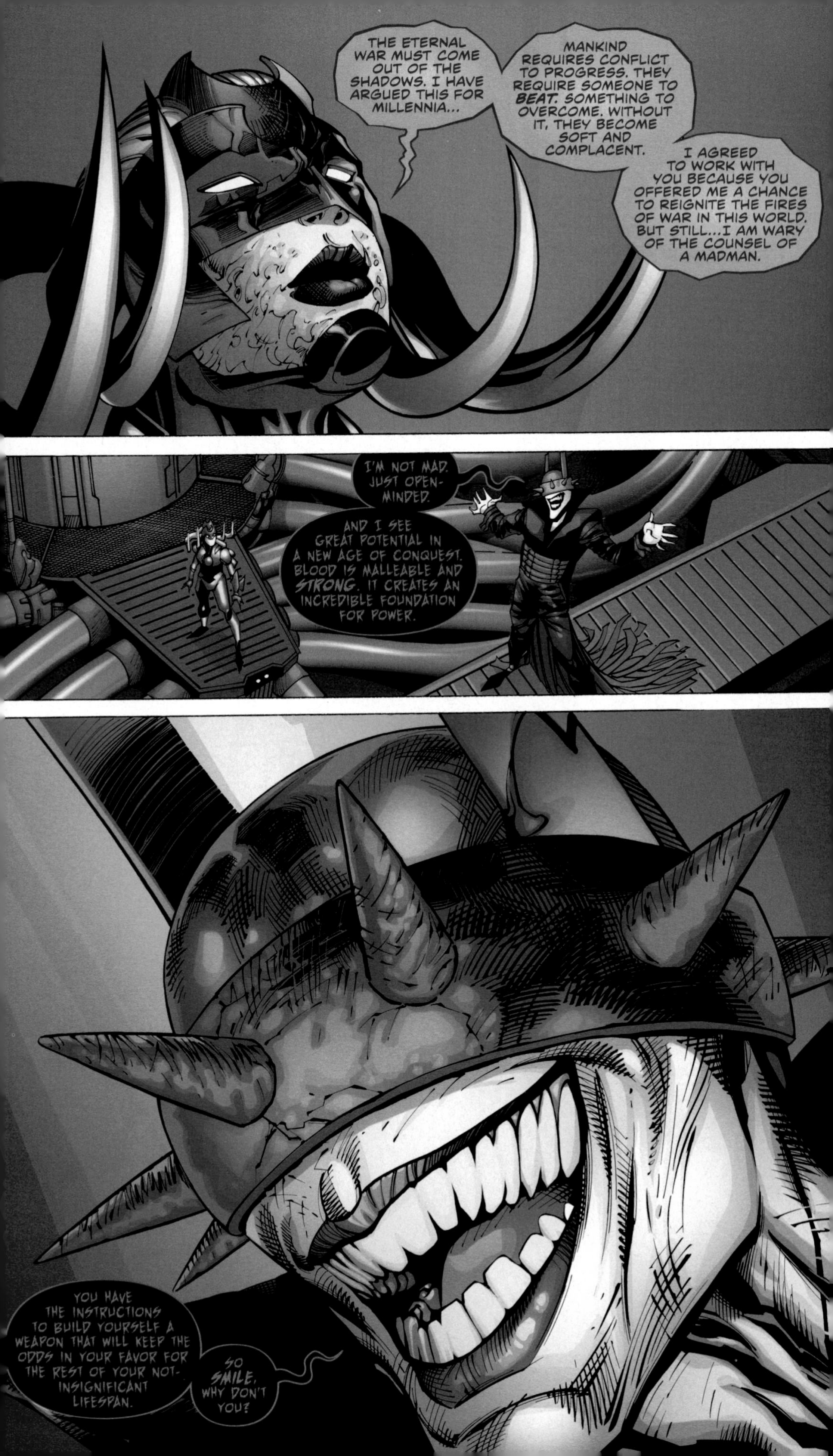
THE ETERNAL WAR MUST COME OUT OF THE SHADOWS. I HAVE ARGUED THIS FOR MILLENNIA...
MANKIND REQUIRES CONFLICT TO PROGRESS. THEY REQUIRE SOMEONE TO BEAT. SOMETHING TO OVERCOME. WITHOUT IT, THEY BECOME SOFT AND COMPLACENT.
I AGREED TO WORK WITH YOU BECAUSE YOU OFFERED ME A CHANCE TO REIGNITE THE FIRES OF WAR IN THIS WORLD. BUT STILL...I AM WARY OF THE COUNSEL OF A MADMAN.
I'M NOT MAD. JUST OPEN-MINDED.
AND I SEE GREAT POTENTIAL IN A NEW AGE OF CONQUEST. BLOOD IS MALLEABLE AND STRONG. IT CREATES AN INCREDIBLE FOUNDATION FOR POWER.
YOU HAVE THE INSTRUCTIONS TO BUILD YOURSELF A WEAPON THAT WILL KEEP THE ODDS IN YOUR FAVOR FOR THE REST OF YOUR NOT-INSIGNIFICANT LIFESPAN.
SO SMILE, WHY DON'T YOU?

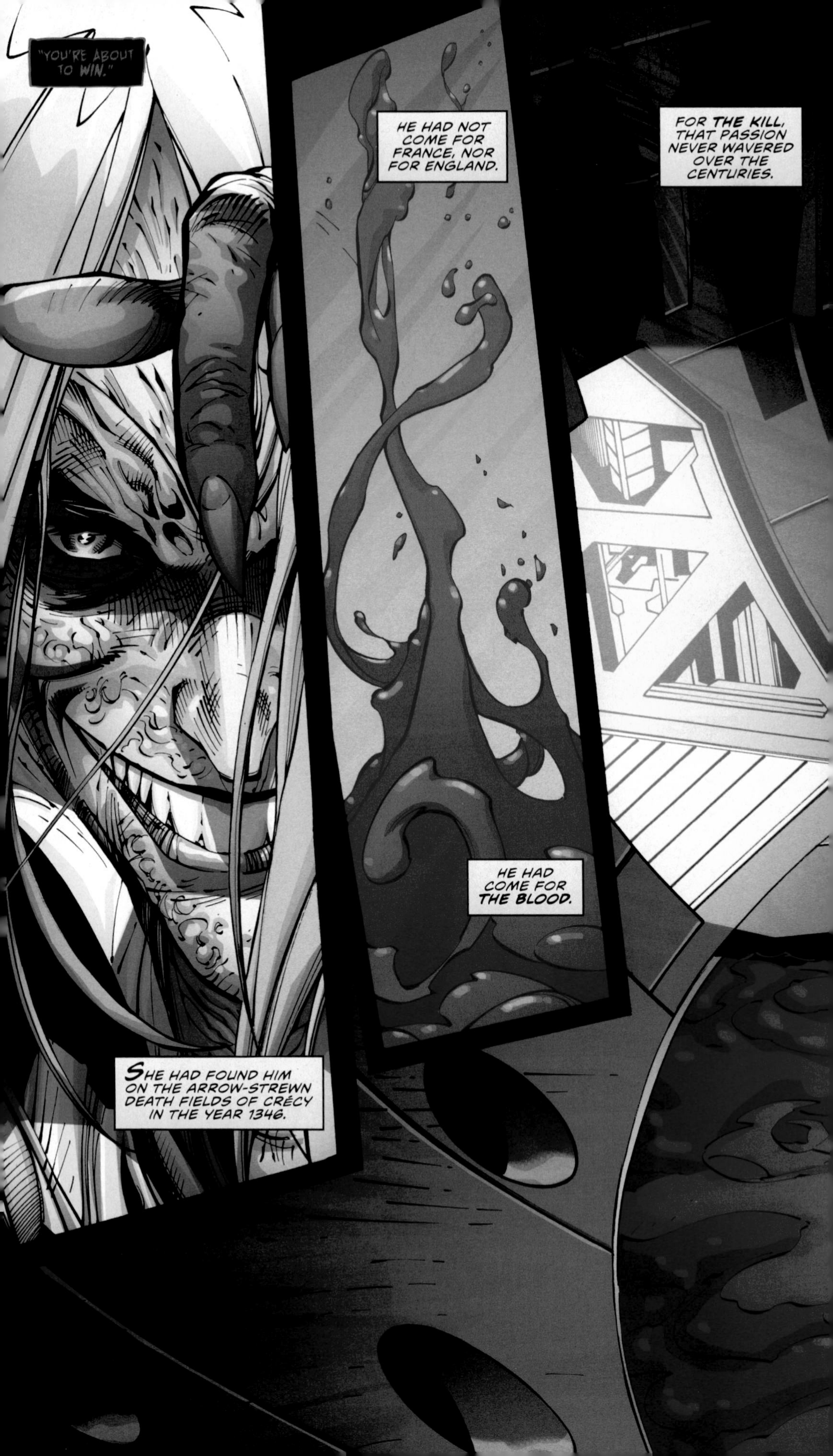
"YOU'RE ABOUT TO WIN."
HE HAD NOT COME FOR FRANCE, NOR FOR ENGLAND.
HE HAD COME FOR THE BLOOD.
FOR THE KILL, THAT PASSION NEVER WAVERED OVER THE CENTURIES.
SHE HAD FOUND HIM ON THE ARROW-STREWN DEATH FIELDS OF CRÉCY IN THE YEAR 1346.

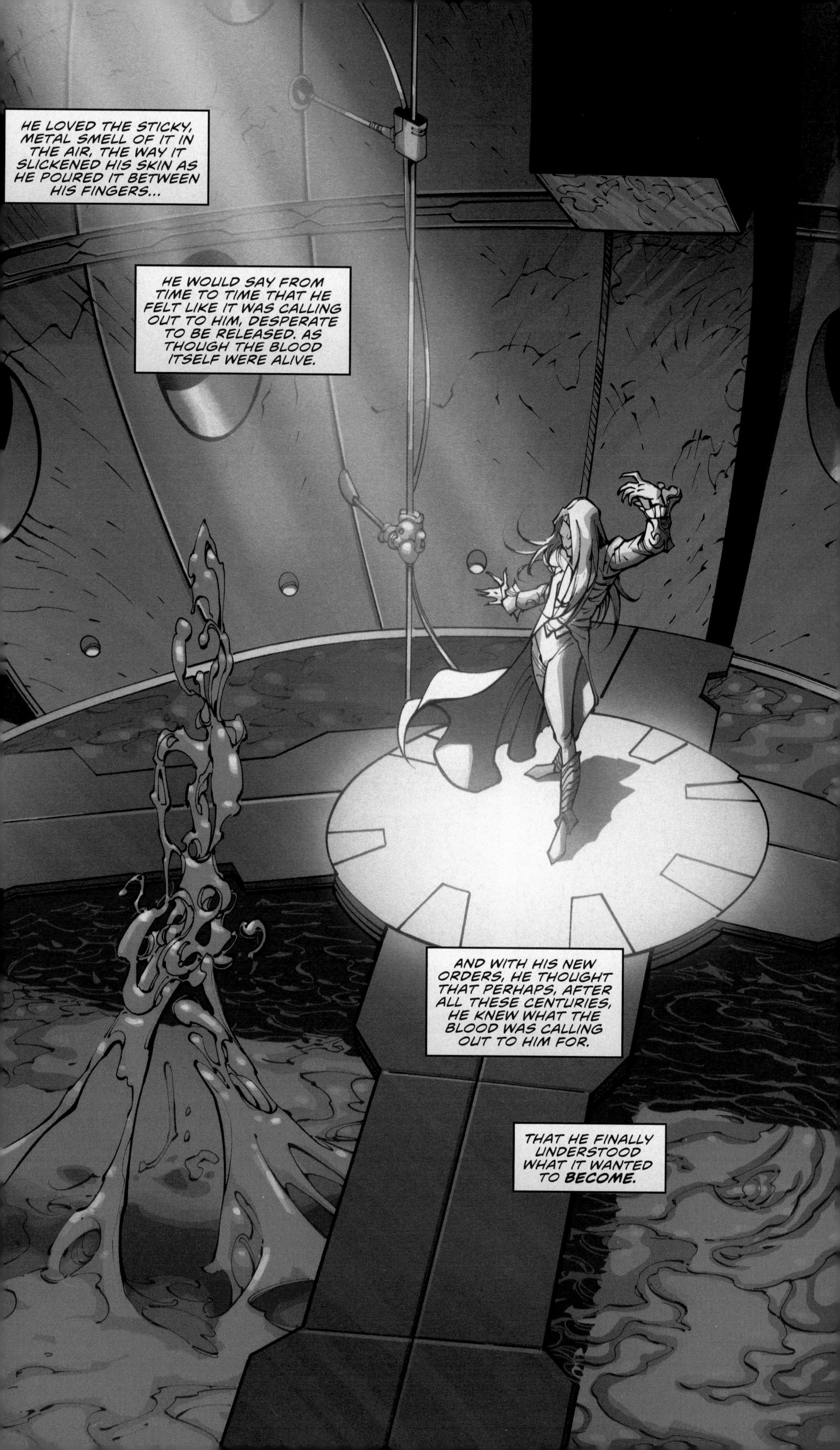
HE LOVED THE STICKY, METAL SMELL OF IT IN THE AIR, THE WAY IT SLICKENED HIS SKIN AS HE POURED IT BETWEEN HIS FINGERS...
HE WOULD SAY FROM TIME TO TIME THAT HE FELT LIKE IT WAS CALLING OUT TO HIM, DESPERATE TO BE RELEASED. AS THOUGH THE BLOOD ITSELF WERE ALIVE.
AND WITH HIS NEW ORDERS, HE THOUGHT THAT PERHAPS, AFTER ALL THESE CENTURIES, HE KNEW WHAT THE BLOOD WAS CALLING OUT TO HIM FOR.
THAT HE FINALLY UNDERSTOOD WHAT IT WANTED TO **BECOME.**

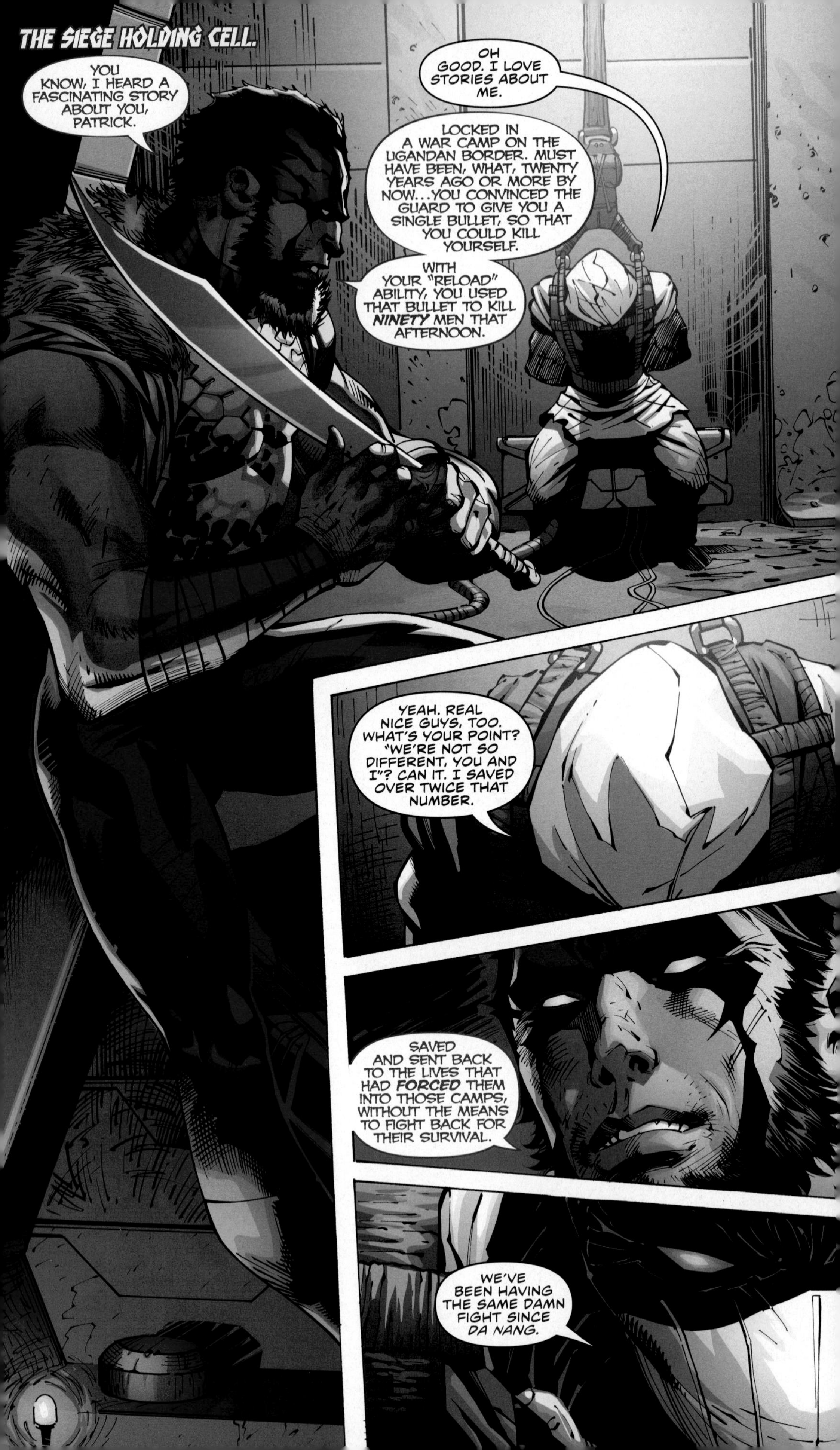
THE SIEGE HOLDING CELL.
YOU KNOW, I HEARD A FASCINATING STORY ABOUT YOU, PATRICK.
OH GOOD. I LOVE STORIES ABOUT ME.
LOCKED IN A WAR CAMP ON THE UGANDAN BORDER. MUST HAVE BEEN, WHAT, TWENTY YEARS AGO OR MORE BY NOW...YOU CONVINCED THE GUARD TO GIVE YOU A SINGLE BULLET, SO THAT YOU COULD KILL YOURSELF.
WITH YOUR "RELOAD" ABILITY, YOU USED THAT BULLET TO KILL NINETY MEN THAT AFTERNOON.
YEAH. REAL NICE GUYS, TOO. WHAT'S YOUR POINT? "WE'RE NOT SO DIFFERENT, YOU AND I"? CAN IT. I SAVED OVER TWICE THAT NUMBER.
SAVED AND SENT BACK TO THE LIVES THAT HAD FORCED THEM INTO THOSE CAMPS, WITHOUT THE MEANS TO FIGHT BACK FOR THEIR SURVIVAL.
WE'VE BEEN HAVING THE SAME DAMN FIGHT SINCE DA NANG.

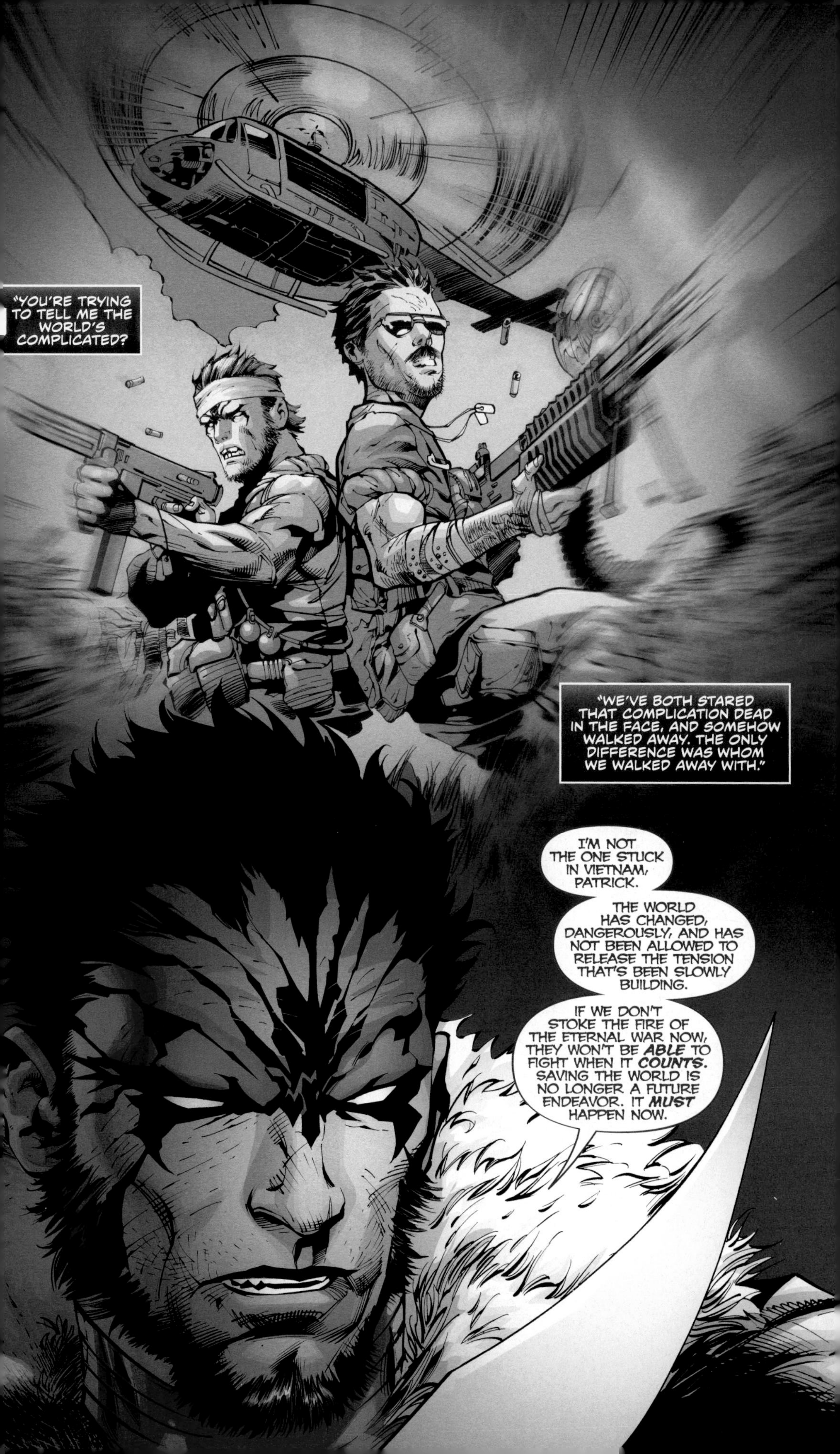
"YOU'RE TRYING TO TELL ME THE WORLD'S COMPLICATED?
"WE'VE BOTH STARED THAT COMPLICATION DEAD IN THE FACE, AND SOMEHOW WALKED AWAY. THE ONLY DIFFERENCE WAS WHOM WE WALKED AWAY WITH."
I'M NOT THE ONE STUCK IN VIETNAM, PATRICK.
THE WORLD HAS CHANGED, DANGEROUSLY, AND HAS NOT BEEN ALLOWED TO RELEASE THE TENSION THAT'S BEEN SLOWLY BUILDING.
IF WE DON'T STOKE THE FIRE OF THE ETERNAL WAR NOW, THEY WON'T BE *ABLE* TO FIGHT WHEN IT *COUNTS*. SAVING THE WORLD IS NO LONGER A FUTURE ENDEAVOR. IT *MUST* HAPPEN NOW.

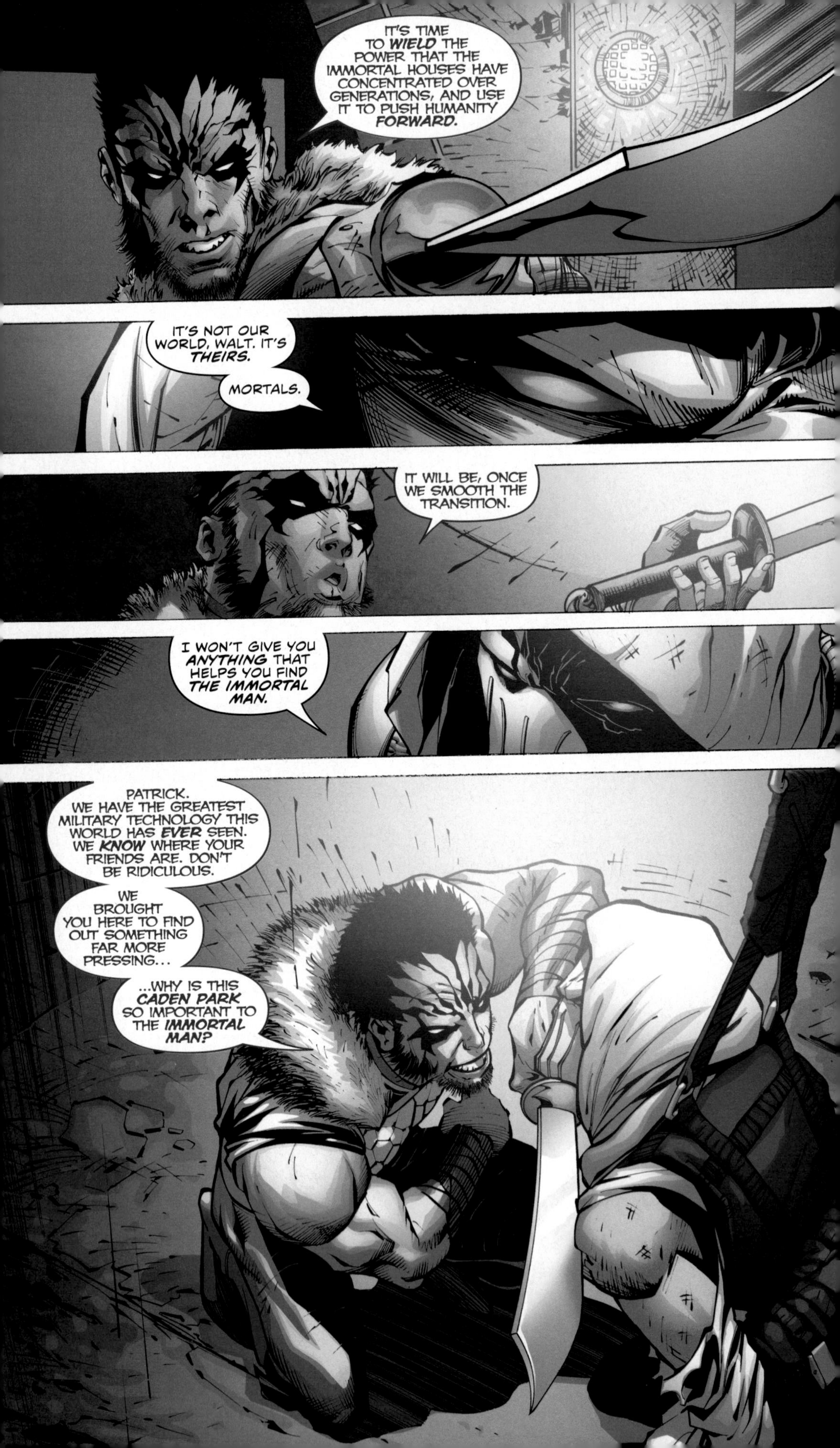
IT'S TIME TO WIELD THE POWER THAT THE IMMORTAL HOUSES HAVE CONCENTRATED OVER GENERATIONS, AND USE IT TO PUSH HUMANITY FORWARD.
IT'S NOT OUR WORLD, WALT. IT'S THEIRS.
MORTALS.
IT WILL BE, ONCE WE SMOOTH THE TRANSITION.
I WON'T GIVE YOU ANYTHING THAT HELPS YOU FIND THE IMMORTAL MAN.
PATRICK. WE HAVE THE GREATEST MILITARY TECHNOLOGY THIS WORLD HAS EVER SEEN. WE KNOW WHERE YOUR FRIENDS ARE. DON'T BE RIDICULOUS.
WE BROUGHT YOU HERE TO FIND OUT SOMETHING FAR MORE PRESSING...
...WHY IS THIS CADEN PARK SO IMPORTANT TO THE IMMORTAL MAN?

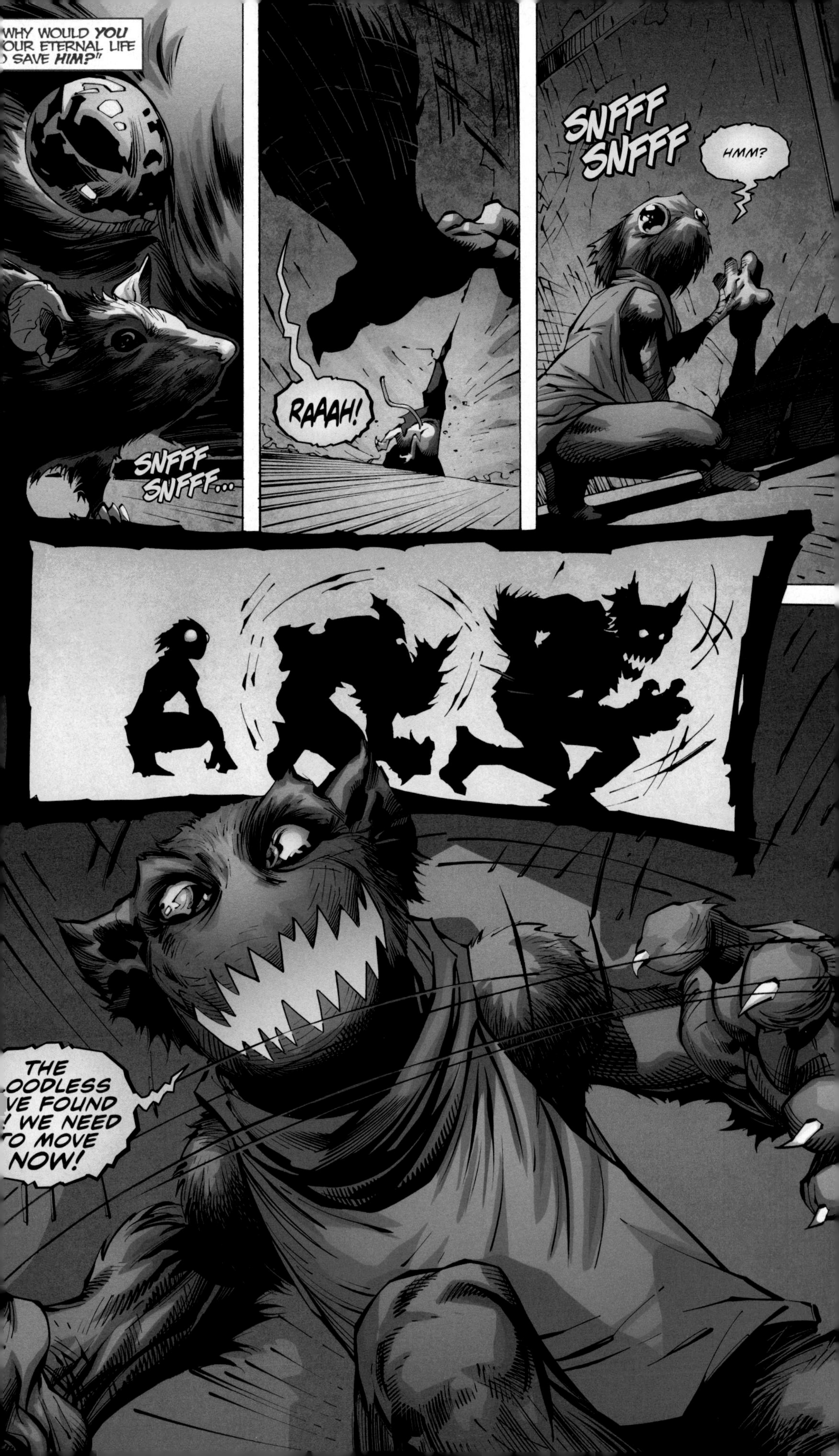
WHY WOULD YOU OUR ETERNAL LIFE SAVE HIM?"
SNFFF SNFFF...
RAAAH!
SNFFF SNFFF
HMM?
THE OODLESS VE FOUND WE NEED TO MOVE NOW!

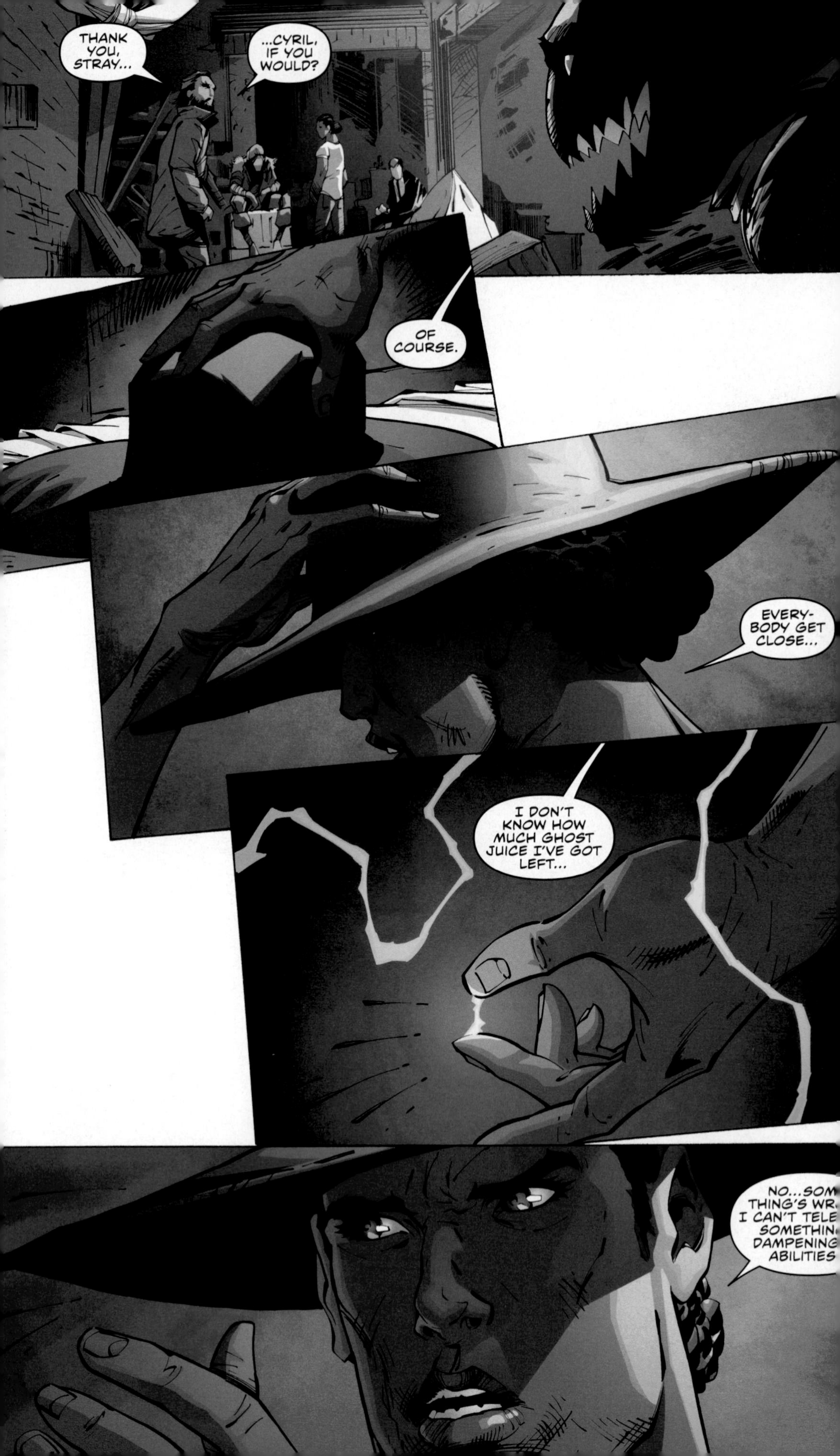
THANK YOU, STRAY...
...CYRIL, IF YOU WOULD?
OF COURSE.
EVERY-BODY GET CLOSE...
I DON'T KNOW HOW MUCH GHOST JUICE I'VE GOT LEFT...
NO...SOM THING'S WR I CAN'T TELE SOMETHIN DAMPENING ABILITIES

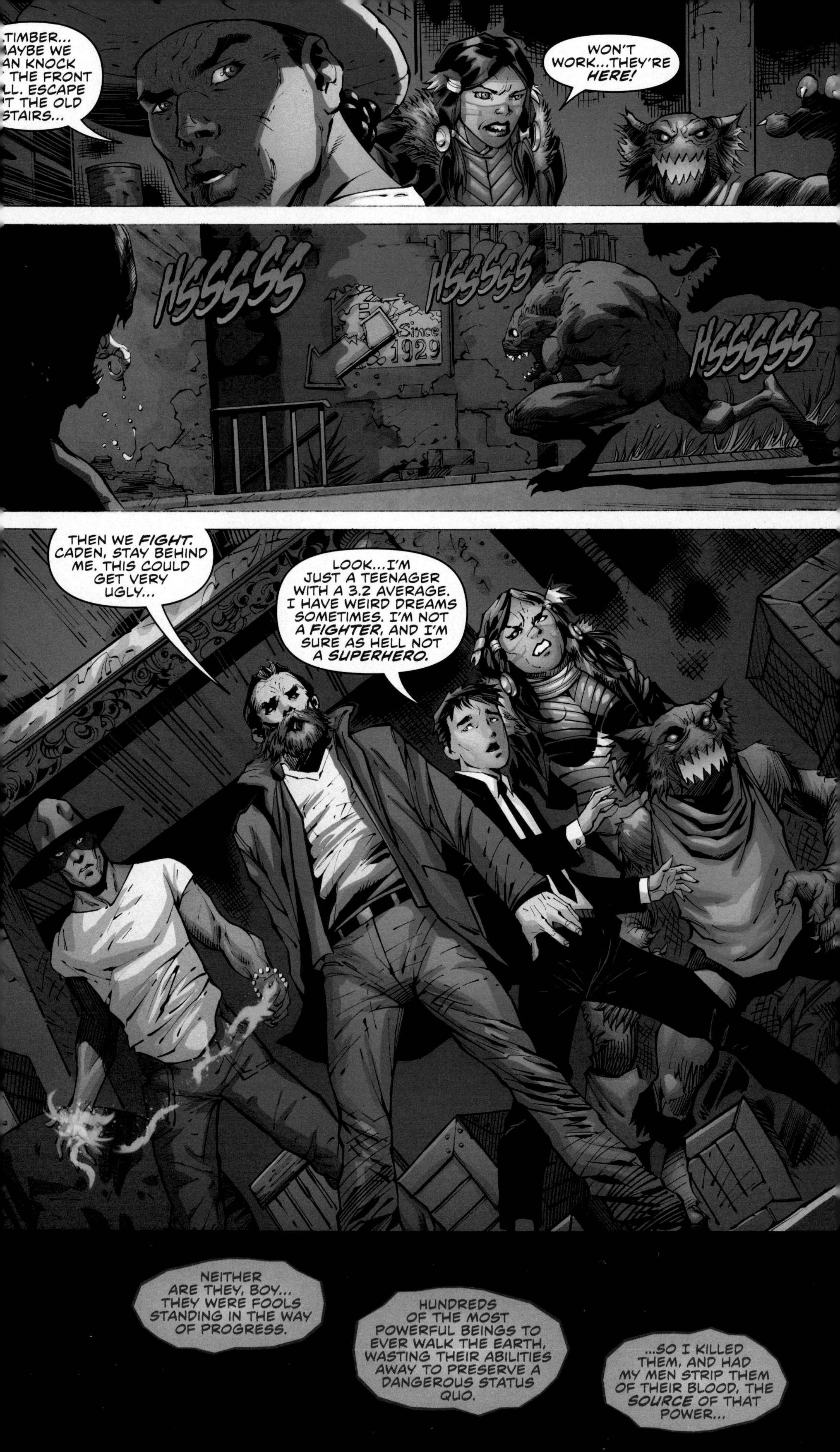

TIMBER... AYBE WE AN KNOCK THE FRONT LL. ESCAPE T THE OLD STAIRS...
WON'T WORK...THEY'RE *HERE!*
HSSSSS
HSSSSS
Since 1929
HSSSSS
THEN WE *FIGHT.* CADEN, STAY BEHIND ME. THIS COULD GET VERY UGLY...
LOOK...I'M JUST A TEENAGER WITH A 3.2 AVERAGE. I HAVE WEIRD DREAMS SOMETIMES. I'M NOT A *FIGHTER*, AND I'M SURE AS HELL NOT A *SUPERHERO.*
NEITHER ARE THEY, BOY... THEY WERE FOOLS STANDING IN THE WAY OF PROGRESS.
HUNDREDS OF THE MOST POWERFUL BEINGS TO EVER WALK THE EARTH, WASTING THEIR ABILITIES AWAY TO PRESERVE A DANGEROUS STATUS QUO.
...SO I KILLED THEM, AND HAD MY MEN STRIP THEM OF THEIR BLOOD, THE *SOURCE* OF THAT POWER...

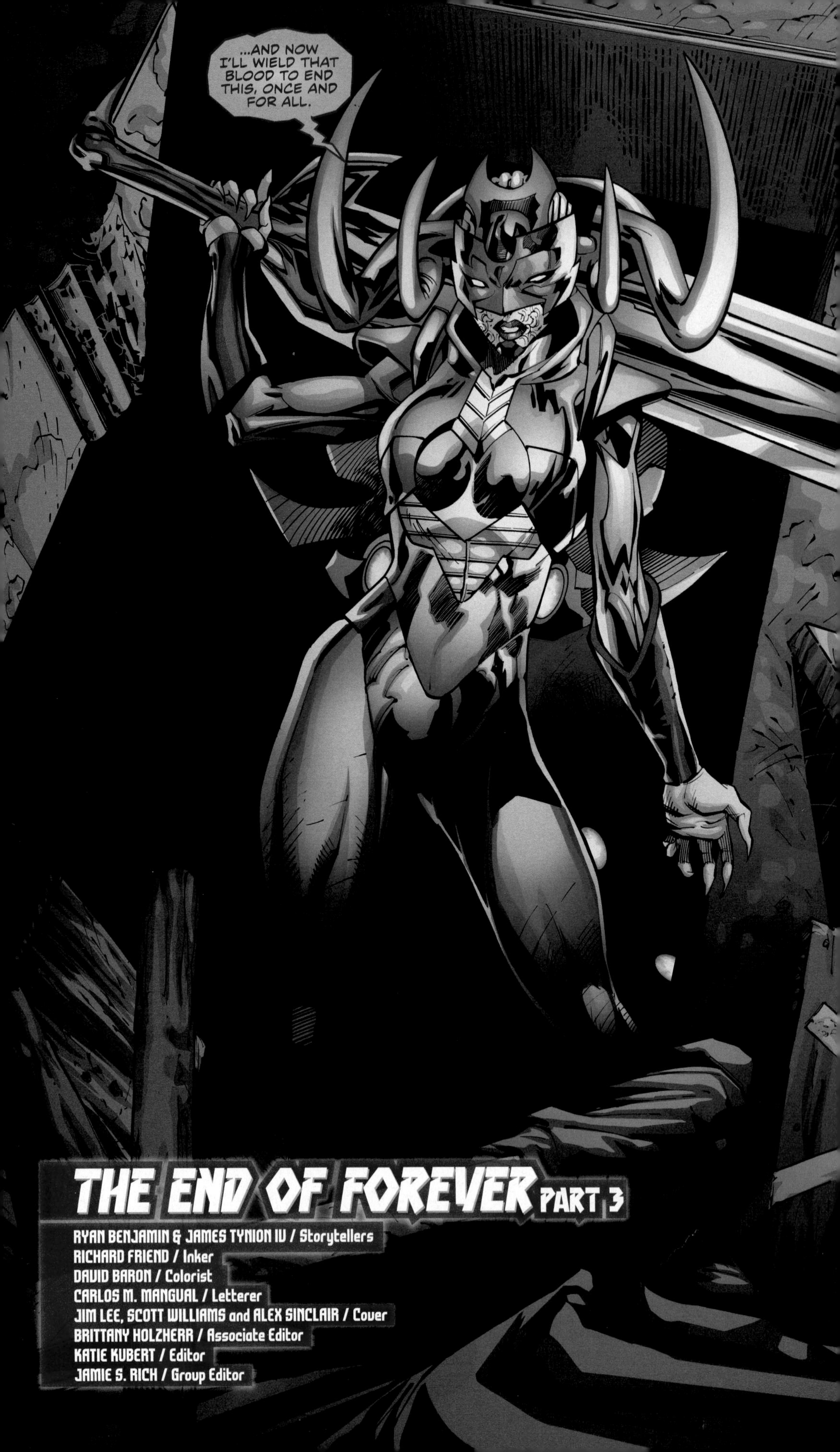
...AND NOW I'LL WIELD THAT BLOOD TO END THIS, ONCE AND FOR ALL.
THE END OF FOREVER PART 3
RYAN BENJAMIN & JAMES TYNION IV / Storytellers
RICHARD FRIEND / Inker
DAVID BARON / Colorist
CARLOS M. MANGUAL / Letterer
JIM LEE, SCOTT WILLIAMS and ALEX SINCLAIR / Cover
BRITTANY HOLZHERR / Associate Editor
KATIE KUBERT / Editor
JAMIE S. RICH / Group Editor

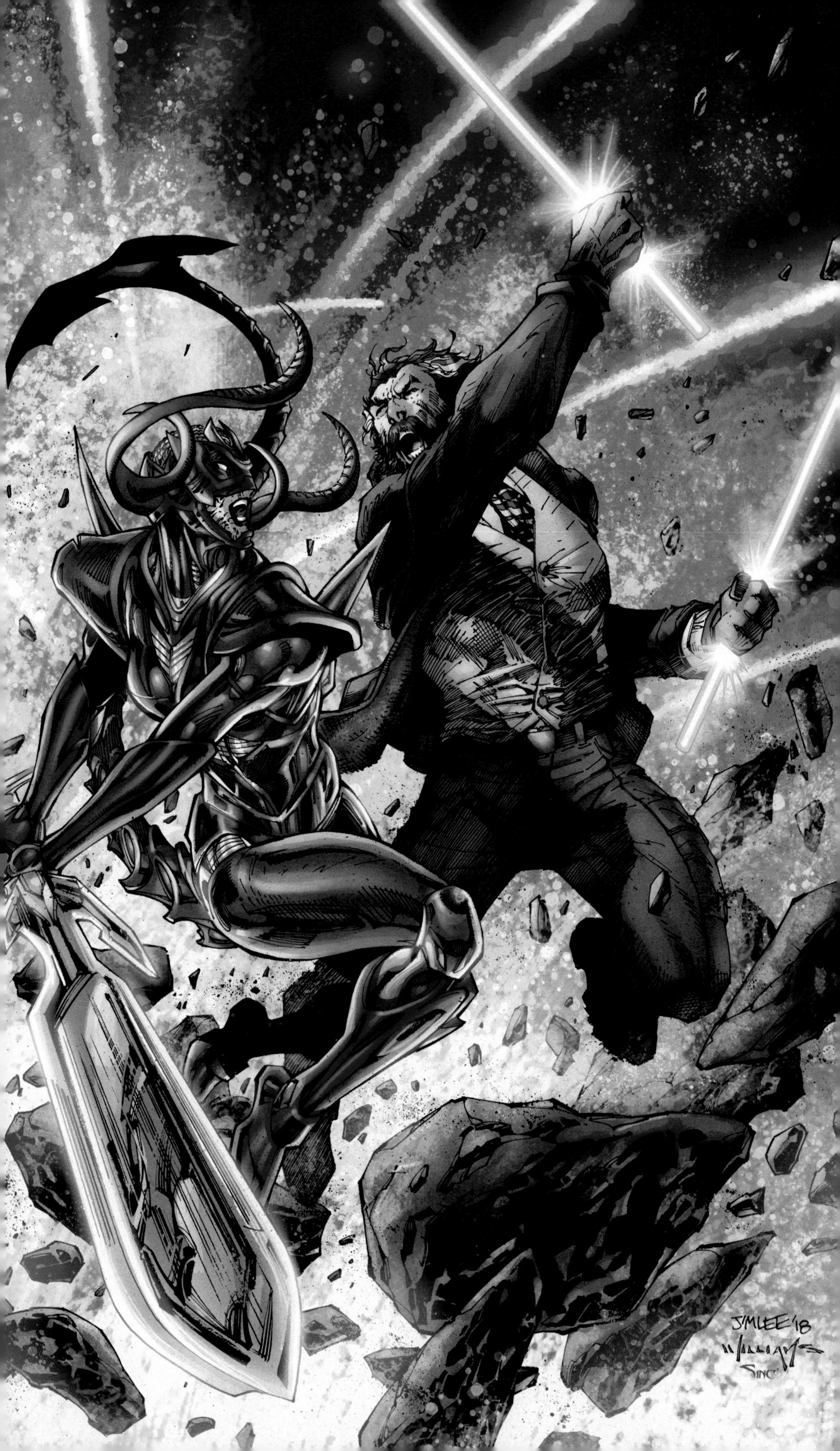
JIMLEE'18

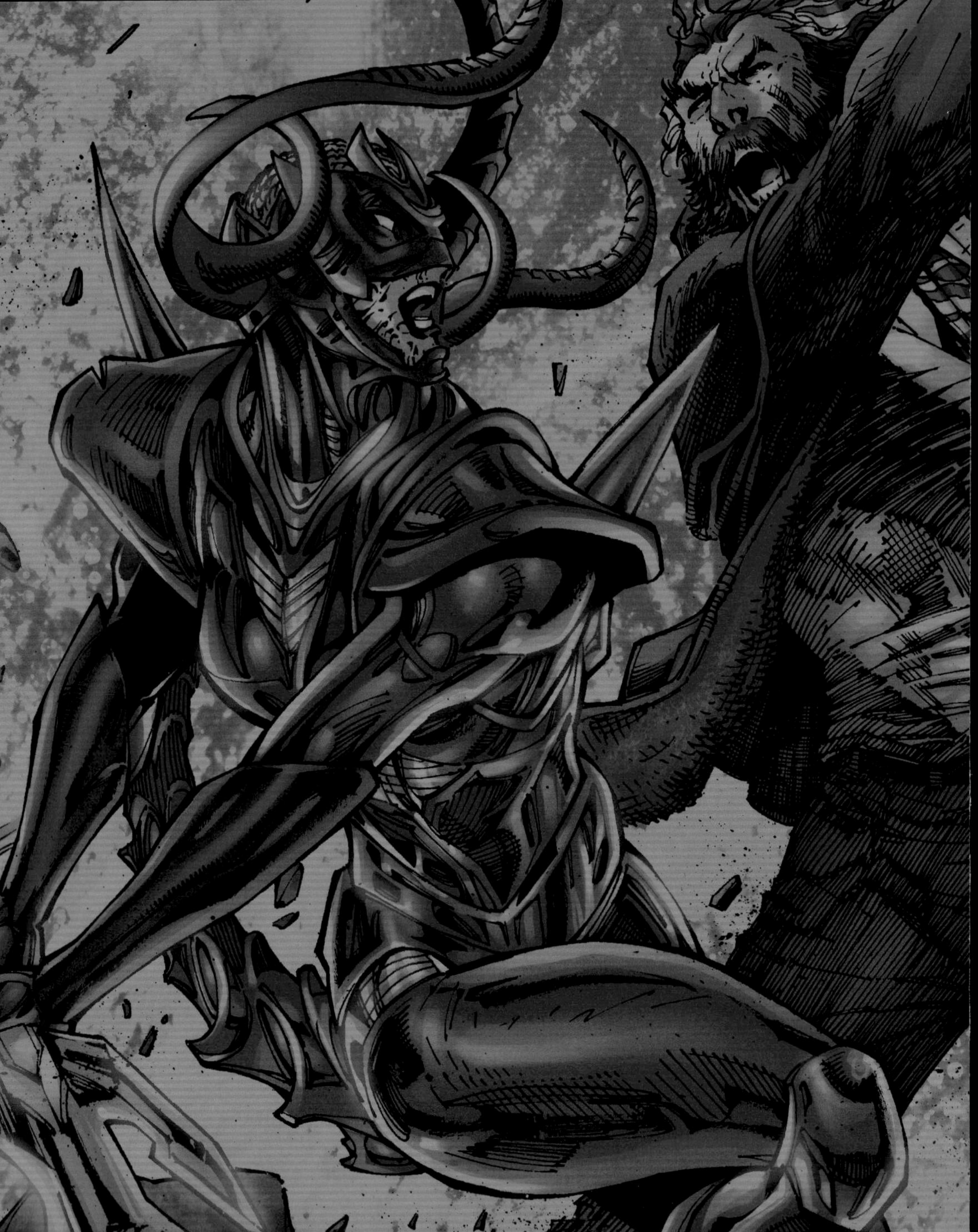

THE IMMORTAL MEN
#4

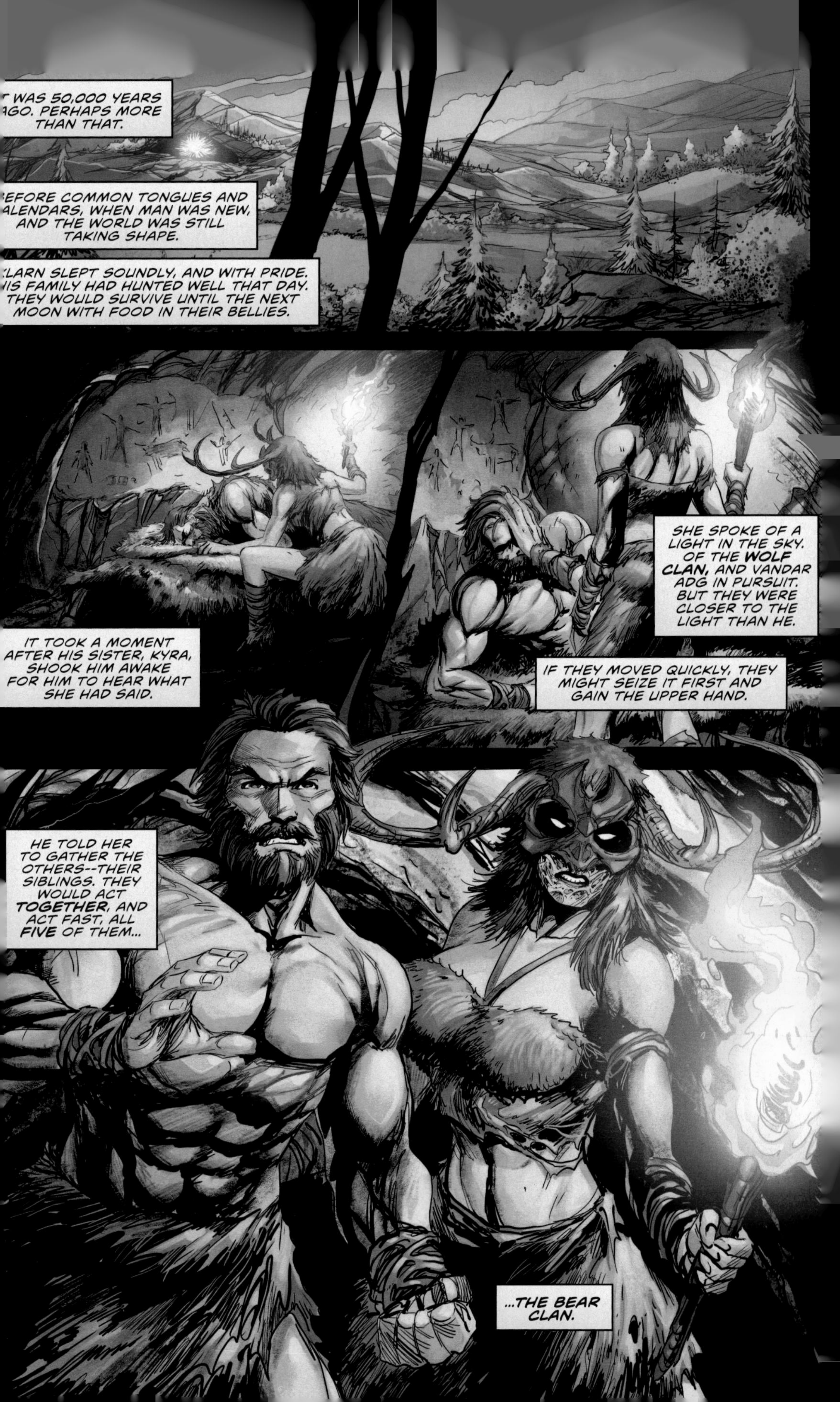

T WAS 50,000 YEARS AGO. PERHAPS MORE THAN THAT.
EFORE COMMON TONGUES AND ALENDARS, WHEN MAN WAS NEW, AND THE WORLD WAS STILL TAKING SHAPE.
LARN SLEPT SOUNDLY, AND WITH PRIDE. IS FAMILY HAD HUNTED WELL THAT DAY. THEY WOULD SURVIVE UNTIL THE NEXT MOON WITH FOOD IN THEIR BELLIES.
IT TOOK A MOMENT AFTER HIS SISTER, KYRA, SHOOK HIM AWAKE FOR HIM TO HEAR WHAT SHE HAD SAID.
SHE SPOKE OF A LIGHT IN THE SKY. OF THE WOLF CLAN, AND VANDAR ADG IN PURSUIT. BUT THEY WERE CLOSER TO THE LIGHT THAN HE.
IF THEY MOVED QUICKLY, THEY MIGHT SEIZE IT FIRST AND GAIN THE UPPER HAND.
HE TOLD HER TO GATHER THE OTHERS--THEIR SIBLINGS. THEY WOULD ACT TOGETHER, AND ACT FAST, ALL FIVE OF THEM...
...THE BEAR CLAN.

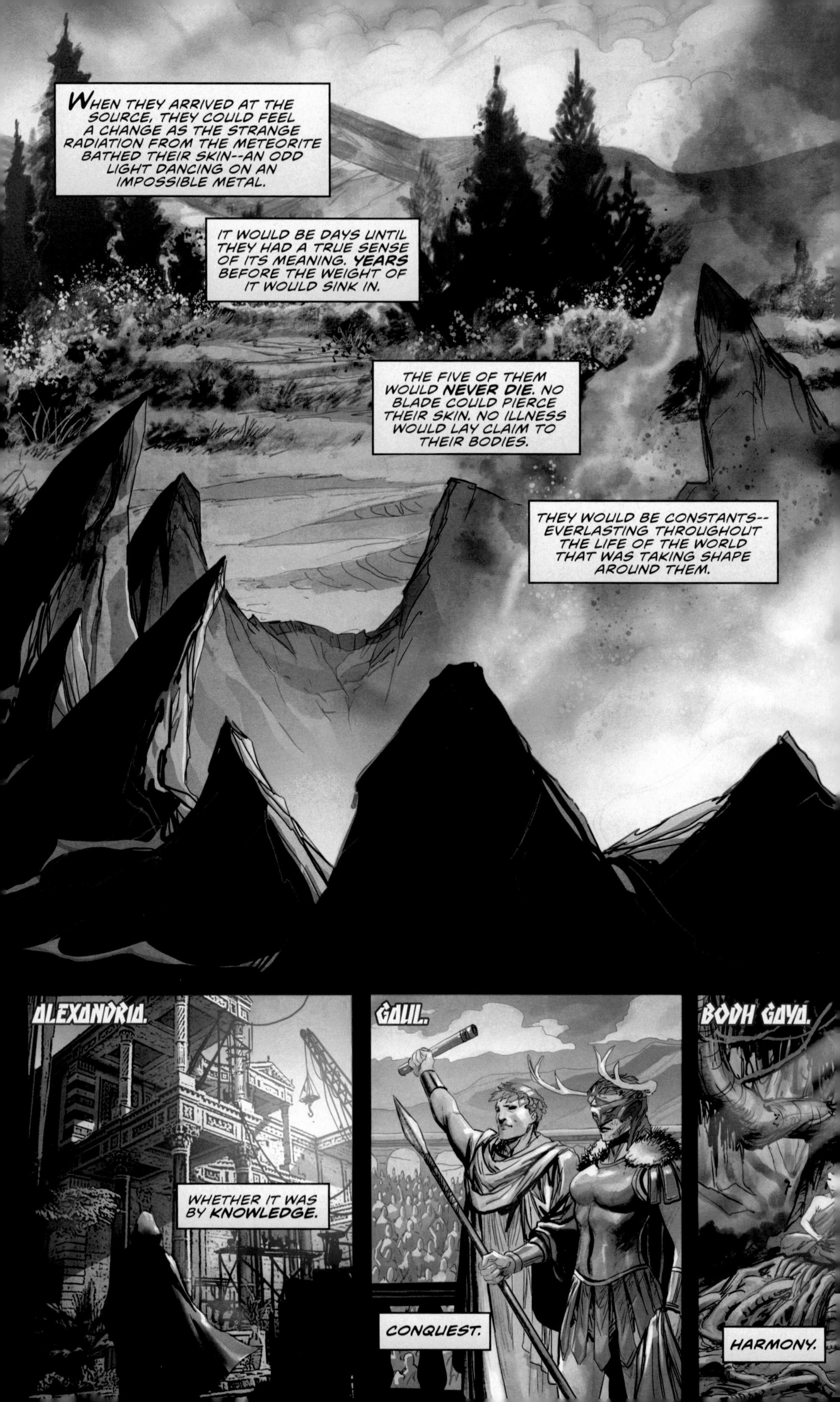
WHEN THEY ARRIVED AT THE SOURCE, THEY COULD FEEL A CHANGE AS THE STRANGE RADIATION FROM THE METEORITE BATHED THEIR SKIN--AN ODD LIGHT DANCING ON AN IMPOSSIBLE METAL.
IT WOULD BE DAYS UNTIL THEY HAD A TRUE SENSE OF ITS MEANING. YEARS BEFORE THE WEIGHT OF IT WOULD SINK IN.
THE FIVE OF THEM WOULD NEVER DIE. NO BLADE COULD PIERCE THEIR SKIN. NO ILLNESS WOULD LAY CLAIM TO THEIR BODIES.
THEY WOULD BE CONSTANTS-- EVERLASTING THROUGHOUT THE LIFE OF THE WORLD THAT WAS TAKING SHAPE AROUND THEM.
ALEXANDRIA.
WHETHER IT WAS BY KNOWLEDGE.
GAUL.
CONQUEST.
BODH GAYA.
HARMONY.

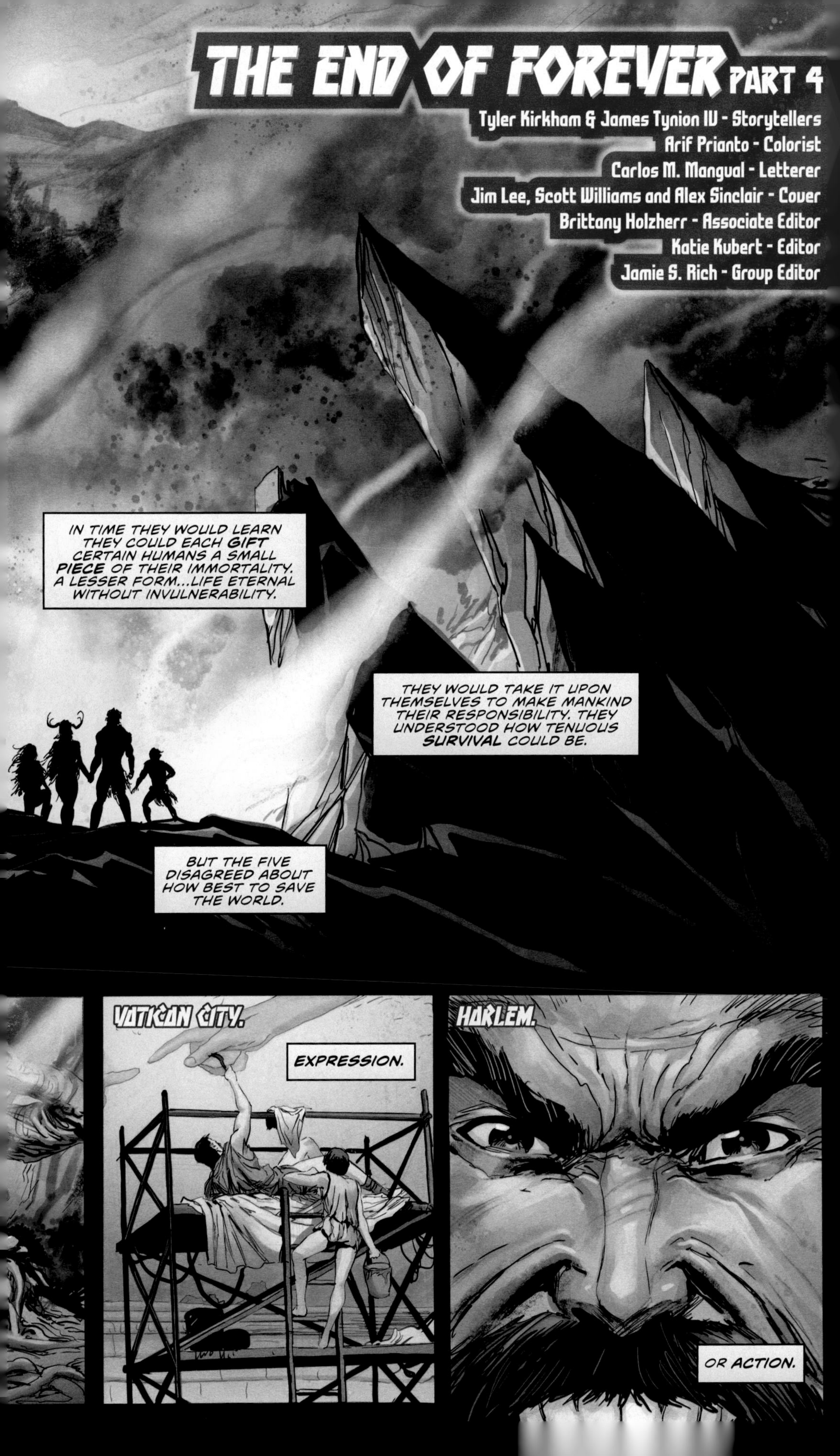
THE END OF FOREVER PART 4
Tyler Kirkham & James Tynion IV - Storytellers
Arif Prianto - Colorist
Carlos M. Mangual - Letterer
Jim Lee, Scott Williams and Alex Sinclair - Cover
Brittany Holzherr - Associate Editor
Katie Kubert - Editor
Jamie S. Rich - Group Editor
IN TIME THEY WOULD LEARN THEY COULD EACH GIFT CERTAIN HUMANS A SMALL PIECE OF THEIR IMMORTALITY. A LESSER FORM...LIFE ETERNAL WITHOUT INVULNERABILITY.
THEY WOULD TAKE IT UPON THEMSELVES TO MAKE MANKIND THEIR RESPONSIBILITY. THEY UNDERSTOOD HOW TENUOUS SURVIVAL COULD BE.
BUT THE FIVE DISAGREED ABOUT HOW BEST TO SAVE THE WORLD.
VATICAN CITY.
EXPRESSION.
HARLEM.
OR ACTION.

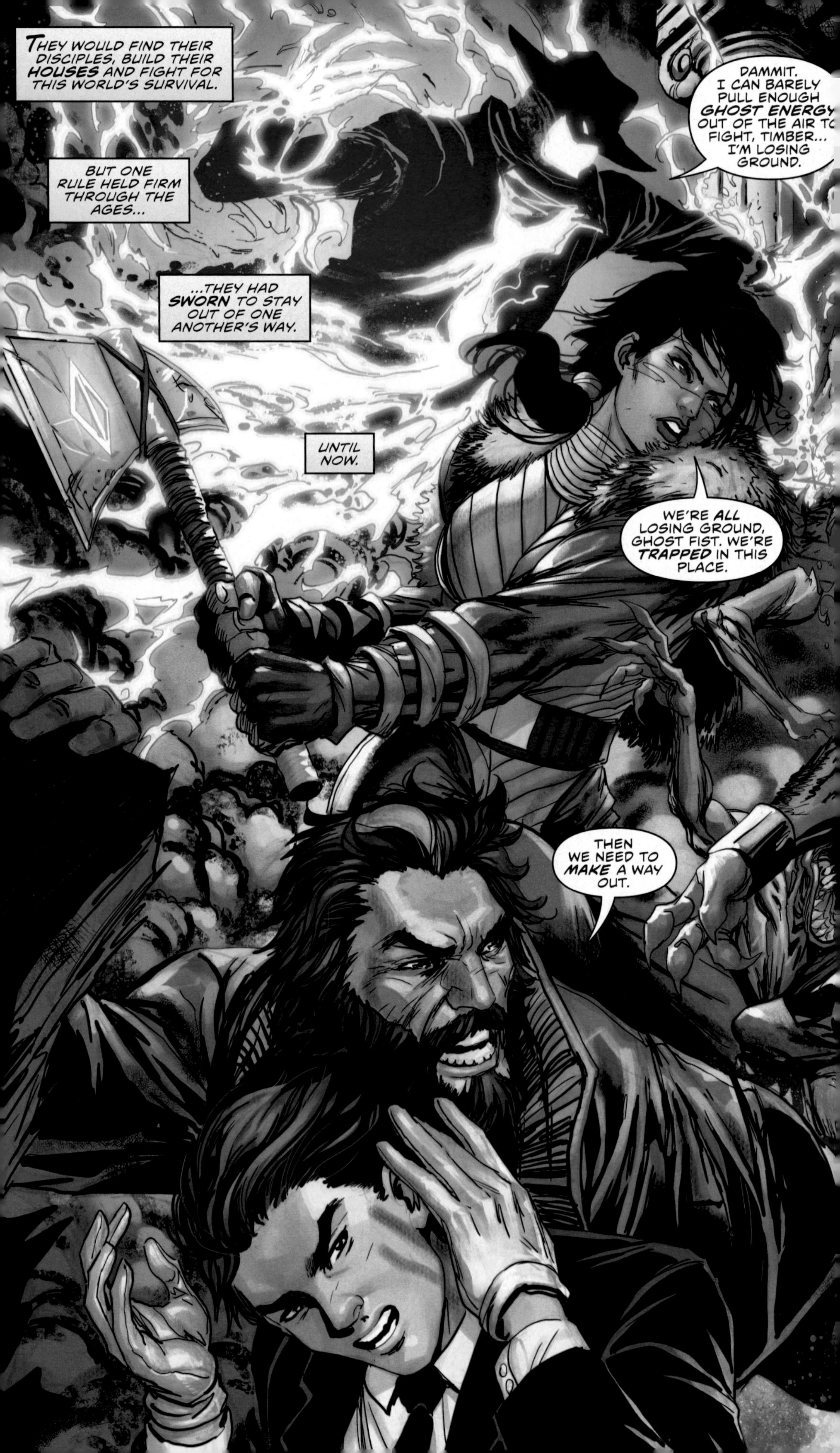
THEY WOULD FIND THEIR DISCIPLES, BUILD THEIR HOUSES AND FIGHT FOR THIS WORLD'S SURVIVAL.
BUT ONE RULE HELD FIRM THROUGH THE AGES...
...THEY HAD SWORN TO STAY OUT OF ONE ANOTHER'S WAY.
UNTIL NOW.
DAMMIT. I CAN BARELY PULL ENOUGH GHOST ENERGY OUT OF THE AIR TO FIGHT, TIMBER... I'M LOSING GROUND.
WE'RE ALL LOSING GROUND, GHOST FIST. WE'RE TRAPPED IN THIS PLACE.
THEN WE NEED TO MAKE A WAY OUT.

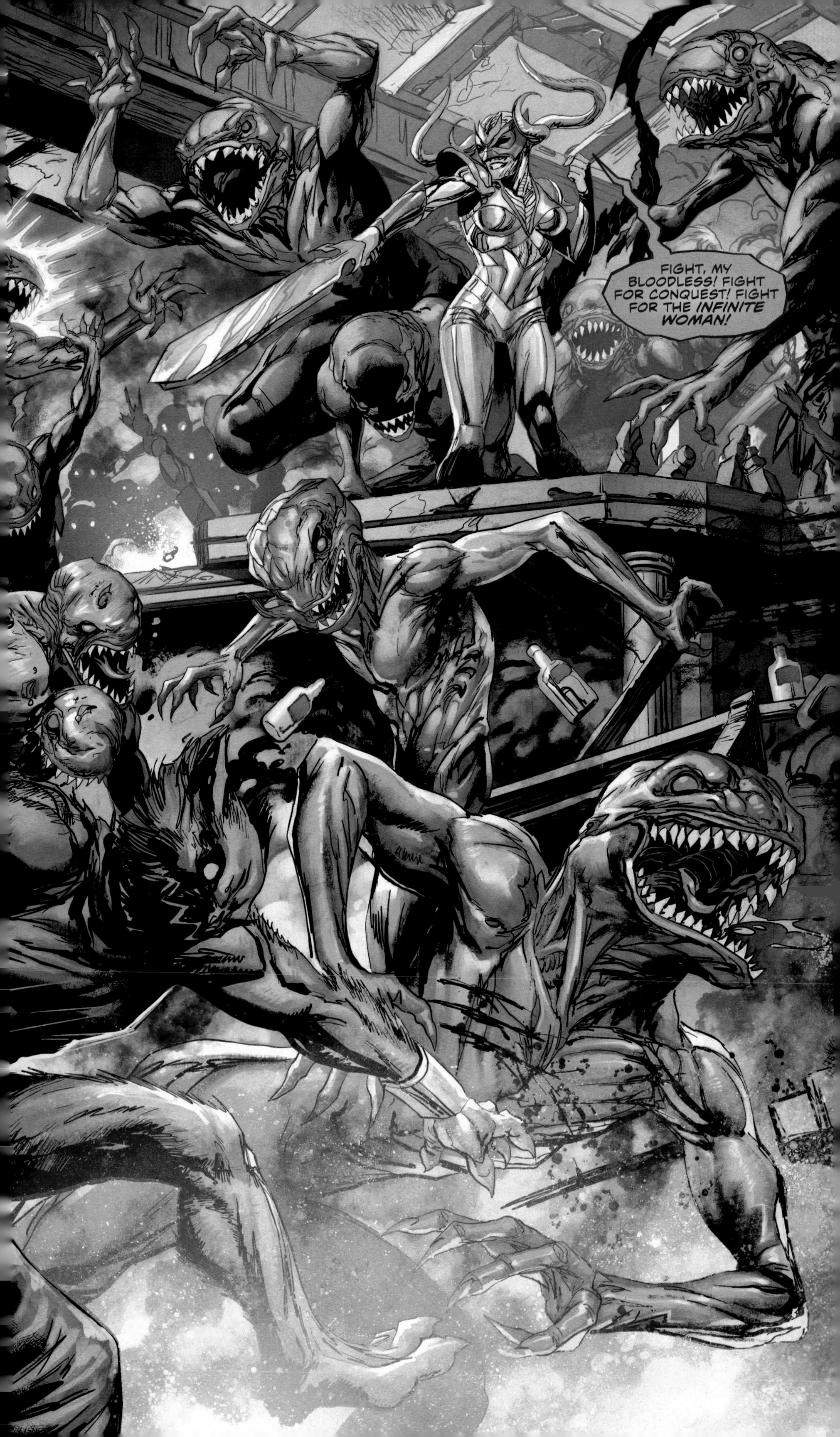
FIGHT, MY BLOODLESS! FIGHT FOR CONQUEST! FIGHT FOR THE *INFINITE WOMAN!*

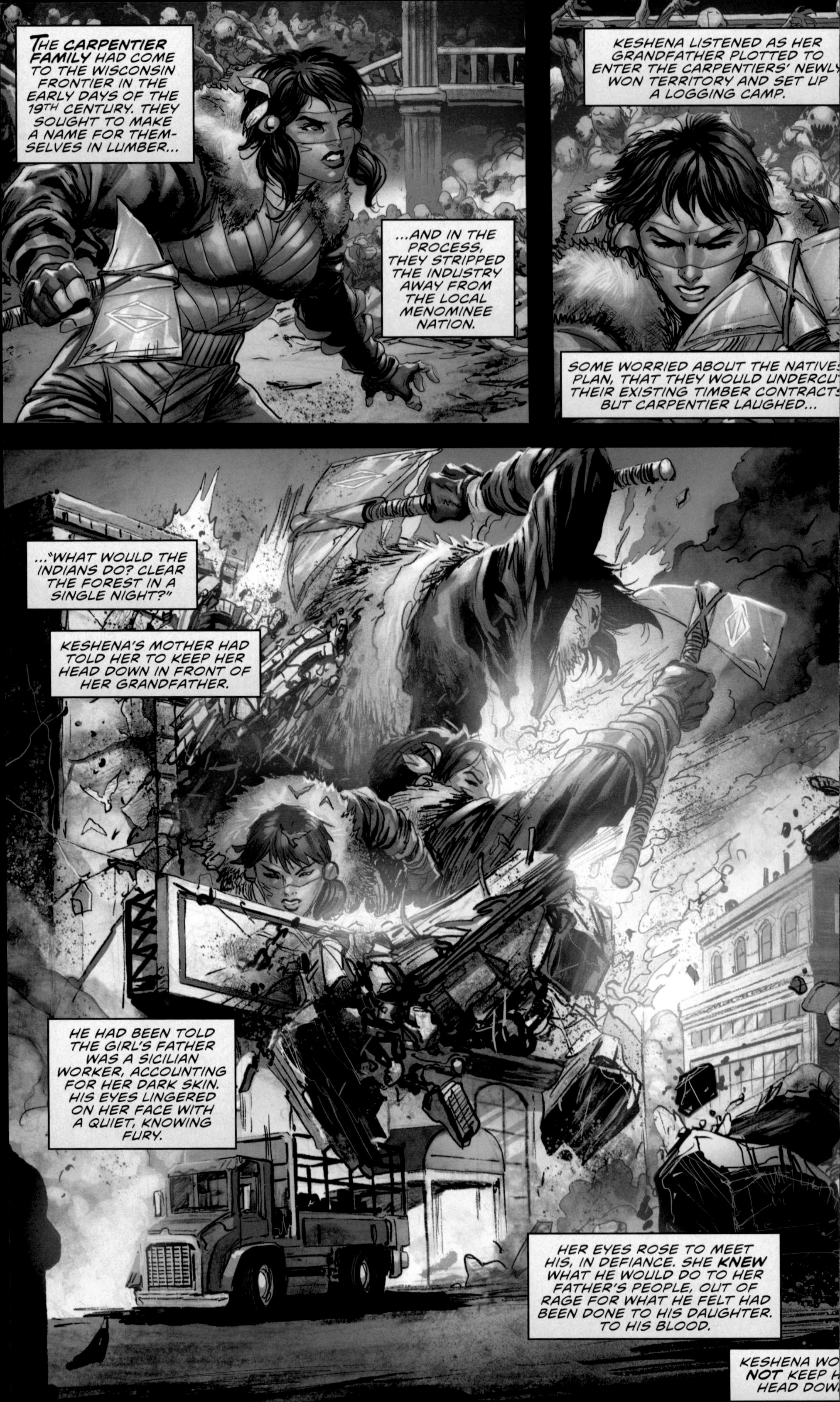
THE CARPENTIER FAMILY HAD COME TO THE WISCONSIN FRONTIER IN THE EARLY DAYS OF THE 19TH CENTURY. THEY SOUGHT TO MAKE A NAME FOR THEMSELVES IN LUMBER...
...AND IN THE PROCESS, THEY STRIPPED THE INDUSTRY AWAY FROM THE LOCAL MENOMINEE NATION.
KESHENA LISTENED AS HER GRANDFATHER PLOTTED TO ENTER THE CARPENTIERS' NEWLY WON TERRITORY AND SET UP A LOGGING CAMP.
SOME WORRIED ABOUT THE NATIVES' PLAN, THAT THEY WOULD UNDERCUT THEIR EXISTING TIMBER CONTRACTS, BUT CARPENTIER LAUGHED...
..."WHAT WOULD THE INDIANS DO? CLEAR THE FOREST IN A SINGLE NIGHT?"
KESHENA'S MOTHER HAD TOLD HER TO KEEP HER HEAD DOWN IN FRONT OF HER GRANDFATHER.
HE HAD BEEN TOLD THE GIRL'S FATHER WAS A SICILIAN WORKER, ACCOUNTING FOR HER DARK SKIN. HIS EYES LINGERED ON HER FACE WITH A QUIET, KNOWING FURY.
HER EYES ROSE TO MEET HIS, IN DEFIANCE. SHE KNEW WHAT HE WOULD DO TO HER FATHER'S PEOPLE, OUT OF RAGE FOR WHAT HE FELT HAD BEEN DONE TO HIS DAUGHTER. TO HIS BLOOD.
KESHENA WO NOT KEEP H HEAD DOW

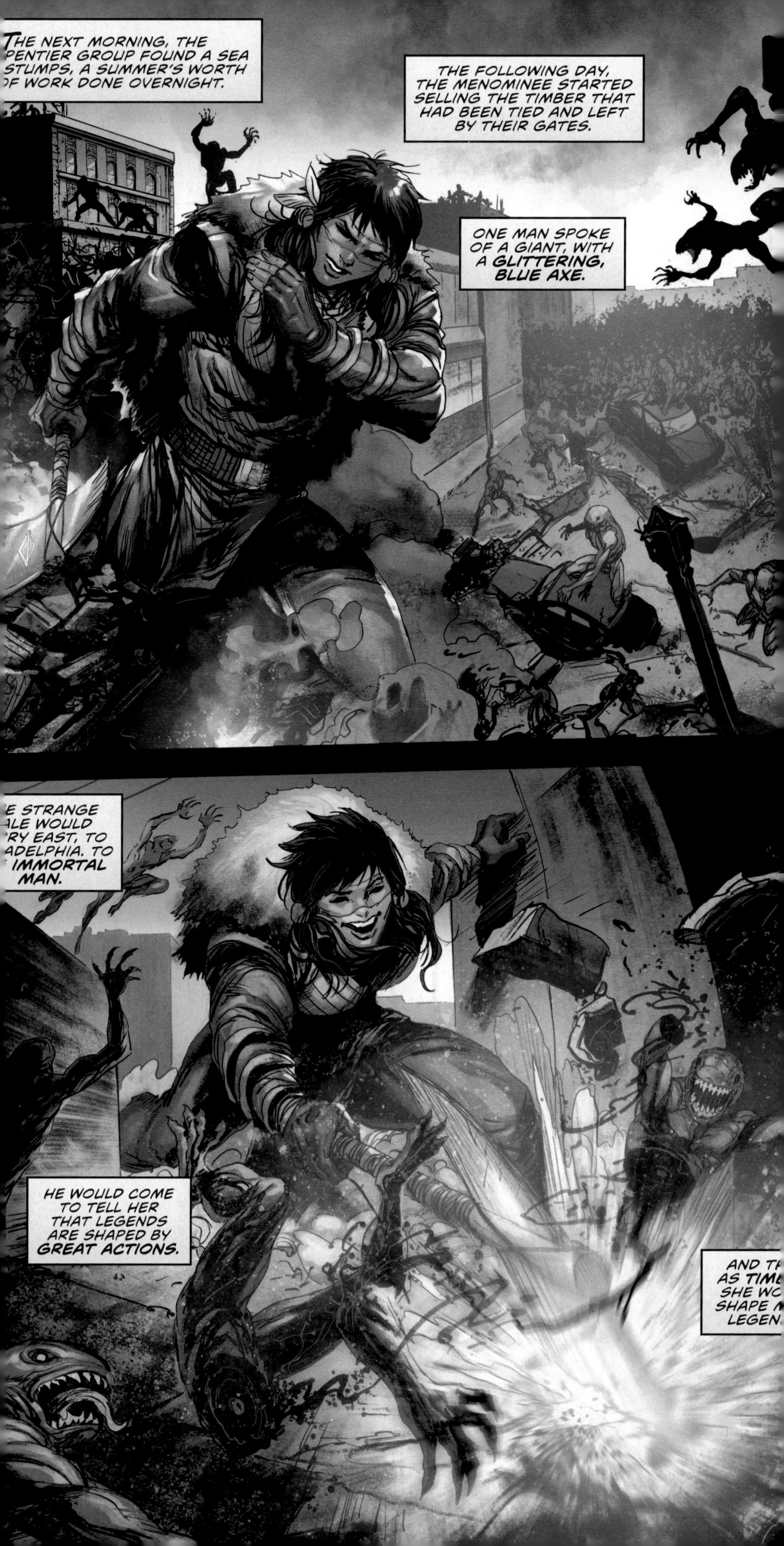

THE NEXT MORNING, THE PENTIER GROUP FOUND A SEA STUMPS, A SUMMER'S WORTH OF WORK DONE OVERNIGHT.
THE FOLLOWING DAY, THE MENOMINEE STARTED SELLING THE TIMBER THAT HAD BEEN TIED AND LEFT BY THEIR GATES.
ONE MAN SPOKE OF A GIANT, WITH A GLITTERING, BLUE AXE.
E STRANGE ALE WOULD RY EAST, TO ADELPHIA. TO IMMORTAL MAN.
HE WOULD COME TO TELL HER THAT LEGENDS ARE SHAPED BY GREAT ACTIONS.
AND TH AS TIME SHE WO SHAPE M LEGEN

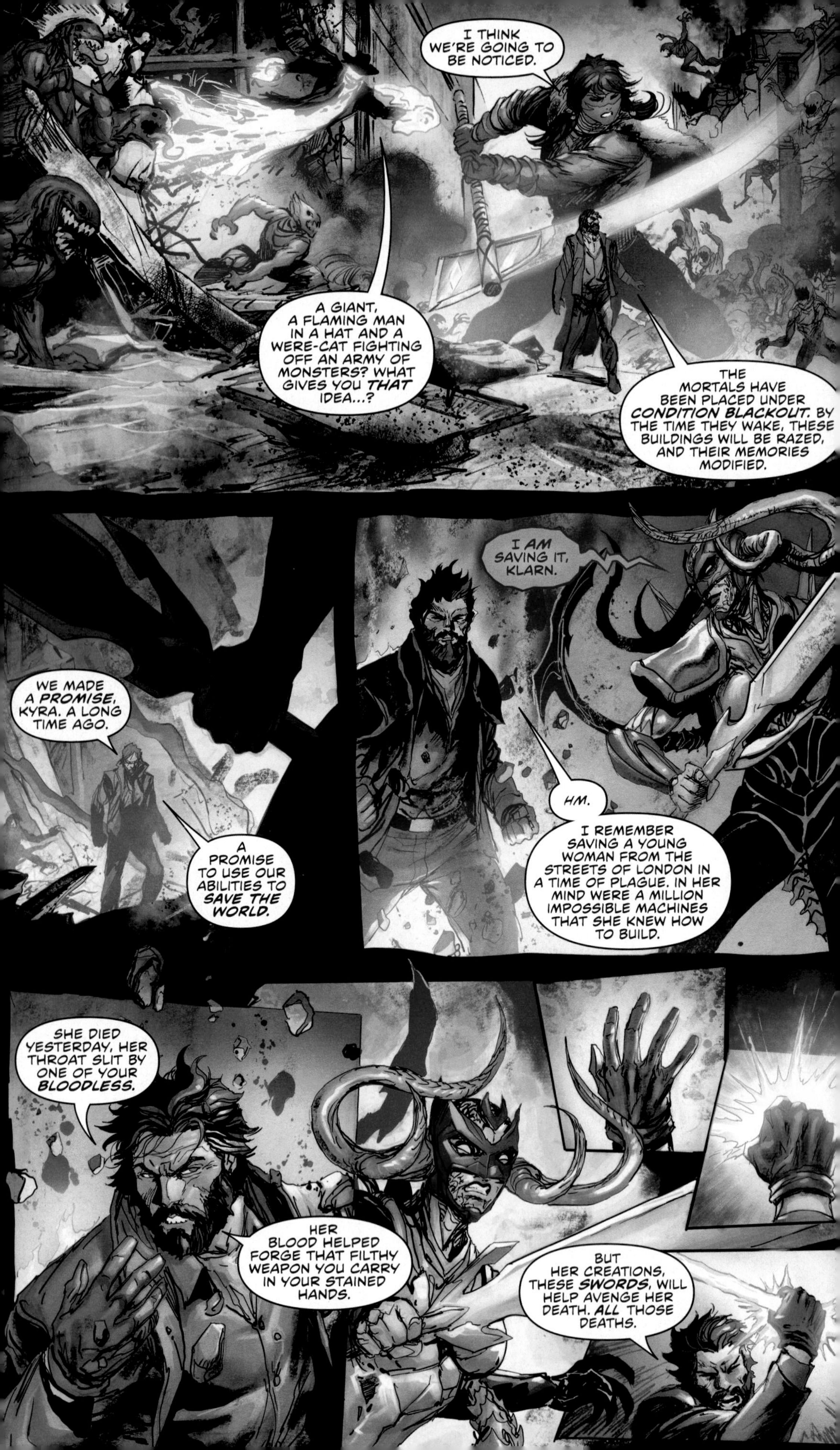
I THINK WE'RE GOING TO BE NOTICED.
A GIANT, A FLAMING MAN IN A HAT AND A WERE-CAT FIGHTING OFF AN ARMY OF MONSTERS? WHAT GIVES YOU THAT IDEA...?
THE MORTALS HAVE BEEN PLACED UNDER CONDITION BLACKOUT. BY THE TIME THEY WAKE, THESE BUILDINGS WILL BE RAZED, AND THEIR MEMORIES MODIFIED.
WE MADE A PROMISE, KYRA. A LONG TIME AGO.
A PROMISE TO USE OUR ABILITIES TO SAVE THE WORLD.
I AM SAVING IT, KLARN.
HM.
I REMEMBER SAVING A YOUNG WOMAN FROM THE STREETS OF LONDON IN A TIME OF PLAGUE. IN HER MIND WERE A MILLION IMPOSSIBLE MACHINES THAT SHE KNEW HOW TO BUILD.
SHE DIED YESTERDAY, HER THROAT SLIT BY ONE OF YOUR BLOODLESS.
HER BLOOD HELPED FORGE THAT FILTHY WEAPON YOU CARRY IN YOUR STAINED HANDS.
BUT HER CREATIONS, THESE SWORDS, WILL HELP AVENGE HER DEATH. ALL THOSE DEATHS.

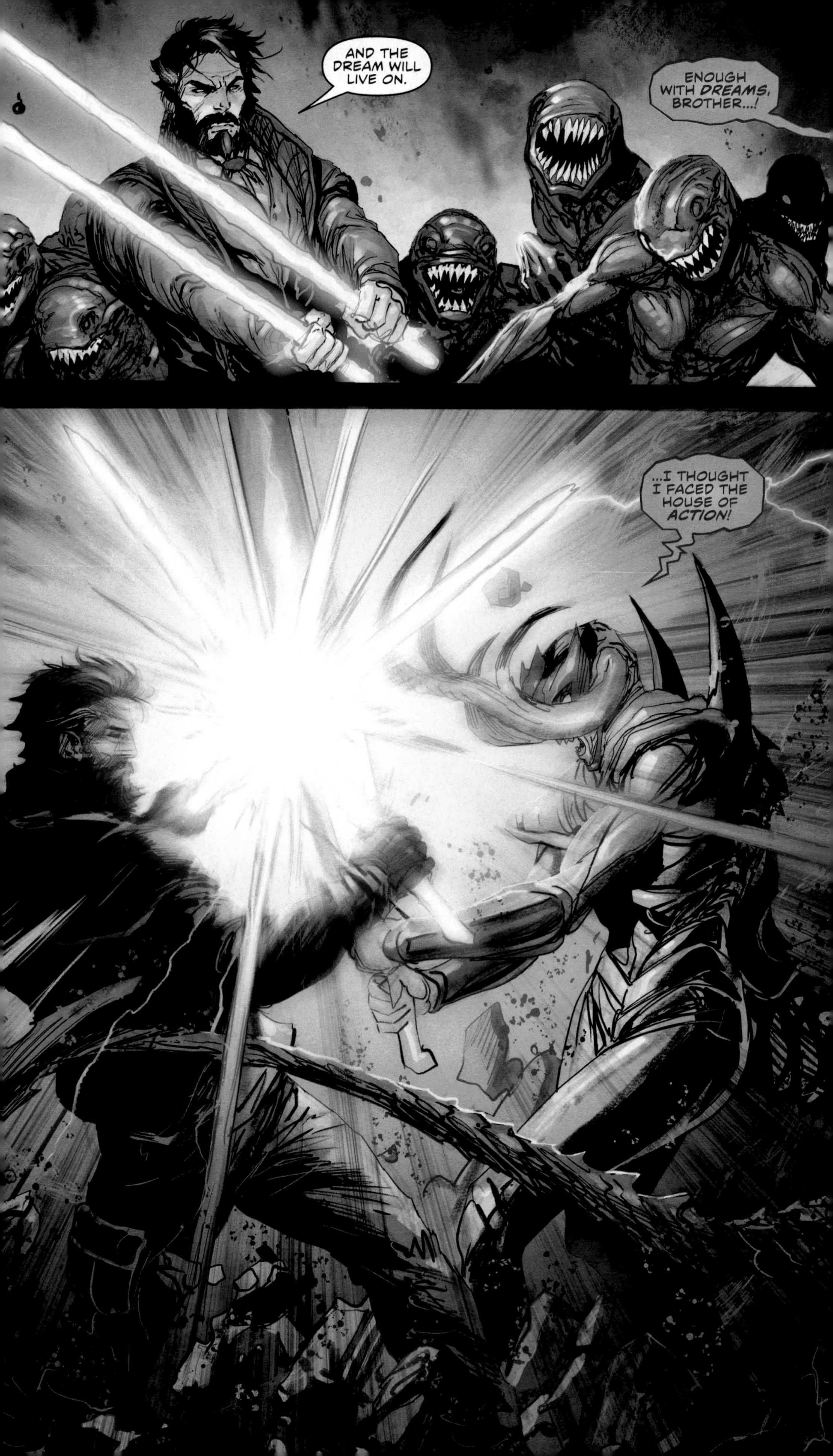
AND THE DREAM WILL LIVE ON.
ENOUGH WITH DREAMS, BROTHER...!
...I THOUGHT I FACED THE HOUSE OF ACTION!

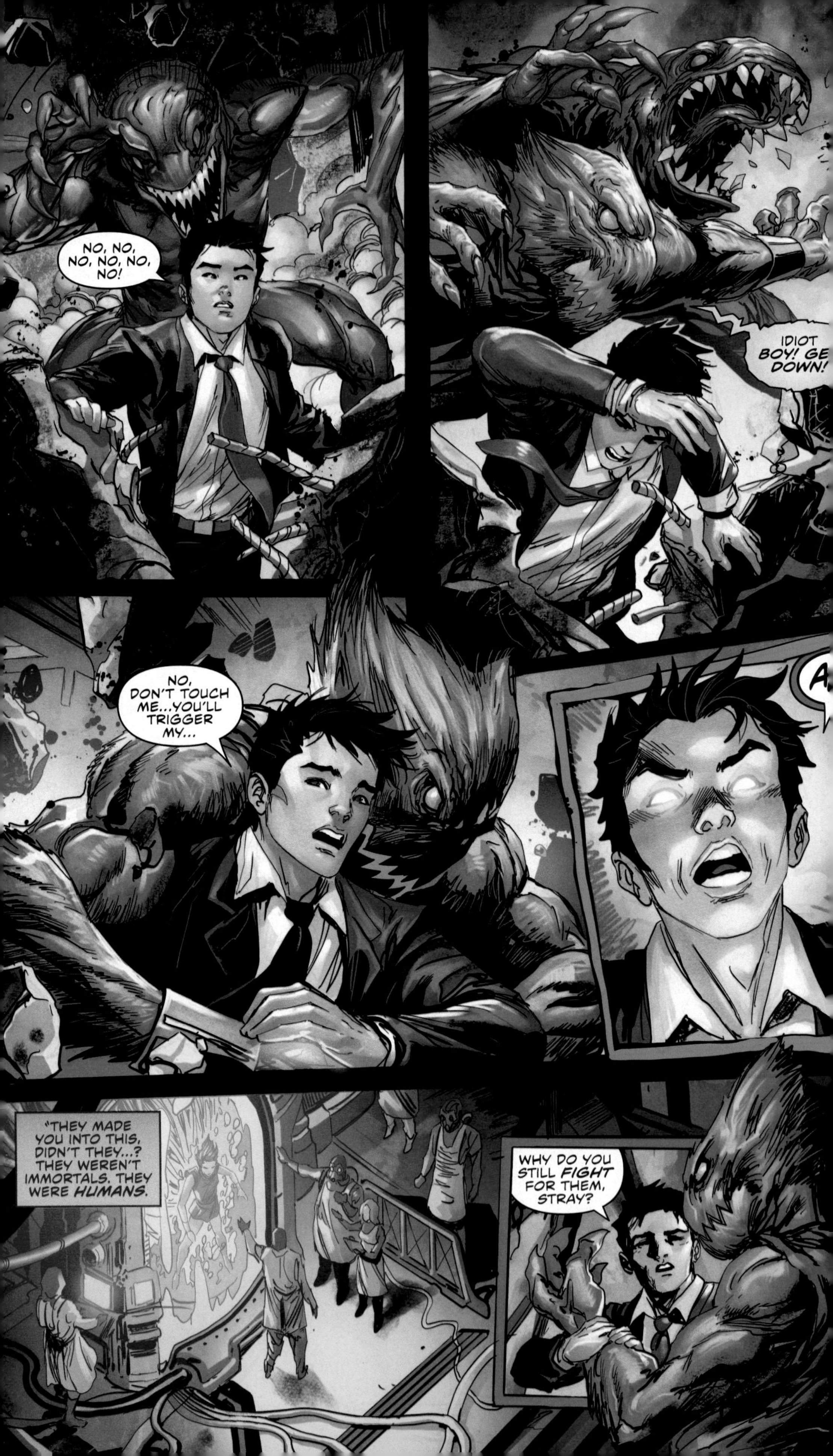
NO, NO, NO, NO, NO, NO!
IDIOT BOY! GE DOWN!
NO, DON'T TOUCH ME...YOU'LL TRIGGER MY...
A
"THEY MADE YOU INTO THIS, DIDN'T THEY...? THEY WEREN'T IMMORTALS. THEY WERE *HUMANS*.
WHY DO YOU STILL *FIGHT* FOR THEM, STRAY?

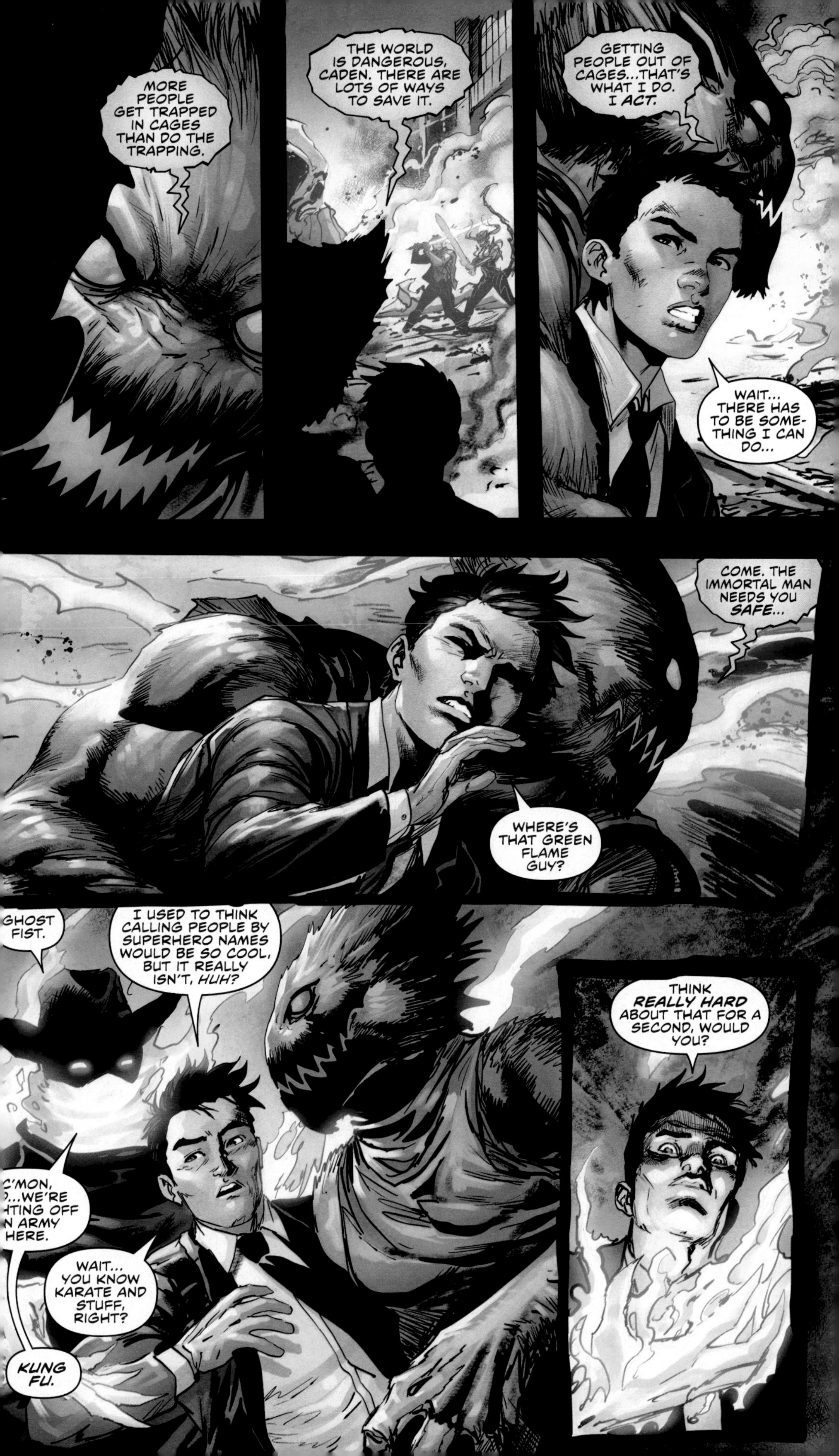
MORE PEOPLE GET TRAPPED IN CAGES THAN DO THE TRAPPING.
THE WORLD IS DANGEROUS, CADEN. THERE ARE LOTS OF WAYS TO SAVE IT.
GETTING PEOPLE OUT OF CAGES...THAT'S WHAT I DO. I *ACT.*
WAIT... THERE HAS TO BE SOME-THING I CAN DO...
COME. THE IMMORTAL MAN NEEDS YOU *SAFE...*
WHERE'S THAT GREEN FLAME GUY?
GHOST FIST.
I USED TO THINK CALLING PEOPLE BY SUPERHERO NAMES WOULD BE SO COOL, BUT IT REALLY ISN'T, *HUH?*
C'MON, ...WE'RE HTING OFF N ARMY HERE.
WAIT... YOU KNOW KARATE AND STUFF, RIGHT?
KUNG FU.
THINK *REALLY HARD* ABOUT THAT FOR A SECOND, WOULD YOU?

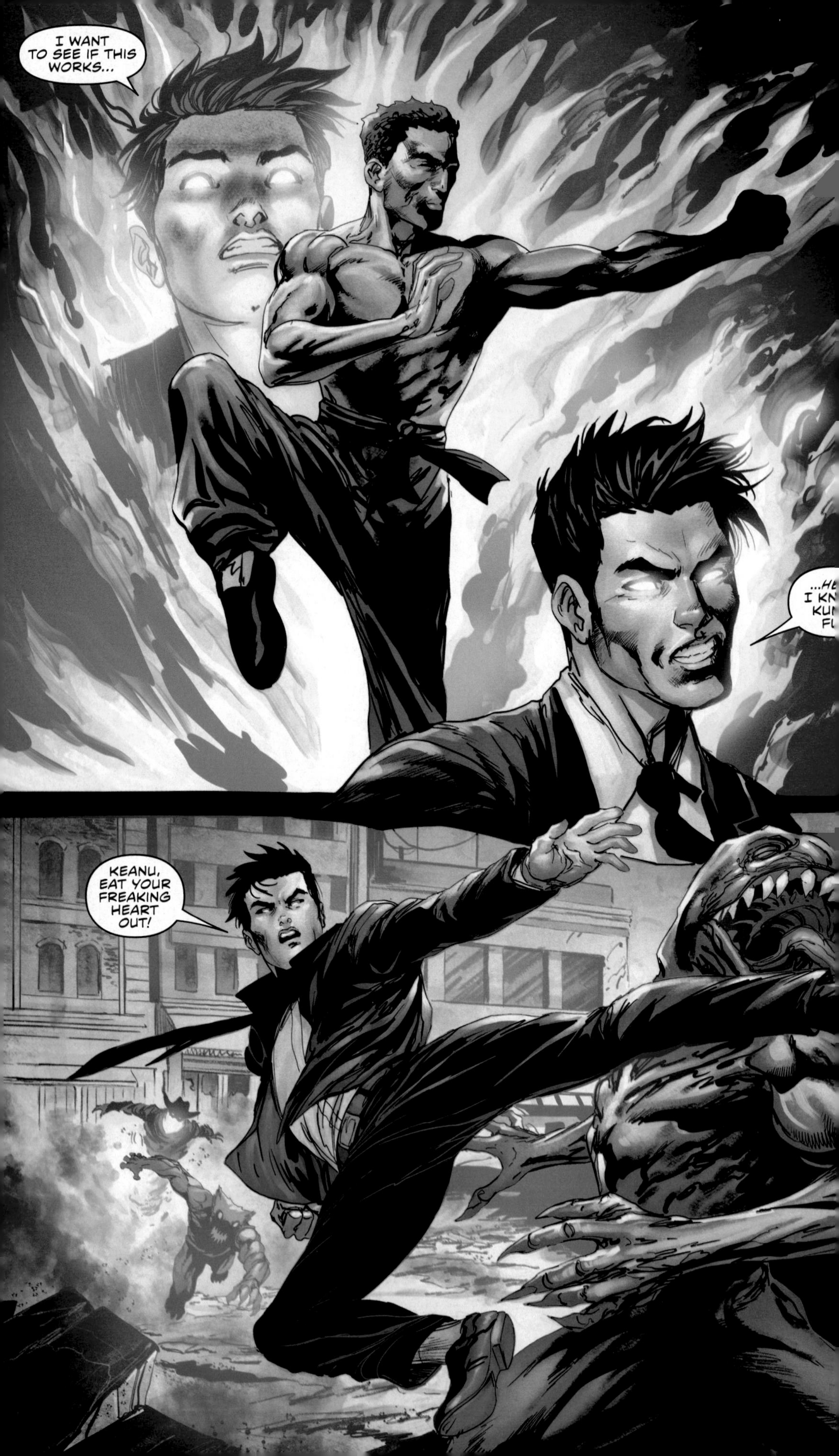
I WANT TO SEE IF THIS WORKS...
KEANU, EAT YOUR FREAKING HEART OUT!

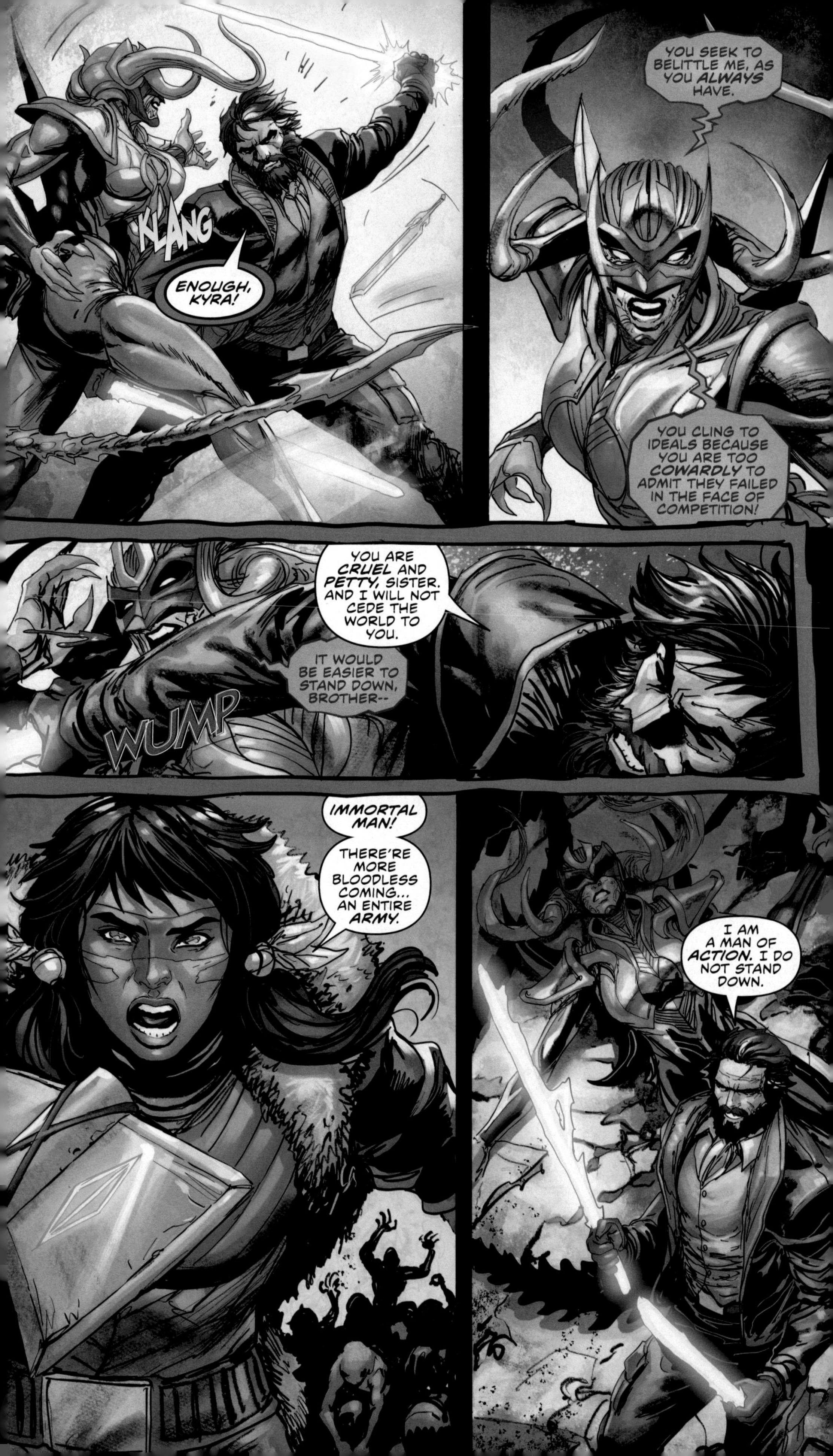
KLANG
ENOUGH, KYRA!
YOU SEEK TO BELITTLE ME, AS YOU ALWAYS HAVE.
YOU CLING TO IDEALS BECAUSE YOU ARE TOO COWARDLY TO ADMIT THEY FAILED IN THE FACE OF COMPETITION!
IT WOULD BE EASIER TO STAND DOWN, BROTHER--
WUMP
YOU ARE CRUEL AND PETTY, SISTER. AND I WILL NOT CEDE THE WORLD TO YOU.
IMMORTAL MAN!
THERE'RE MORE BLOODLESS COMING... AN ENTIRE ARMY.
I AM A MAN OF ACTION. I DO NOT STAND DOWN.

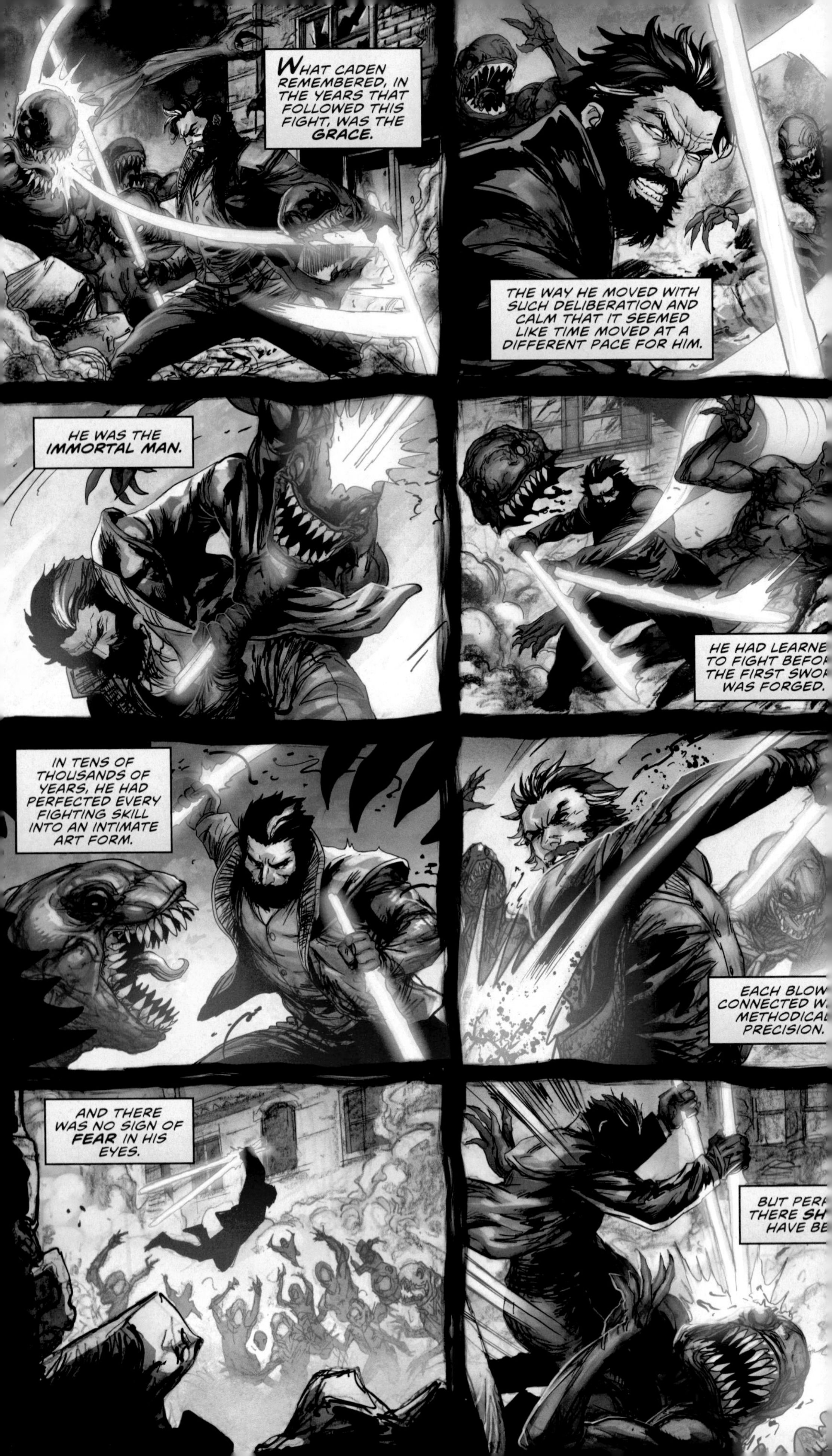
WHAT CADEN REMEMBERED, IN THE YEARS THAT FOLLOWED THIS FIGHT, WAS THE GRACE.
THE WAY HE MOVED WITH SUCH DELIBERATION AND CALM THAT IT SEEMED LIKE TIME MOVED AT A DIFFERENT PACE FOR HIM.
HE WAS THE IMMORTAL MAN.
HE HAD LEARNE TO FIGHT BEFOR THE FIRST SWOR WAS FORGED.
IN TENS OF THOUSANDS OF YEARS, HE HAD PERFECTED EVERY FIGHTING SKILL INTO AN INTIMATE ART FORM.
EACH BLOW CONNECTED W METHODICAL PRECISION.
AND THERE WAS NO SIGN OF FEAR IN HIS EYES.
BUT PER THERE SH HAVE BE

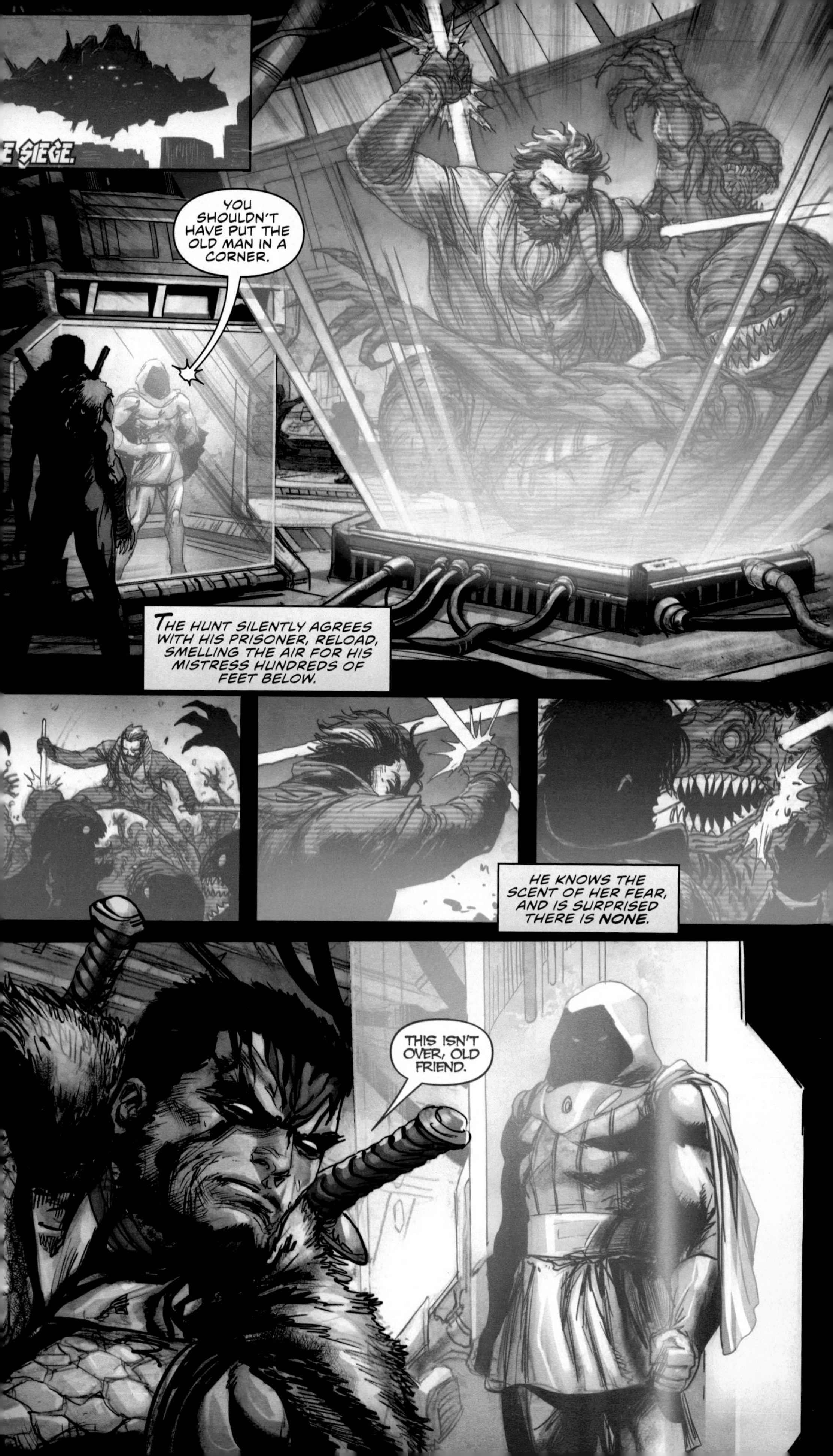
E SIEGE.
YOU SHOULDN'T HAVE PUT THE OLD MAN IN A CORNER.
THE HUNT SILENTLY AGREES WITH HIS PRISONER, RELOAD, SMELLING THE AIR FOR HIS MISTRESS HUNDREDS OF FEET BELOW.
HE KNOWS THE SCENT OF HER FEAR, AND IS SURPRISED THERE IS NONE.
THIS ISN'T OVER, OLD FRIEND.

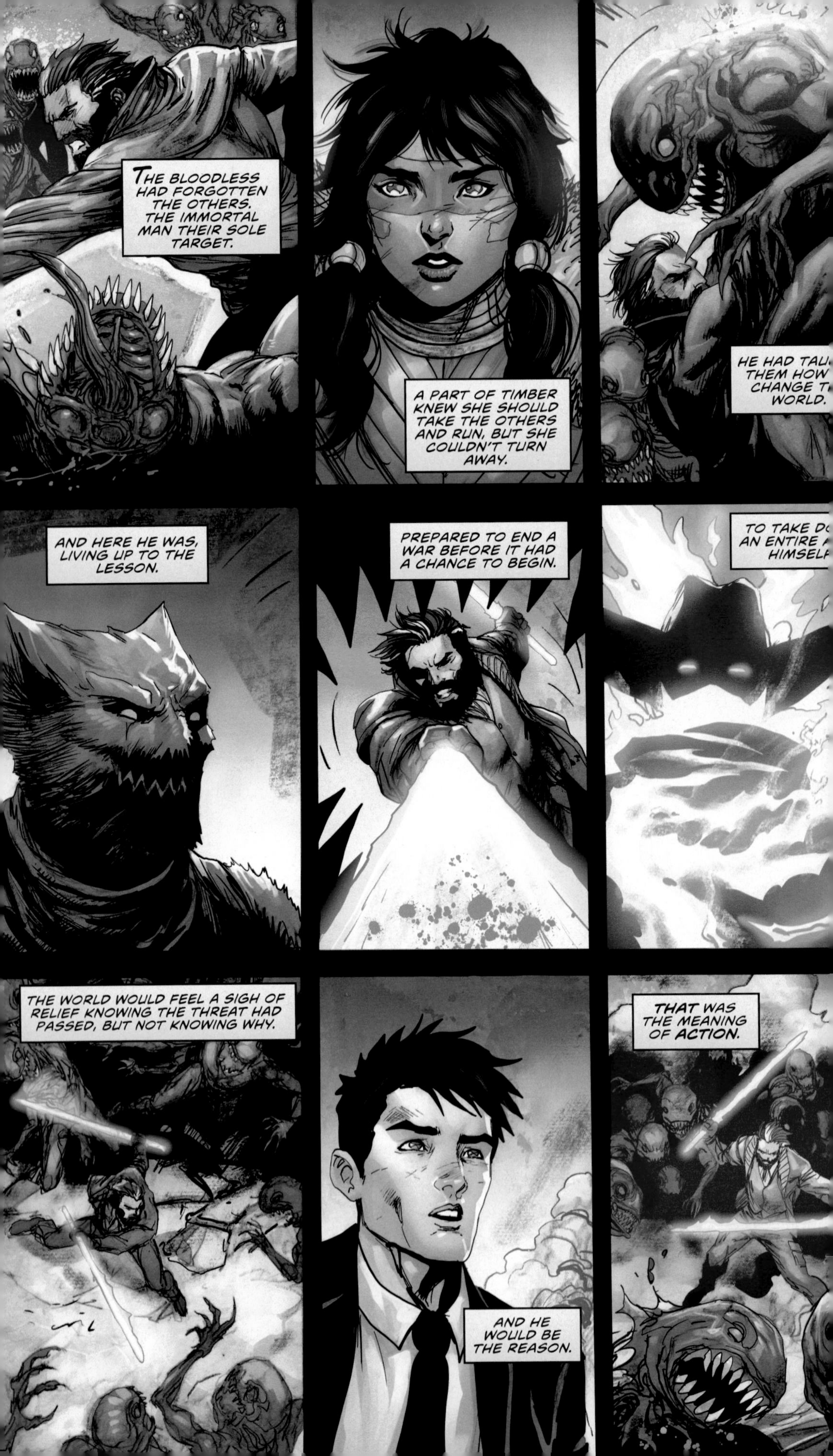
THE BLOODLESS HAD FORGOTTEN THE OTHERS. THE IMMORTAL MAN THEIR SOLE TARGET.
A PART OF TIMBER KNEW SHE SHOULD TAKE THE OTHERS AND RUN, BUT SHE COULDN'T TURN AWAY.
HE HAD TAU THEM HOW CHANGE T WORLD.
AND HERE HE WAS, LIVING UP TO THE LESSON.
PREPARED TO END A WAR BEFORE IT HAD A CHANCE TO BEGIN.
TO TAKE D AN ENTIRE HIMSELF
THE WORLD WOULD FEEL A SIGH OF RELIEF KNOWING THE THREAT HAD PASSED, BUT NOT KNOWING WHY.
AND HE WOULD BE THE REASON.
THAT WAS THE MEANING OF ACTION.

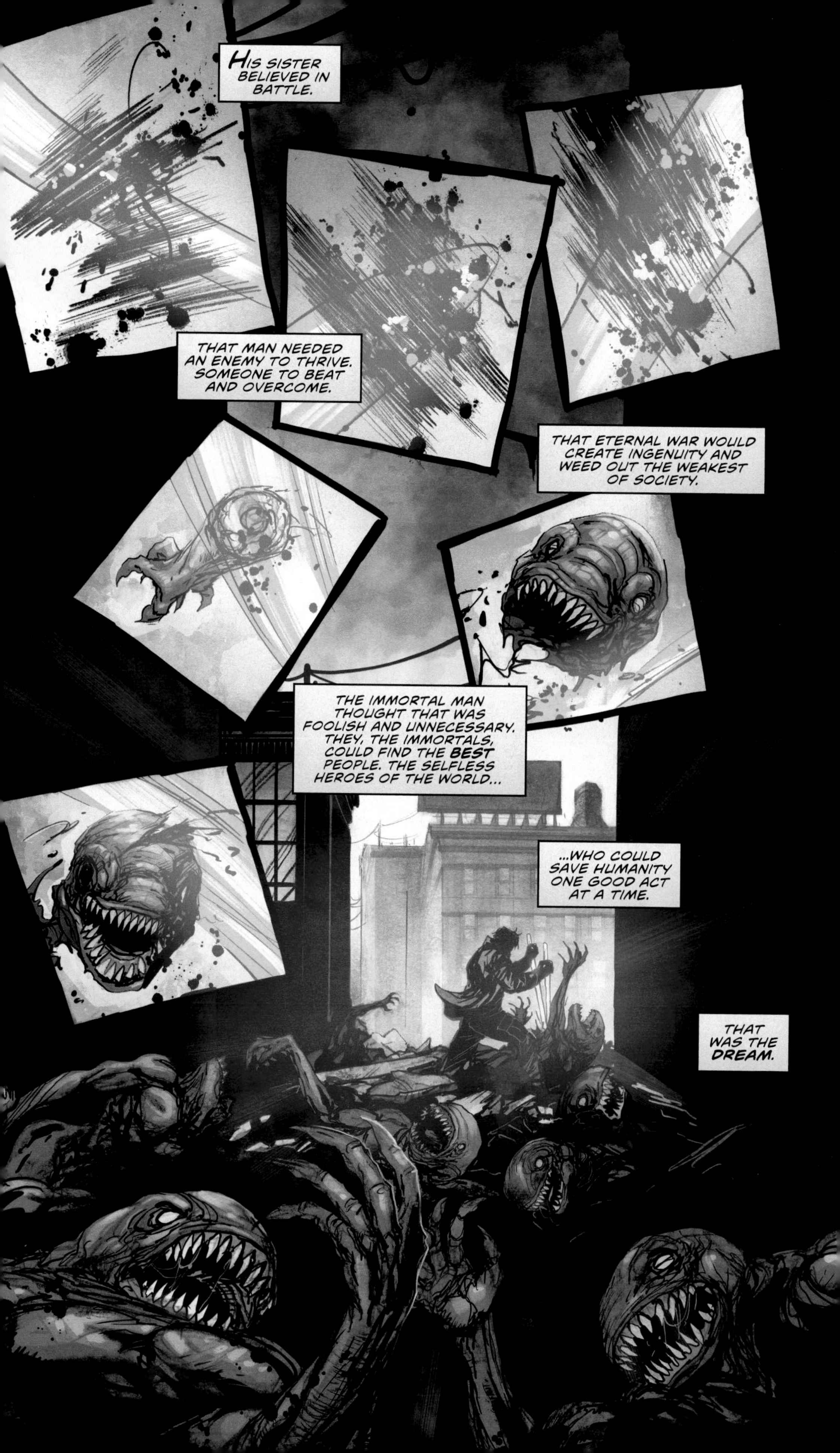
HIS SISTER BELIEVED IN BATTLE.
THAT MAN NEEDED AN ENEMY TO THRIVE. SOMEONE TO BEAT AND OVERCOME.
THAT ETERNAL WAR WOULD CREATE INGENUITY AND WEED OUT THE WEAKEST OF SOCIETY.
THE IMMORTAL MAN THOUGHT THAT WAS FOOLISH AND UNNECESSARY. THEY, THE IMMORTALS, COULD FIND THE BEST PEOPLE. THE SELFLESS HEROES OF THE WORLD...
...WHO COULD SAVE HUMANITY ONE GOOD ACT AT A TIME.
THAT WAS THE DREAM.

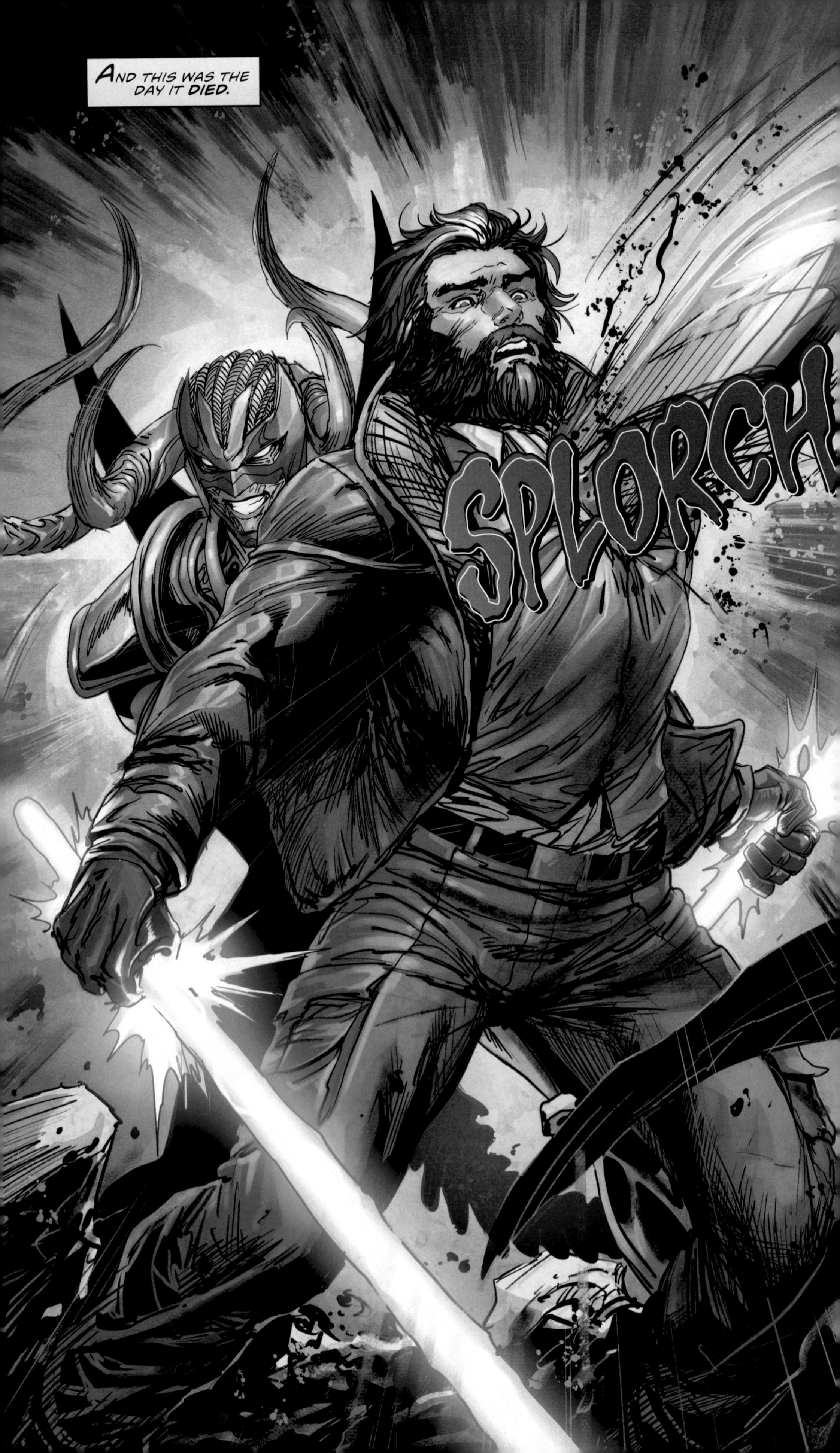
AND THIS WAS THE DAY IT DIED.
SPLORCH

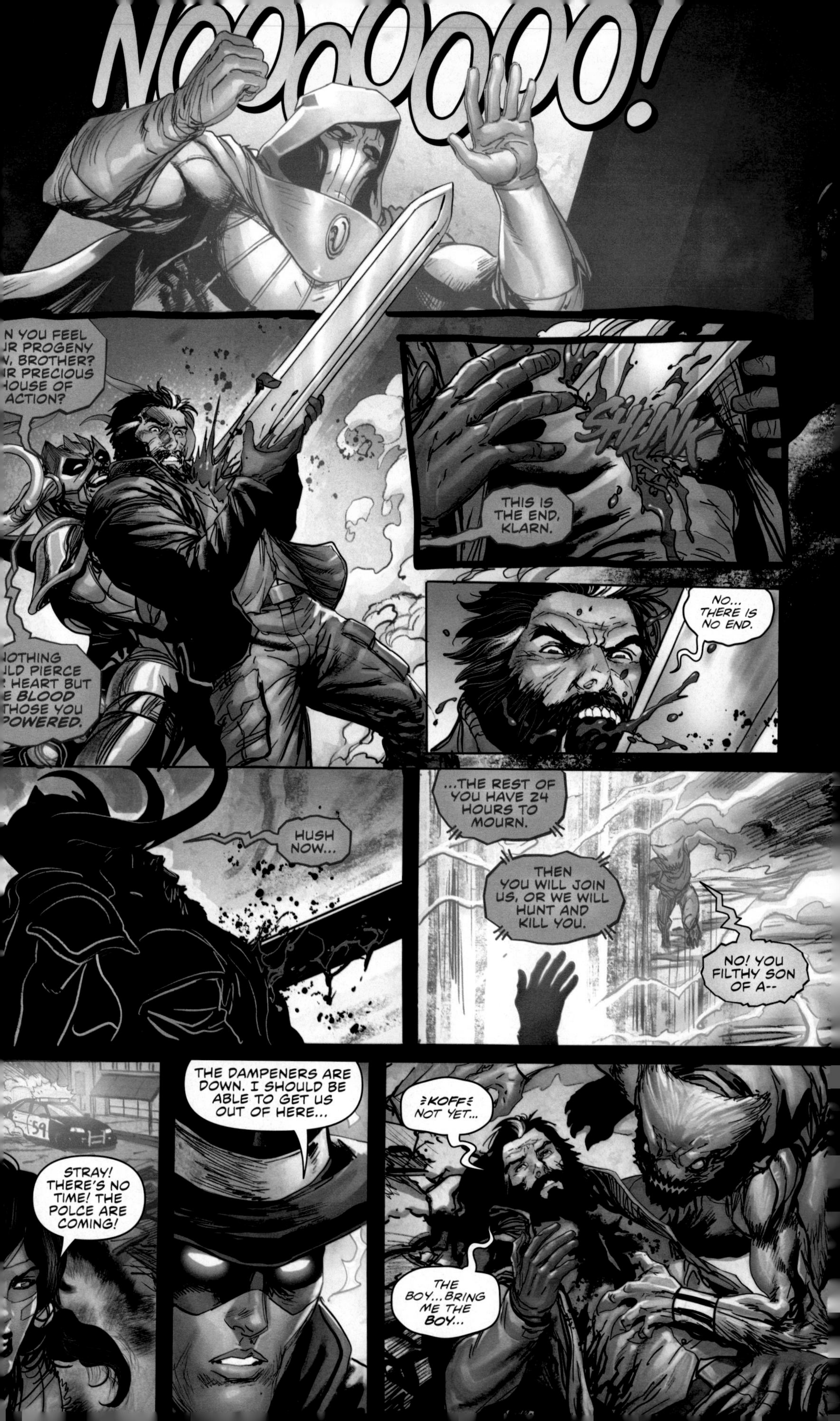
NOOOOOOO!
N YOU FEEL
IR PROGENY
V, BROTHER?
IR PRECIOUS
HOUSE OF
ACTION?
NOTHING
ILD PIERCE
R HEART BUT
E BLOOD
THOSE YOU
POWERED.
SHUNK
THIS IS THE END, KLARN.
NO... THERE IS NO END.
HUSH NOW...
...THE REST OF YOU HAVE 24 HOURS TO MOURN.
THEN YOU WILL JOIN US, OR WE WILL HUNT AND KILL YOU.
NO! YOU FILTHY SON OF A--
STRAY! THERE'S NO TIME! THE POLCE ARE COMING!
THE DAMPENERS ARE DOWN. I SHOULD BE ABLE TO GET US OUT OF HERE...
KOFF NOT YET...
THE BOY...BRING ME THE BOY...

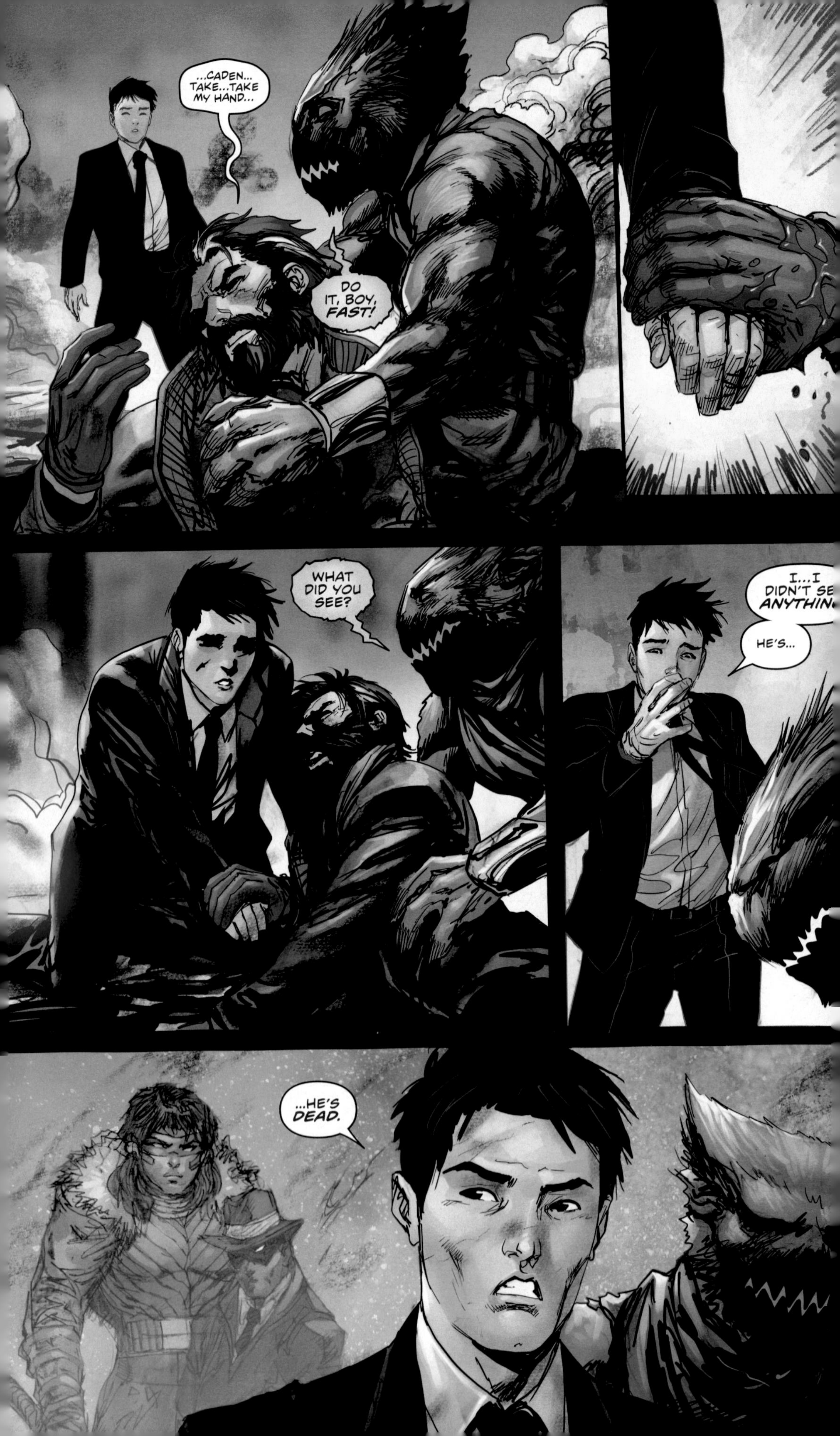
...CADEN... TAKE...TAKE MY HAND...
DO IT, BOY, FAST!
WHAT DID YOU SEE?
I...I DIDN'T SE ANYTHIN
HE'S...
...HE'S DEAD.

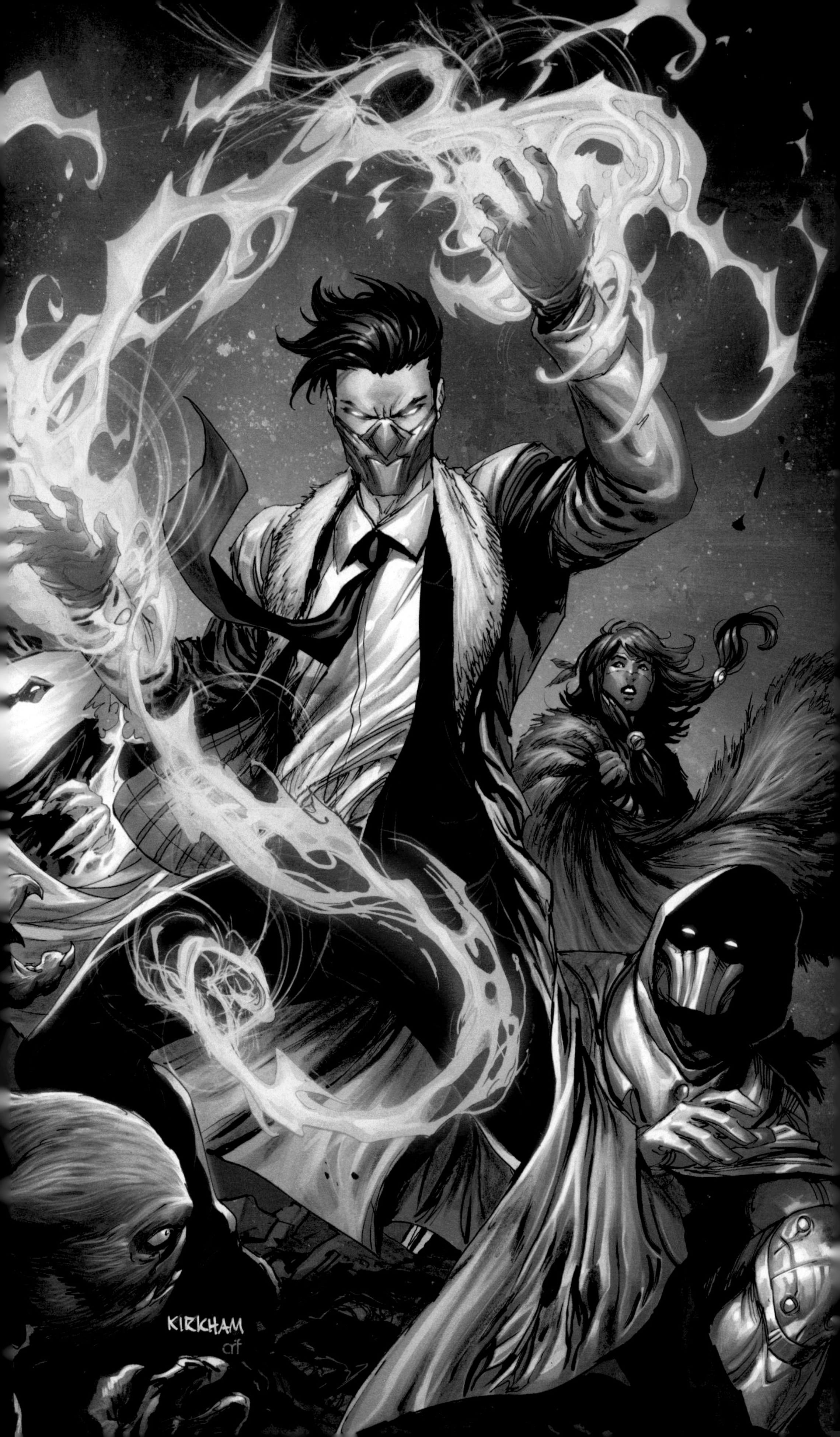
KIRKHAM
crf

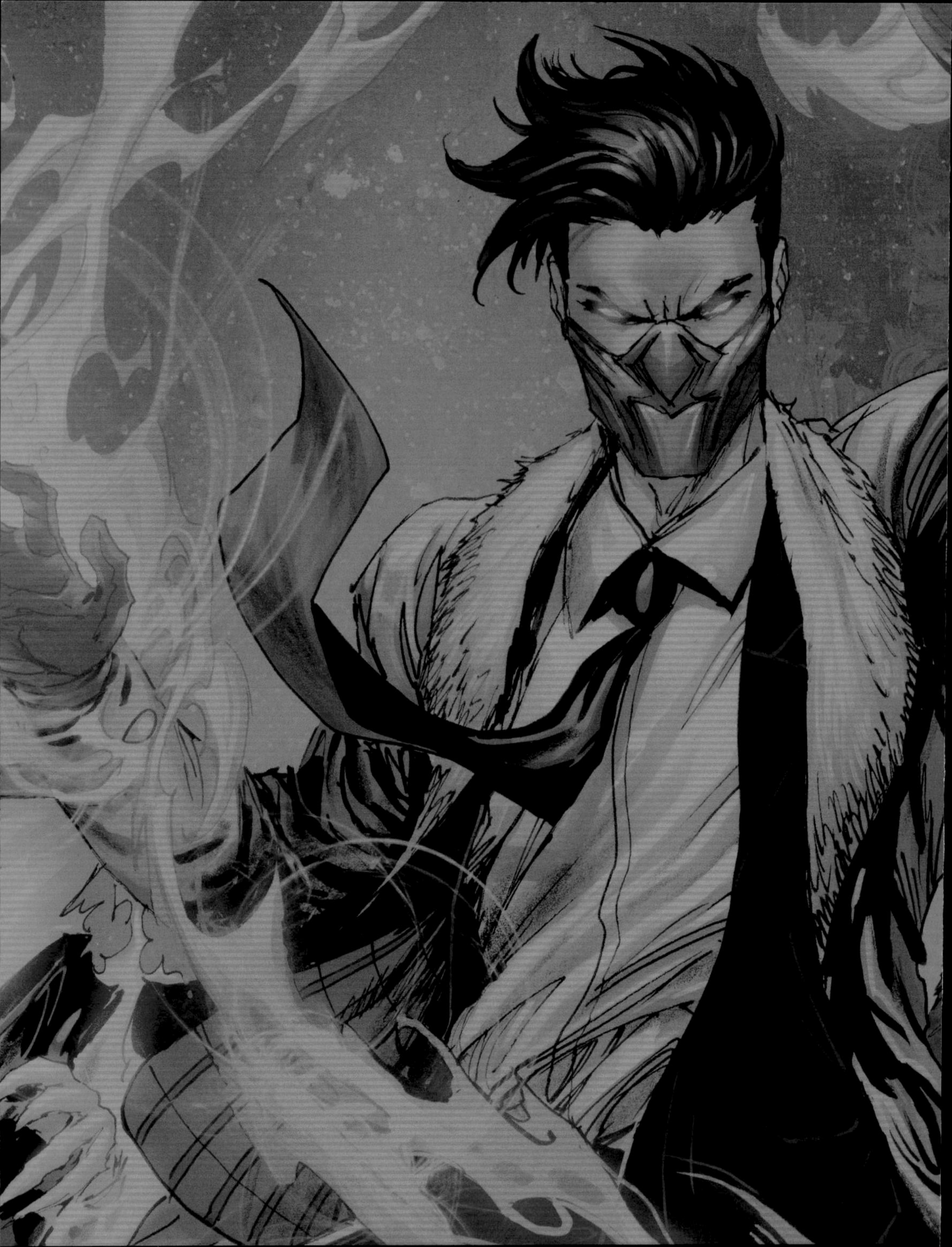

THE IMMORTAL MEN #5

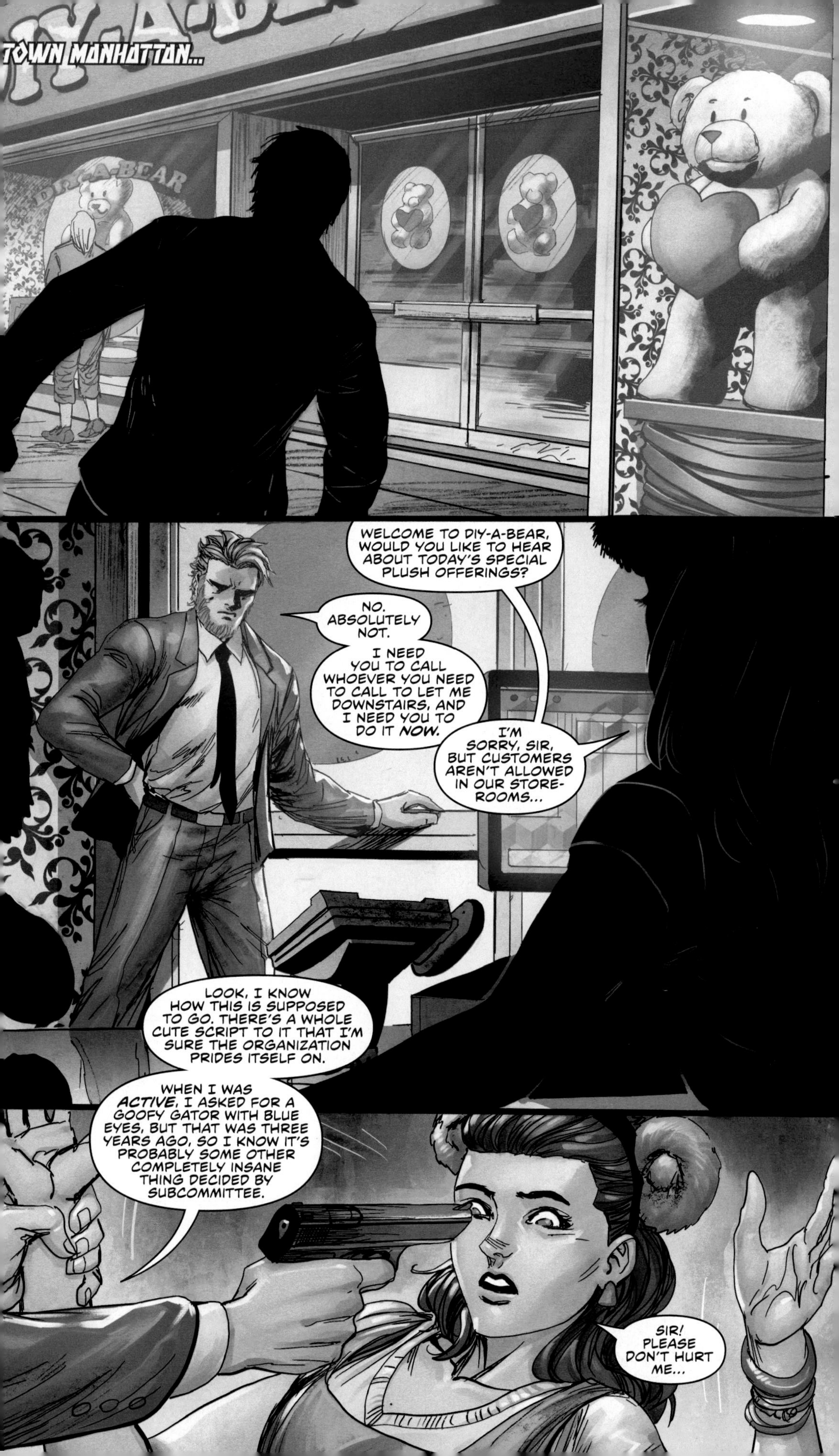
TOWN MANHATTAN...
DIY-A-BEAR
WELCOME TO DIY-A-BEAR, WOULD YOU LIKE TO HEAR ABOUT TODAY'S SPECIAL PLUSH OFFERINGS?
NO. ABSOLUTELY NOT.
I NEED YOU TO CALL WHOEVER YOU NEED TO CALL TO LET ME DOWNSTAIRS, AND I NEED YOU TO DO IT *NOW.*
I'M SORRY, SIR, BUT CUSTOMERS AREN'T ALLOWED IN OUR STORE-ROOMS...
LOOK, I KNOW HOW THIS IS SUPPOSED TO GO. THERE'S A WHOLE CUTE SCRIPT TO IT THAT I'M SURE THE ORGANIZATION PRIDES ITSELF ON.
WHEN I WAS *ACTIVE,* I ASKED FOR A GOOFY GATOR WITH BLUE EYES, BUT THAT WAS THREE YEARS AGO, SO I KNOW IT'S PROBABLY SOME OTHER COMPLETELY INSANE THING DECIDED BY SUBCOMMITTEE.
SIR! PLEASE DON'T HURT ME...

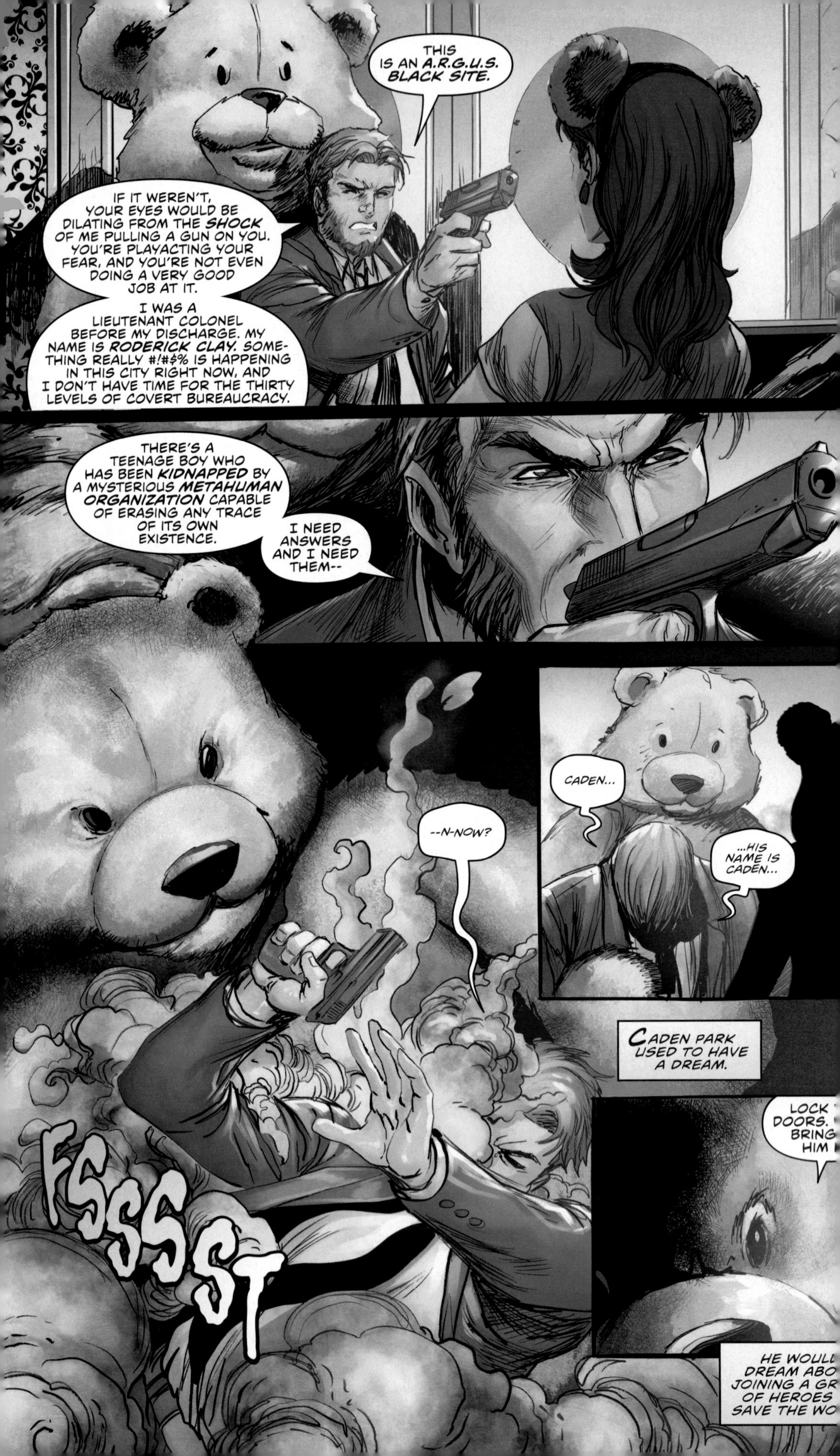
THIS IS AN A.R.G.U.S. BLACK SITE.
IF IT WEREN'T, YOUR EYES WOULD BE DILATING FROM THE SHOCK OF ME PULLING A GUN ON YOU. YOU'RE PLAYACTING YOUR FEAR, AND YOU'RE NOT EVEN DOING A VERY GOOD JOB AT IT.
I WAS A LIEUTENANT COLONEL BEFORE MY DISCHARGE. MY NAME IS RODERICK CLAY. SOMETHING REALLY #!#$% IS HAPPENING IN THIS CITY RIGHT NOW, AND I DON'T HAVE TIME FOR THE THIRTY LEVELS OF COVERT BUREAUCRACY.
THERE'S A TEENAGE BOY WHO HAS BEEN KIDNAPPED BY A MYSTERIOUS METAHUMAN ORGANIZATION CAPABLE OF ERASING ANY TRACE OF ITS OWN EXISTENCE.
I NEED ANSWERS AND I NEED THEM--
--N-NOW?
FSSSST
CADEN...
...HIS NAME IS CADEN...
CADEN PARK USED TO HAVE A DREAM.
LOCK DOORS. BRING HIM
HE WOUL DREAM ABO JOINING A GR OF HEROES SAVE THE WO

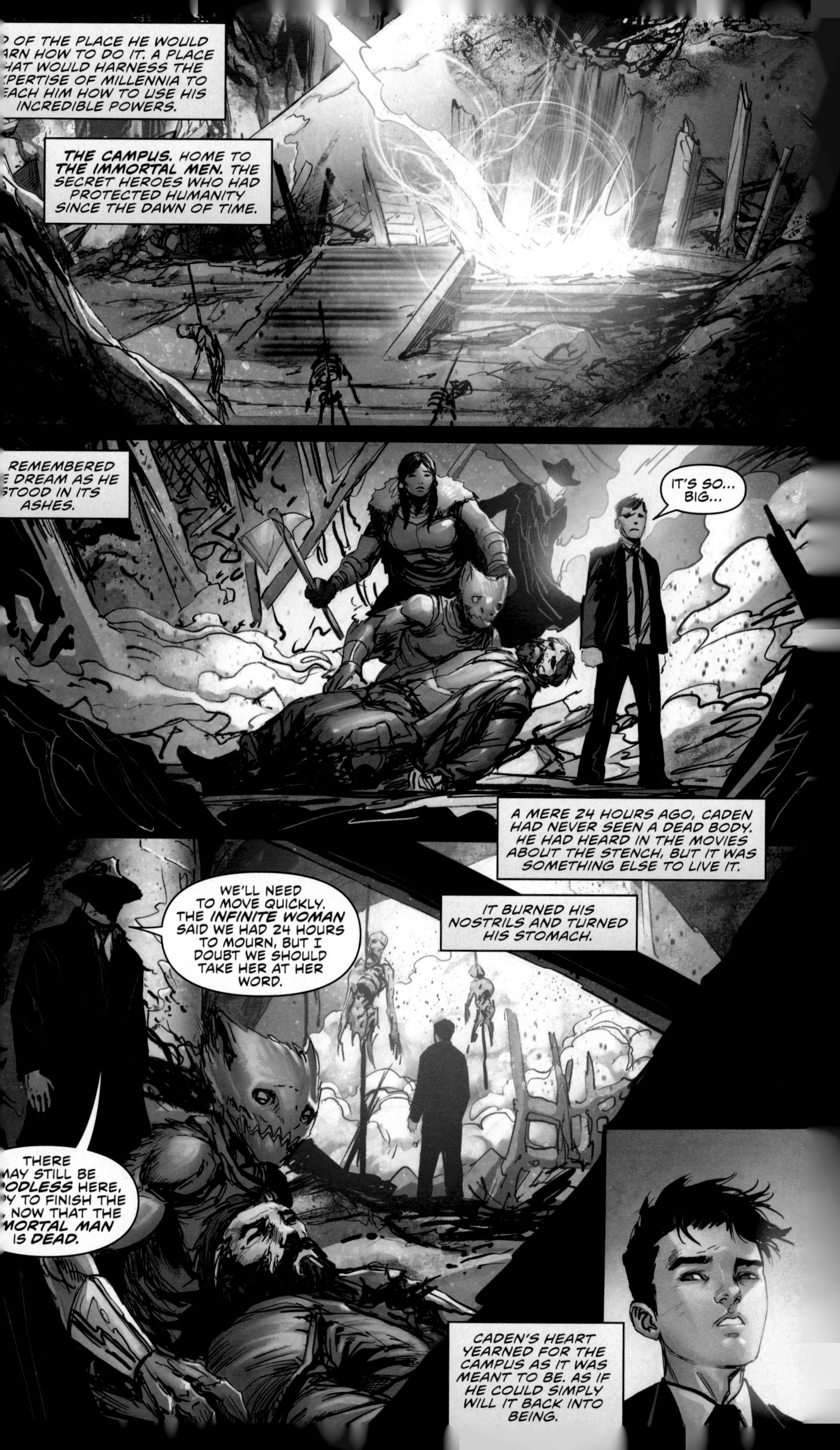

OF THE PLACE HE WOULD ARN HOW TO DO IT. A PLACE HAT WOULD HARNESS THE PERTISE OF MILLENNIA TO EACH HIM HOW TO USE HIS INCREDIBLE POWERS.
THE CAMPUS. HOME TO THE IMMORTAL MEN. THE SECRET HEROES WHO HAD PROTECTED HUMANITY SINCE THE DAWN OF TIME.
REMEMBERED E DREAM AS HE STOOD IN ITS ASHES.
IT'S SO... BIG...
A MERE 24 HOURS AGO, CADEN HAD NEVER SEEN A DEAD BODY. HE HAD HEARD IN THE MOVIES ABOUT THE STENCH, BUT IT WAS SOMETHING ELSE TO LIVE IT.
WE'LL NEED TO MOVE QUICKLY. THE INFINITE WOMAN SAID WE HAD 24 HOURS TO MOURN, BUT I DOUBT WE SHOULD TAKE HER AT HER WORD.
IT BURNED HIS NOSTRILS AND TURNED HIS STOMACH.
THERE MAY STILL BE ODLESS HERE, Y TO FINISH THE , NOW THAT THE MORTAL MAN IS DEAD.
CADEN'S HEART YEARNED FOR THE CAMPUS AS IT WAS MEANT TO BE. AS IF HE COULD SIMPLY WILL IT BACK INTO BEING.

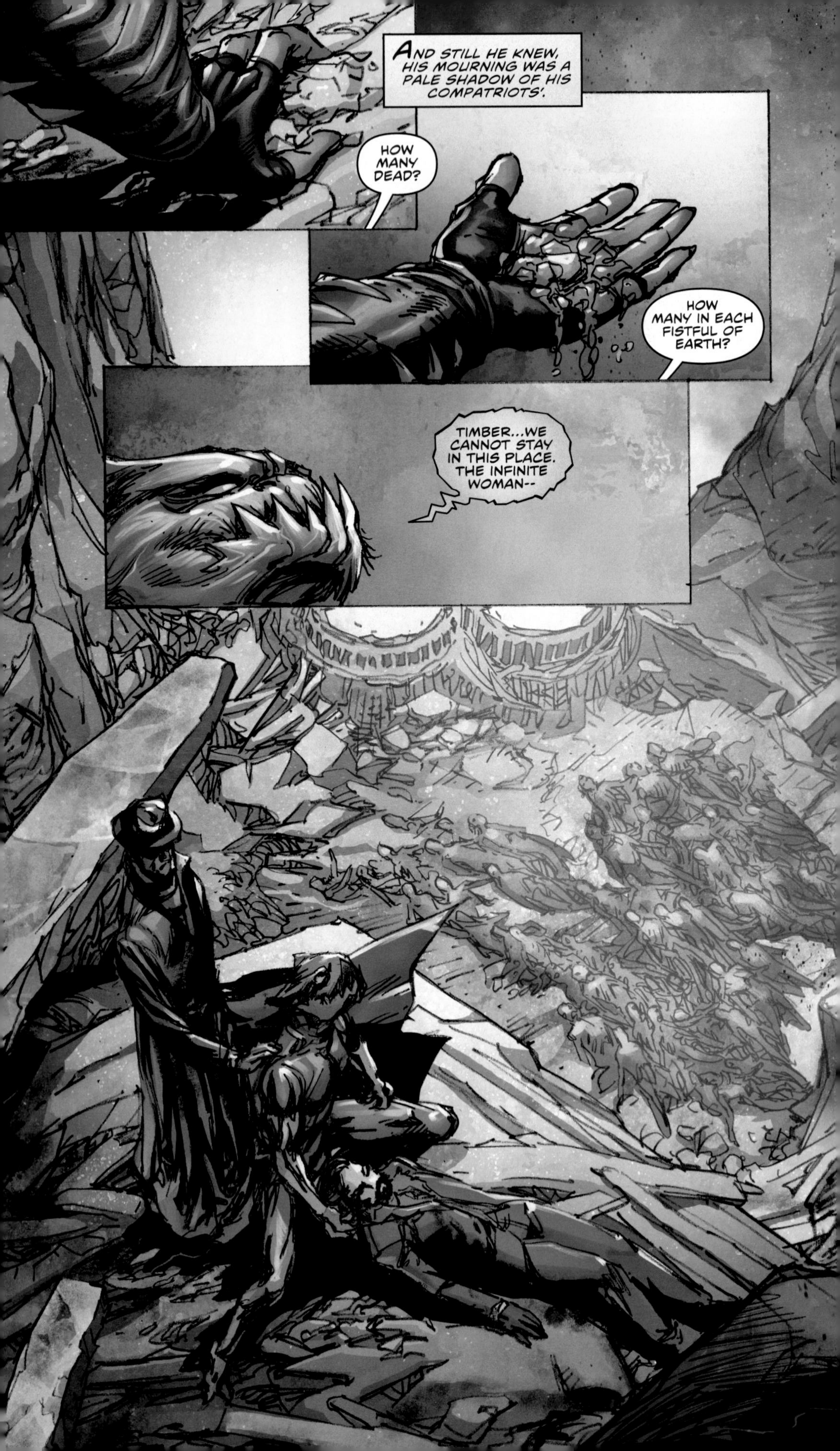
AND STILL HE KNEW, HIS MOURNING WAS A PALE SHADOW OF HIS COMPATRIOTS'.
HOW MANY DEAD?
HOW MANY IN EACH FISTFUL OF EARTH?
TIMBER...WE CANNOT STAY IN THIS PLACE. THE INFINITE WOMAN--

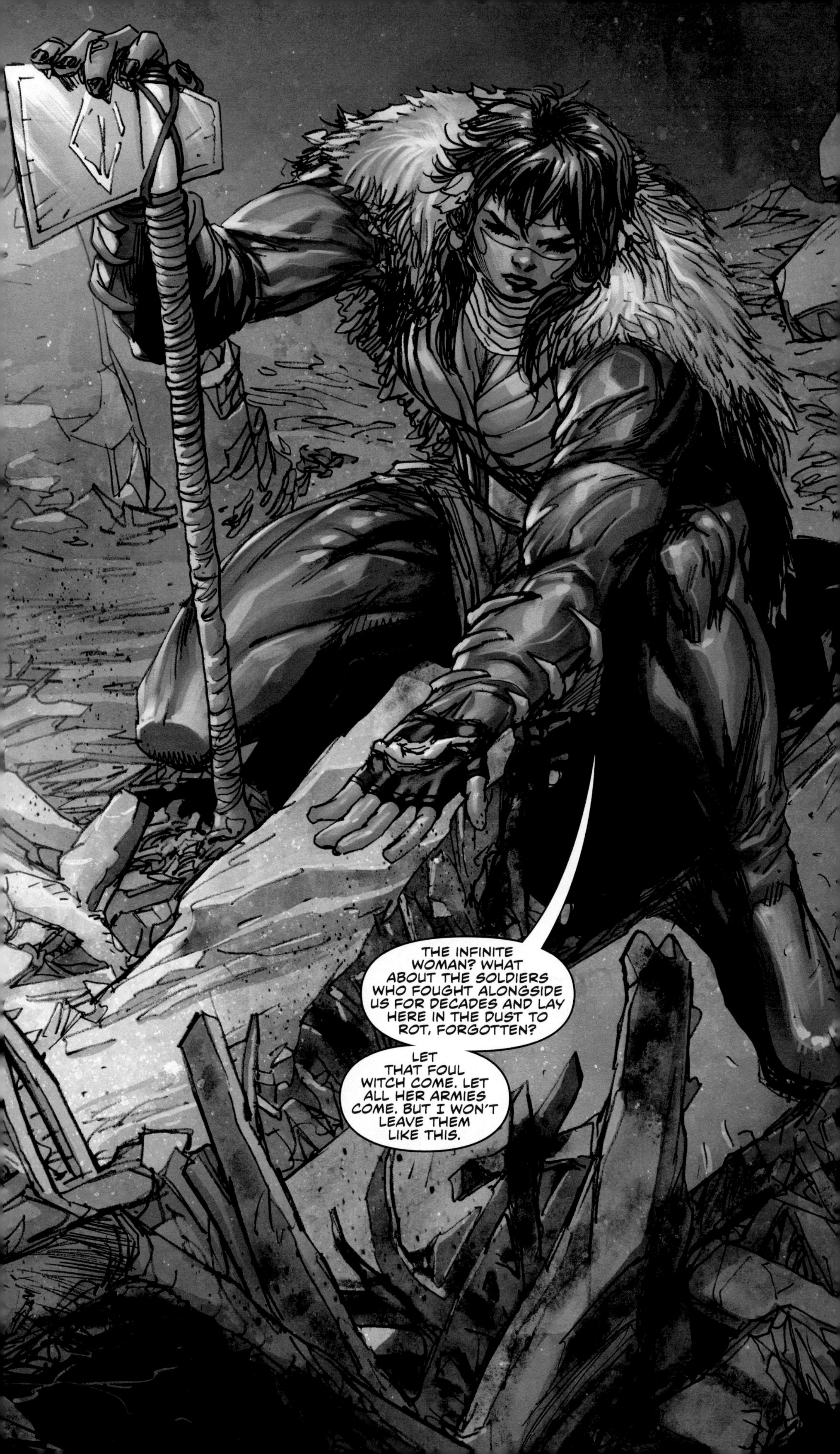
THE INFINITE WOMAN? WHAT ABOUT THE SOLDIERS WHO FOUGHT ALONGSIDE US FOR DECADES AND LAY HERE IN THE DUST TO ROT, FORGOTTEN?
LET THAT FOUL WITCH COME. LET ALL HER ARMIES COME. BUT I WON'T LEAVE THEM LIKE THIS.

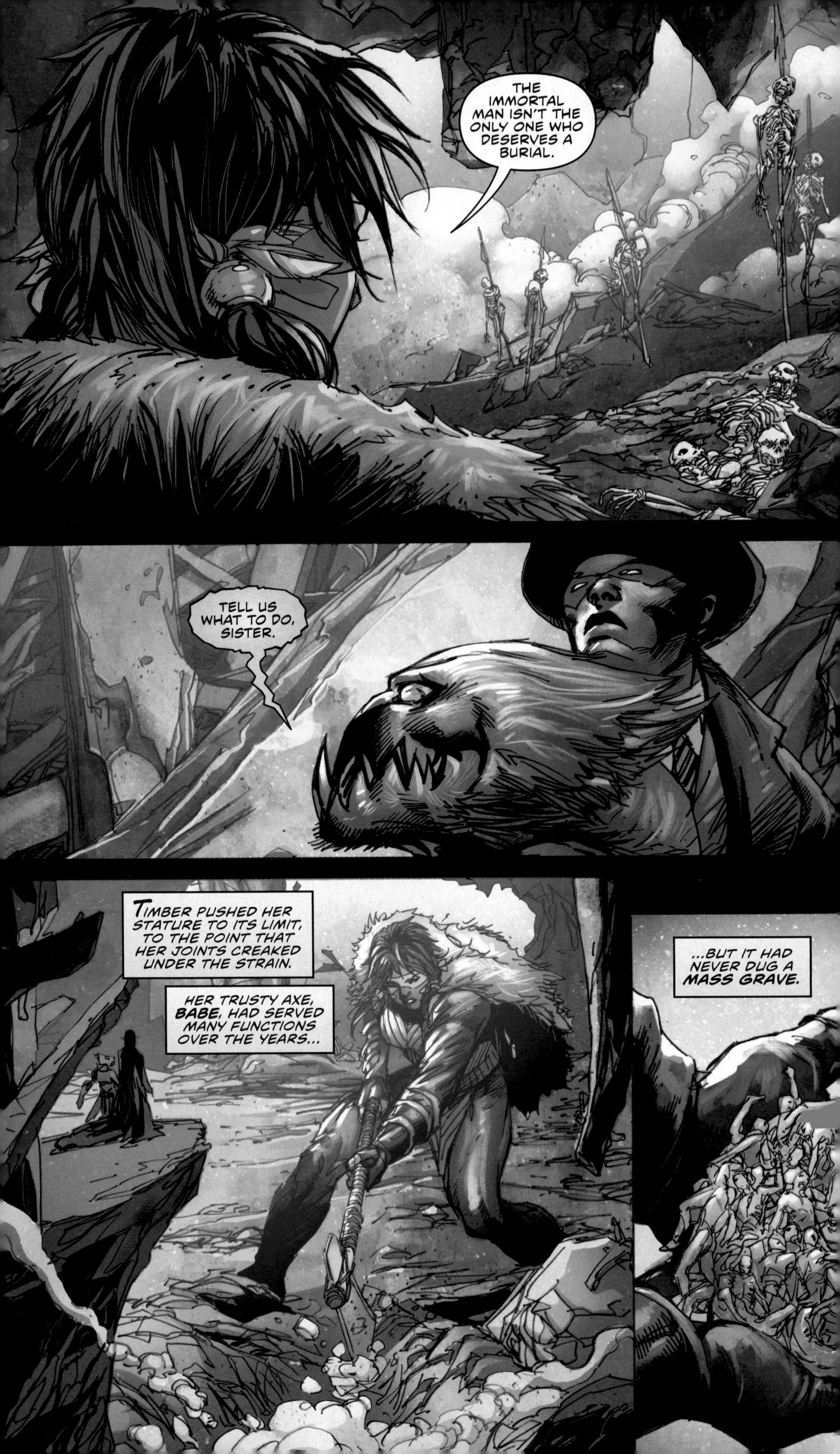
THE IMMORTAL MAN ISN'T THE ONLY ONE WHO DESERVES A BURIAL.
TELL US WHAT TO DO, SISTER.
TIMBER PUSHED HER STATURE TO ITS LIMIT, TO THE POINT THAT HER JOINTS CREAKED UNDER THE STRAIN.
HER TRUSTY AXE, BABE, HAD SERVED MANY FUNCTIONS OVER THE YEARS...
...BUT IT HAD NEVER DUG A MASS GRAVE.

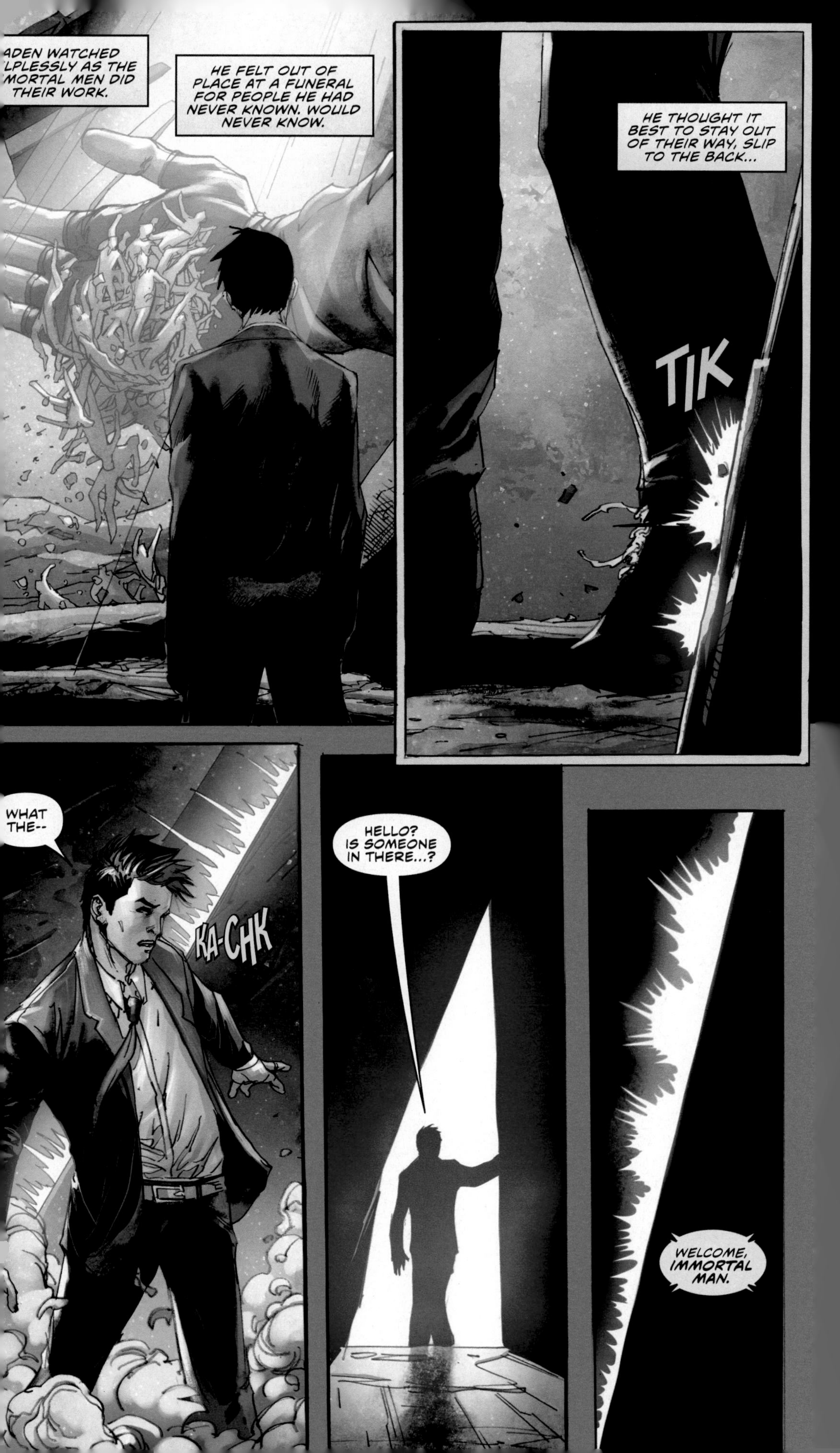

ADEN WATCHED
LPLESSLY AS THE
MORTAL MEN DID
THEIR WORK.
HE FELT OUT OF PLACE AT A FUNERAL FOR PEOPLE HE HAD NEVER KNOWN. WOULD NEVER KNOW.
HE THOUGHT IT BEST TO STAY OUT OF THEIR WAY, SLIP TO THE BACK...
TIK
WHAT THE--
KA-CHK
HELLO? IS SOMEONE IN THERE...?
WELCOME, IMMORTAL MAN.

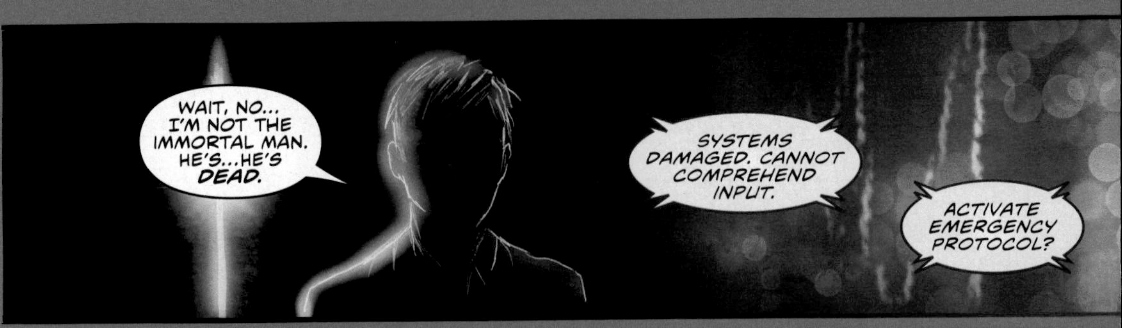
WAIT, NO... I'M NOT THE IMMORTAL MAN. HE'S...HE'S DEAD.
SYSTEMS DAMAGED. CANNOT COMPREHEND INPUT.
ACTIVATE EMERGENCY PROTOCOL?

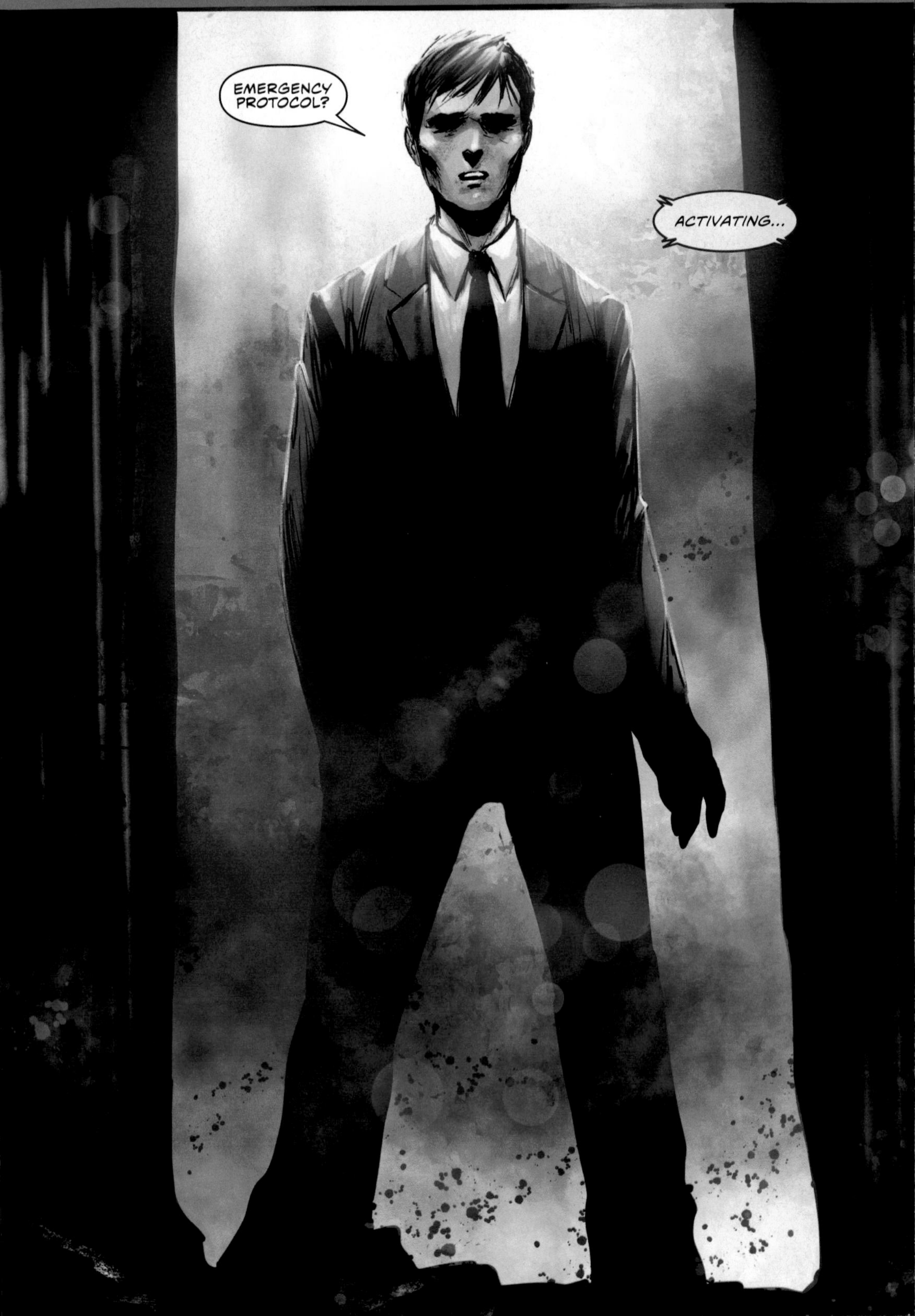
EMERGENCY PROTOCOL?
ACTIVATING...

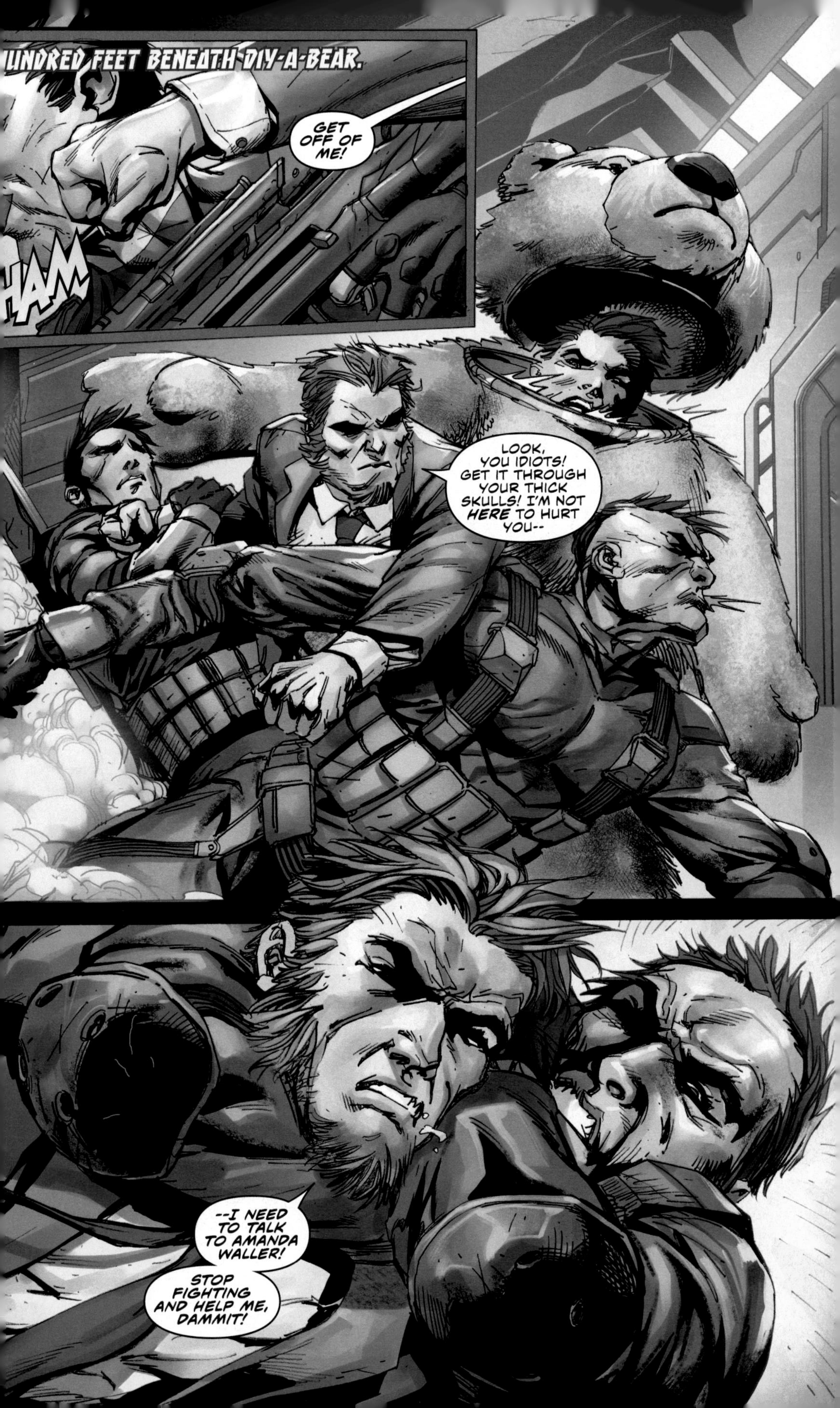
UNDRED FEET BENEATH DIY-A-BEAR.
GET OFF OF ME!
HAM
LOOK, YOU IDIOTS! GET IT THROUGH YOUR THICK SKULLS! I'M NOT HERE TO HURT YOU--
--I NEED TO TALK TO AMANDA WALLER!
STOP FIGHTING AND HELP ME, DAMMIT!

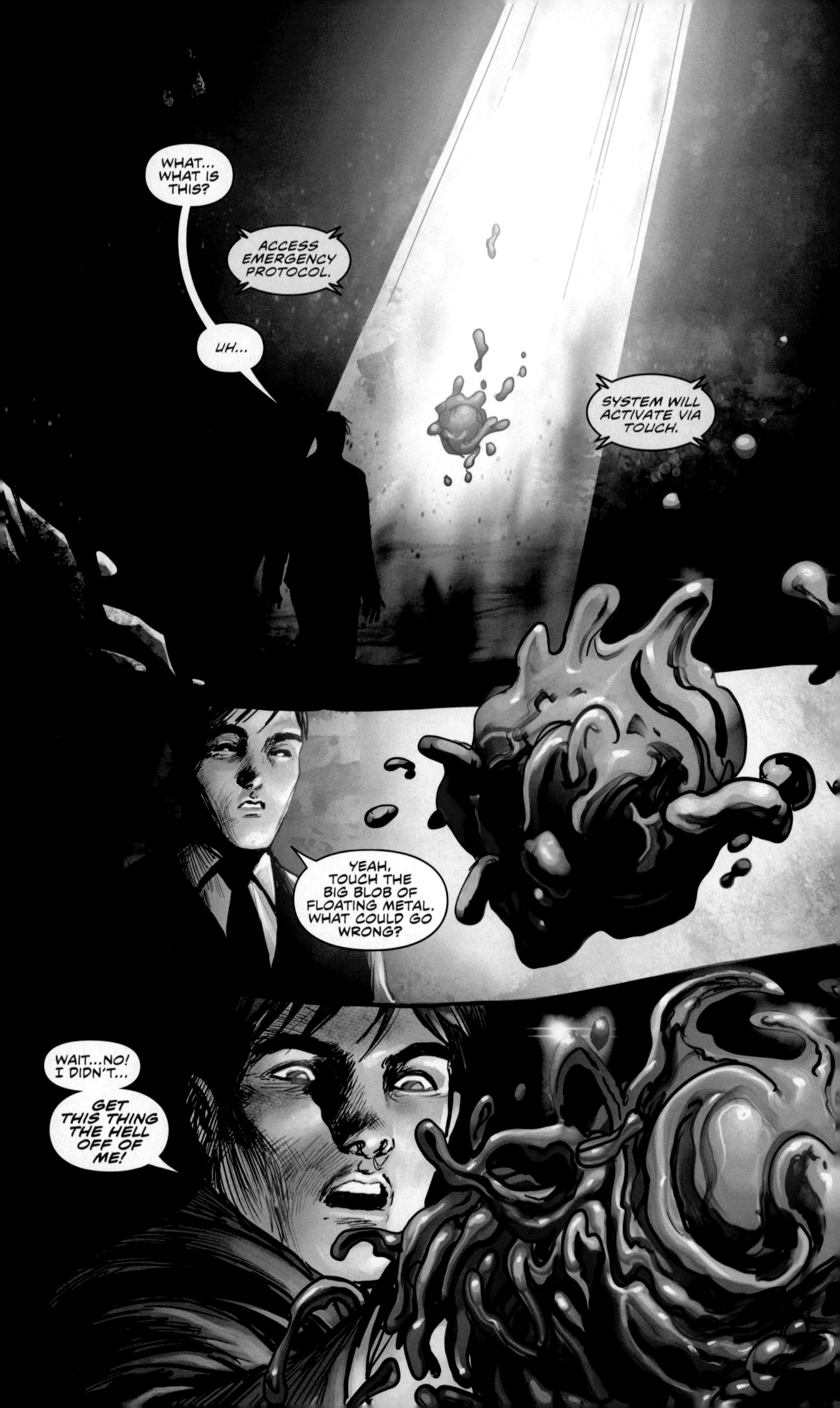

WHAT... WHAT IS THIS?
ACCESS EMERGENCY PROTOCOL.
UH...
SYSTEM WILL ACTIVATE VIA TOUCH.
YEAH, TOUCH THE BIG BLOB OF FLOATING METAL. WHAT COULD GO WRONG?
WAIT...NO! I DIDN'T...
GET THIS THING THE HELL OFF OF ME!

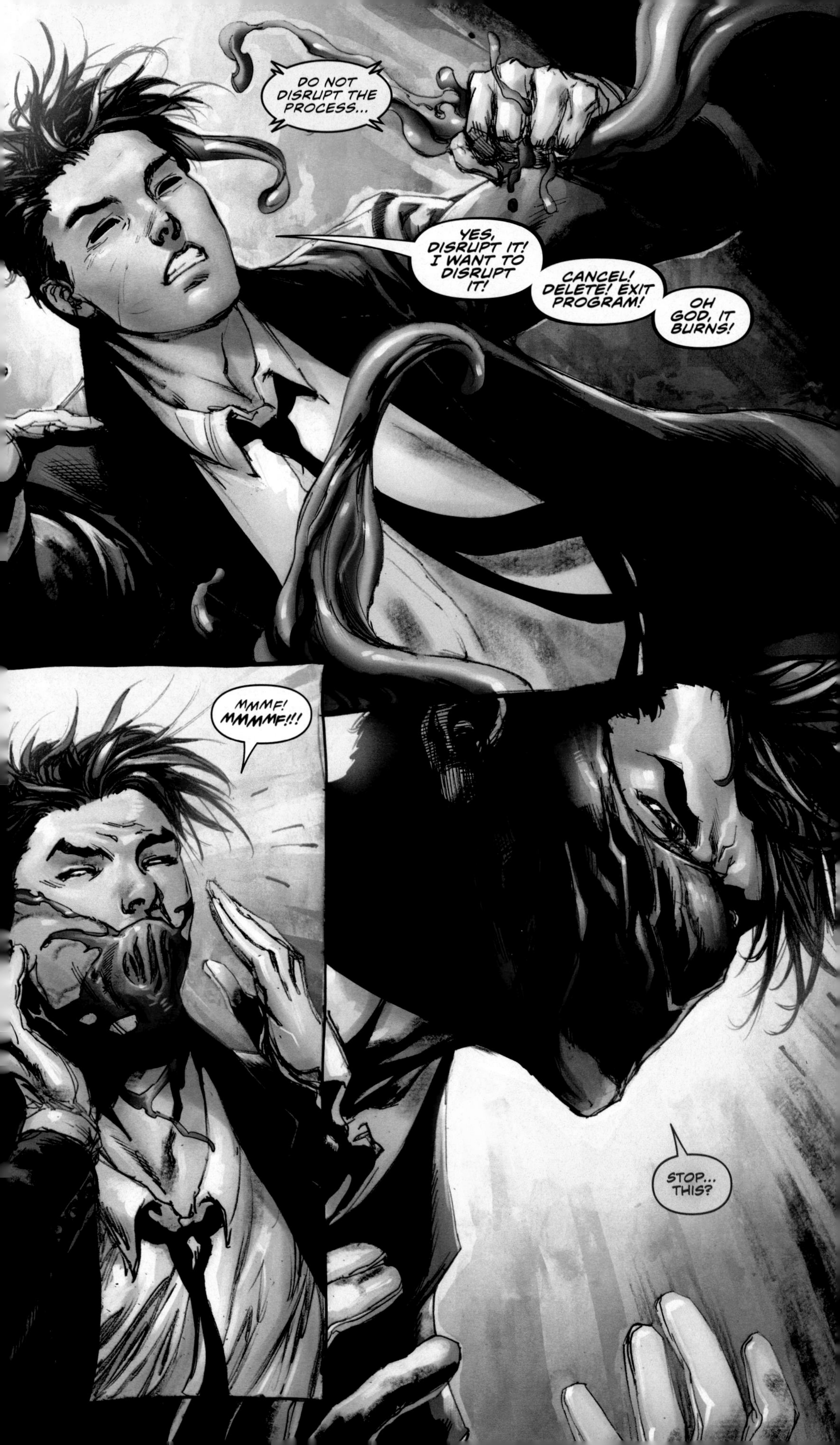
DO NOT DISRUPT THE PROCESS...
YES, DISRUPT IT! I WANT TO DISRUPT IT!
CANCEL! DELETE! EXIT PROGRAM!
OH GOD, IT BURNS!
MMMF! MMMMF!!!
STOP... THIS?

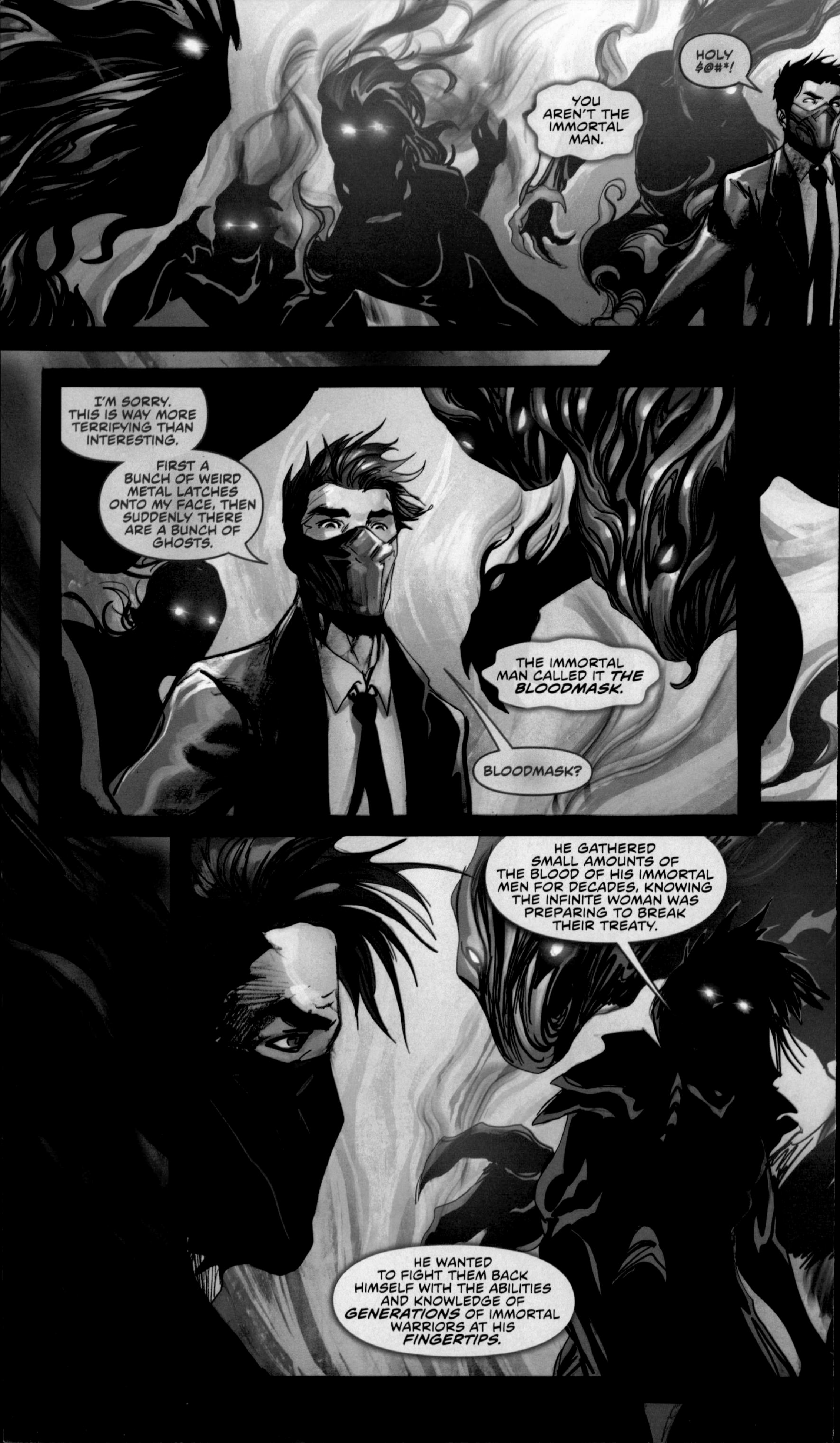
HOLY $@#*!
YOU AREN'T THE IMMORTAL MAN.
I'M SORRY. THIS IS WAY MORE TERRIFYING THAN INTERESTING.
FIRST A BUNCH OF WEIRD METAL LATCHES ONTO MY FACE, THEN SUDDENLY THERE ARE A BUNCH OF GHOSTS.
THE IMMORTAL MAN CALLED IT THE BLOODMASK.
BLOODMASK?
HE GATHERED SMALL AMOUNTS OF THE BLOOD OF HIS IMMORTAL MEN FOR DECADES, KNOWING THE INFINITE WOMAN WAS PREPARING TO BREAK THEIR TREATY.
HE WANTED TO FIGHT THEM BACK HIMSELF WITH THE ABILITIES AND KNOWLEDGE OF GENERATIONS OF IMMORTAL WARRIORS AT HIS FINGERTIPS.

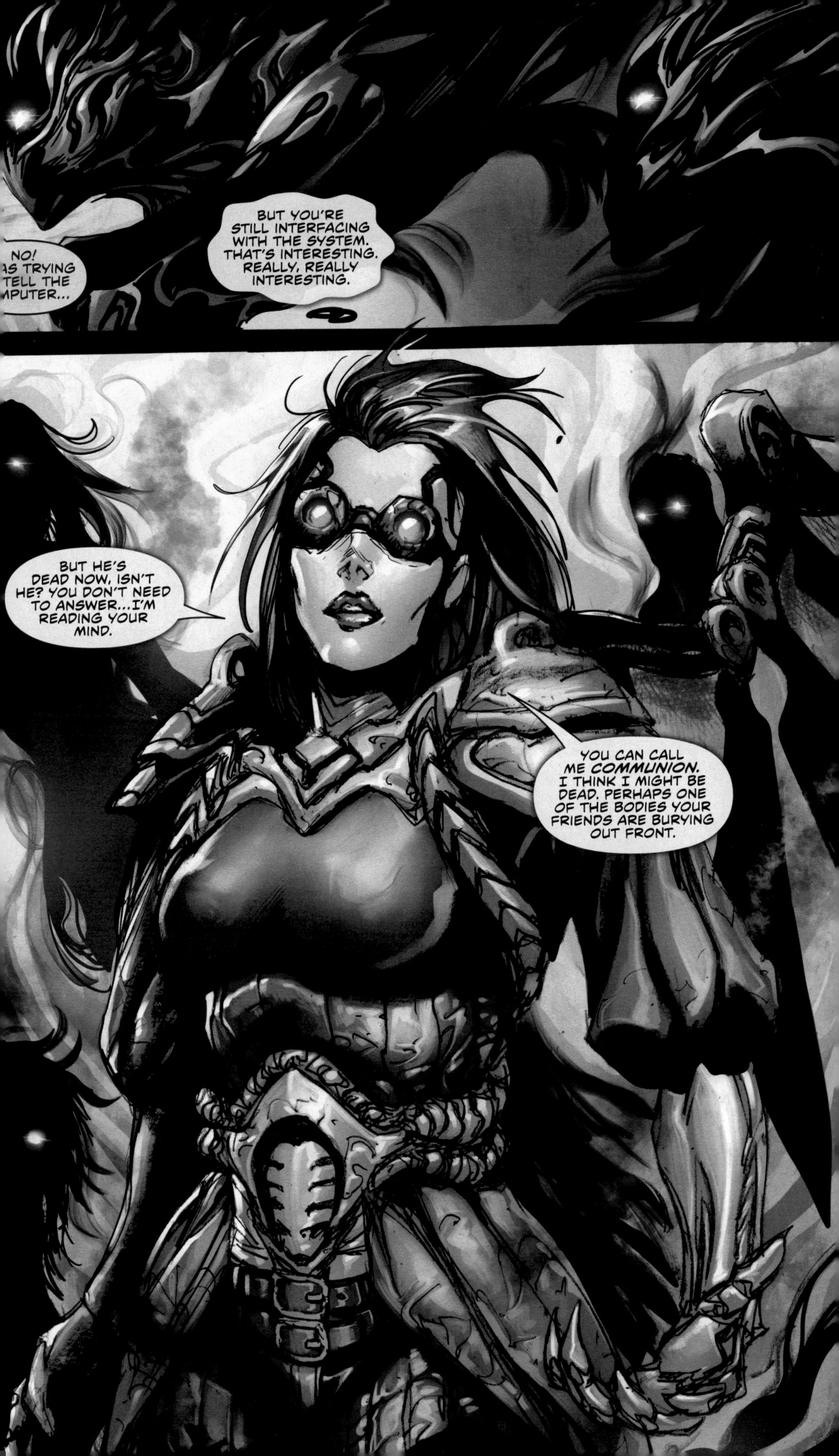
NO!
AS TRYING
TELL THE
MPUTER...
BUT YOU'RE STILL INTERFACING WITH THE SYSTEM. THAT'S INTERESTING. REALLY, REALLY INTERESTING.
BUT HE'S DEAD NOW, ISN'T HE? YOU DON'T NEED TO ANSWER...I'M READING YOUR MIND.
YOU CAN CALL ME *COMMUNION*. I THINK I MIGHT BE DEAD. PERHAPS ONE OF THE BODIES YOUR FRIENDS ARE BURYING OUT FRONT.

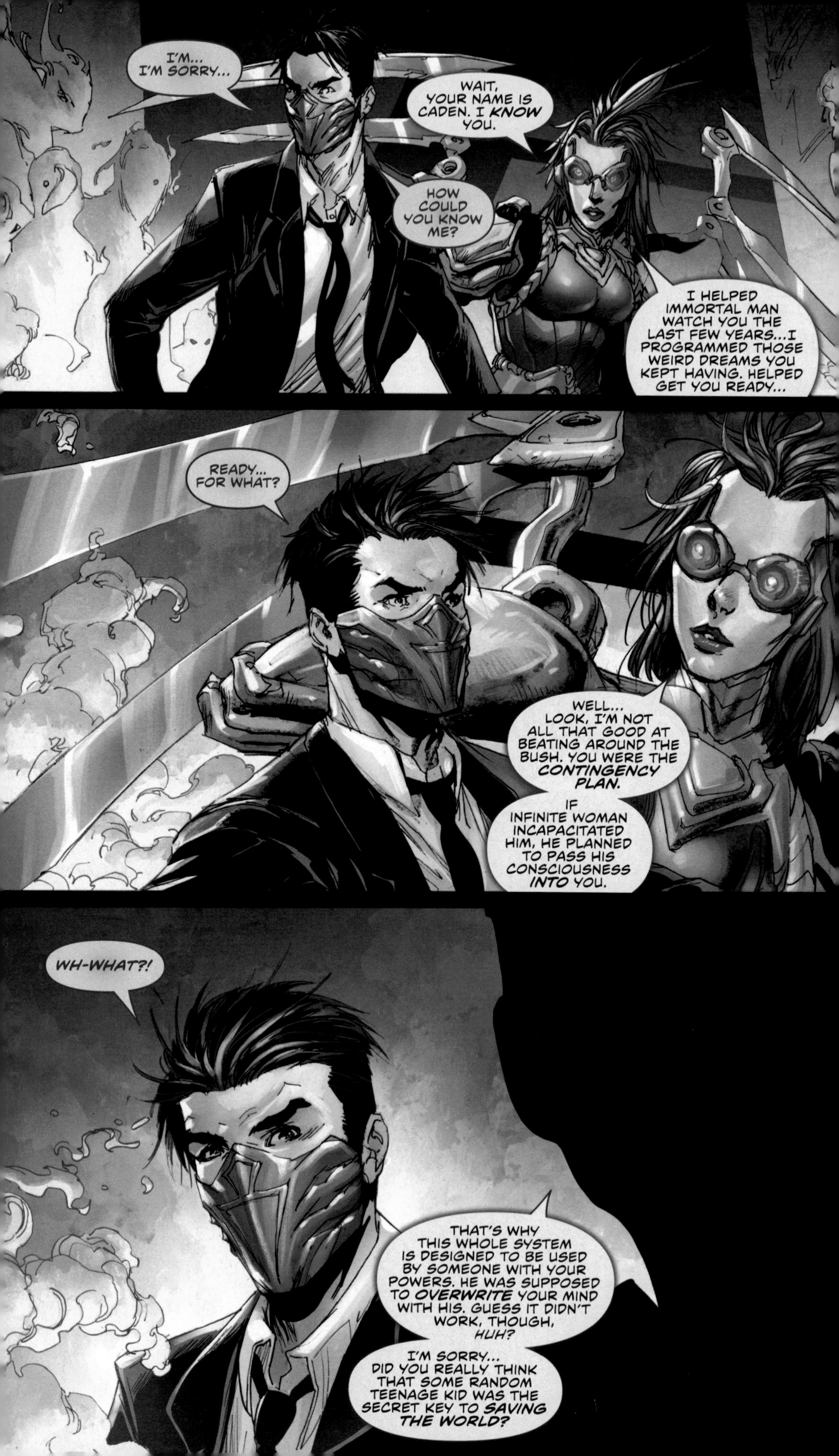
I'M... I'M SORRY...
WAIT, YOUR NAME IS CADEN. I KNOW YOU.
HOW COULD YOU KNOW ME?
I HELPED IMMORTAL MAN WATCH YOU THE LAST FEW YEARS...I PROGRAMMED THOSE WEIRD DREAMS YOU KEPT HAVING. HELPED GET YOU READY...
READY... FOR WHAT?
WELL... LOOK, I'M NOT ALL THAT GOOD AT BEATING AROUND THE BUSH. YOU WERE THE CONTINGENCY PLAN.
IF INFINITE WOMAN INCAPACITATED HIM, HE PLANNED TO PASS HIS CONSCIOUSNESS INTO YOU.
WH-WHAT?!
THAT'S WHY THIS WHOLE SYSTEM IS DESIGNED TO BE USED BY SOMEONE WITH YOUR POWERS. HE WAS SUPPOSED TO OVERWRITE YOUR MIND WITH HIS. GUESS IT DIDN'T WORK, THOUGH, HUH?
I'M SORRY... DID YOU REALLY THINK THAT SOME RANDOM TEENAGE KID WAS THE SECRET KEY TO SAVING THE WORLD?

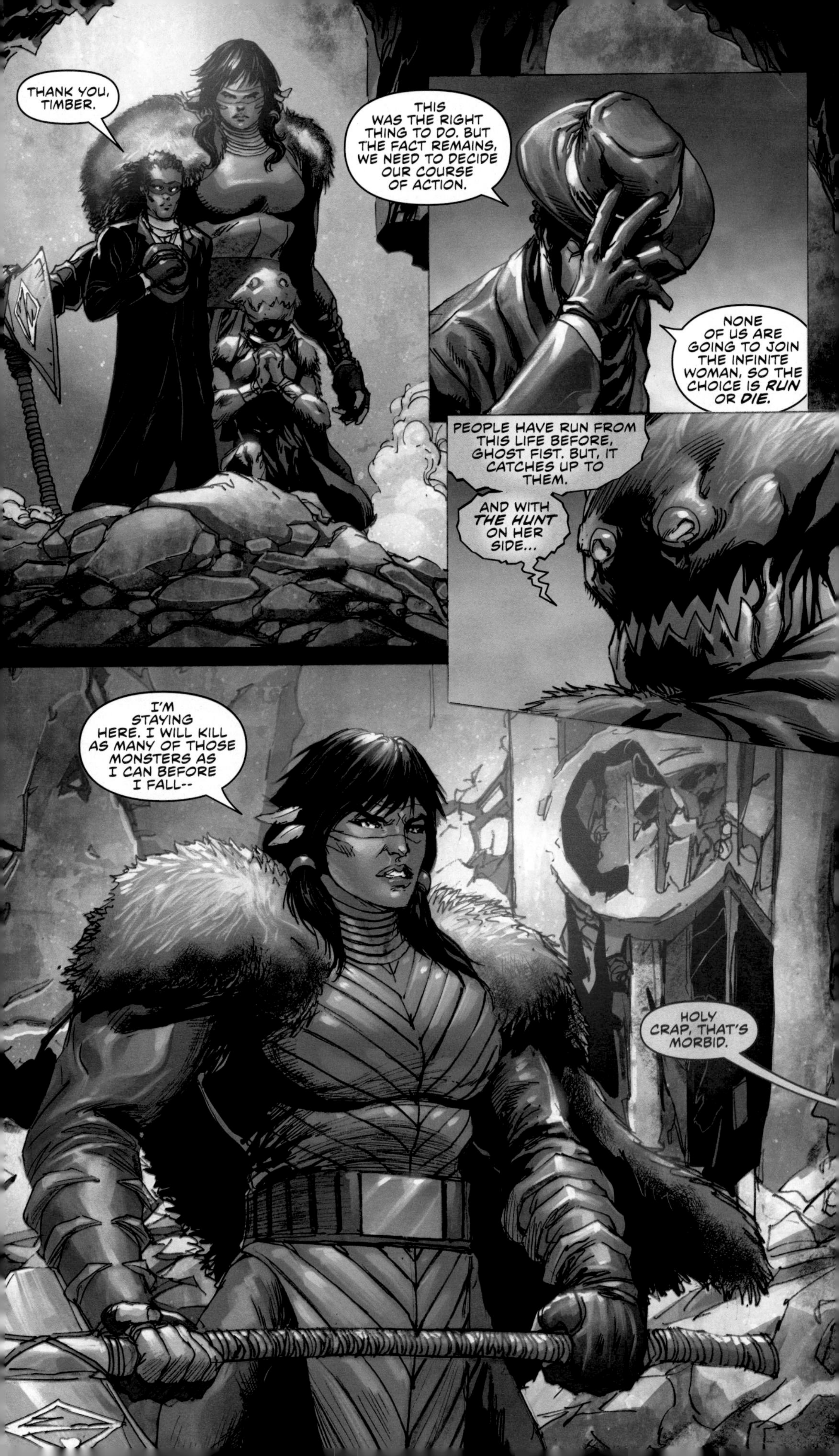
THANK YOU, TIMBER.
THIS WAS THE RIGHT THING TO DO. BUT THE FACT REMAINS, WE NEED TO DECIDE OUR COURSE OF ACTION.
NONE OF US ARE GOING TO JOIN THE INFINITE WOMAN, SO THE CHOICE IS RUN OR DIE.
PEOPLE HAVE RUN FROM THIS LIFE BEFORE, GHOST FIST. BUT, IT CATCHES UP TO THEM.
AND WITH THE HUNT ON HER SIDE...
I'M STAYING HERE. I WILL KILL AS MANY OF THOSE MONSTERS AS I CAN BEFORE I FALL--
HOLY CRAP, THAT'S MORBID.

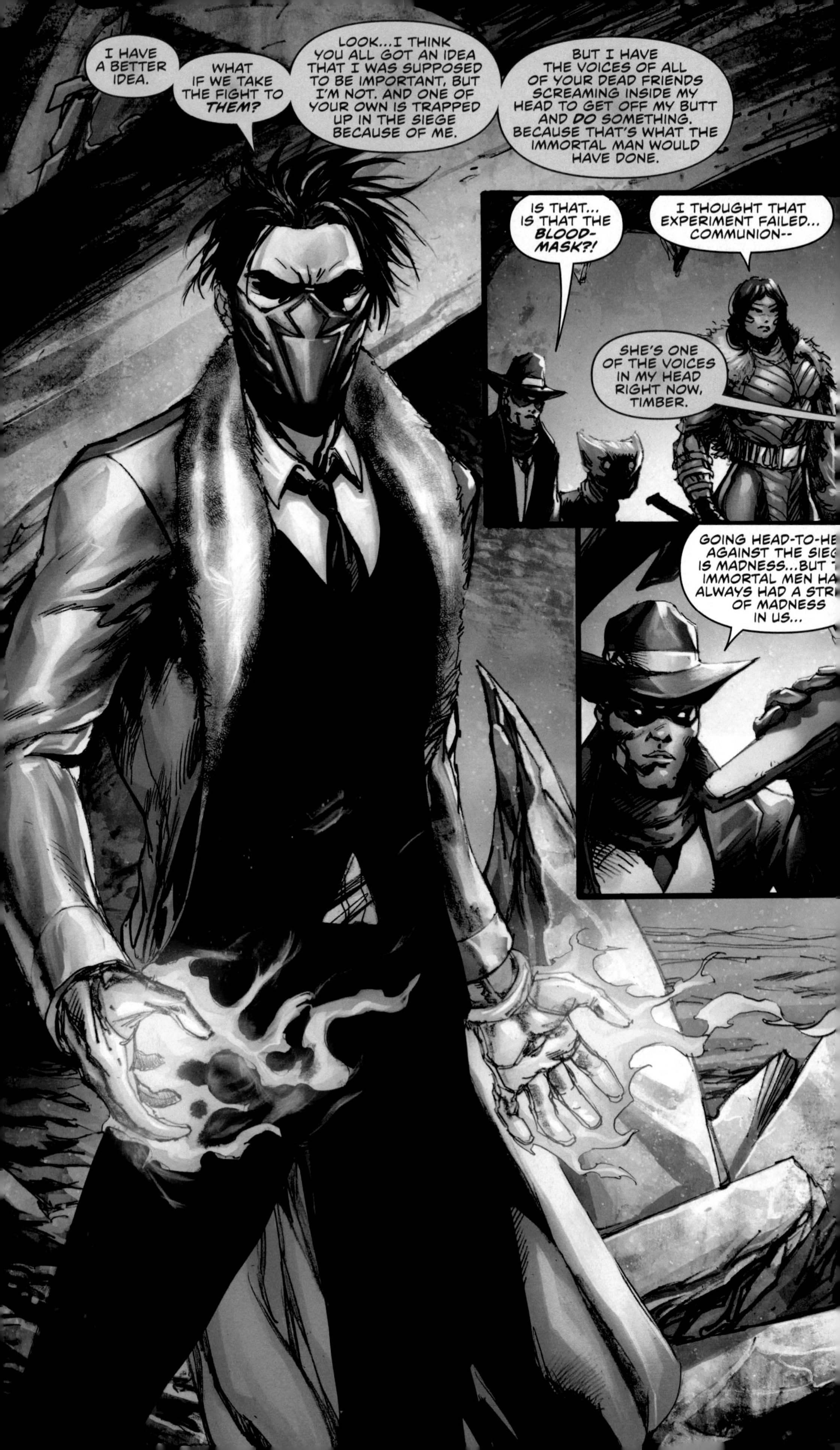
I HAVE A BETTER IDEA.
WHAT IF WE TAKE THE FIGHT TO *THEM?*
LOOK...I THINK YOU ALL GOT AN IDEA THAT I WAS SUPPOSED TO BE IMPORTANT, BUT I'M NOT. AND ONE OF YOUR OWN IS TRAPPED UP IN THE SIEGE BECAUSE OF ME.
BUT I HAVE THE VOICES OF ALL OF YOUR DEAD FRIENDS SCREAMING INSIDE MY HEAD TO GET OFF MY BUTT AND *DO* SOMETHING. BECAUSE THAT'S WHAT THE IMMORTAL MAN WOULD HAVE DONE.
IS THAT... IS THAT THE *BLOOD-MASK?!*
I THOUGHT THAT EXPERIMENT FAILED... COMMUNION--
SHE'S ONE OF THE VOICES IN MY HEAD RIGHT NOW, TIMBER.

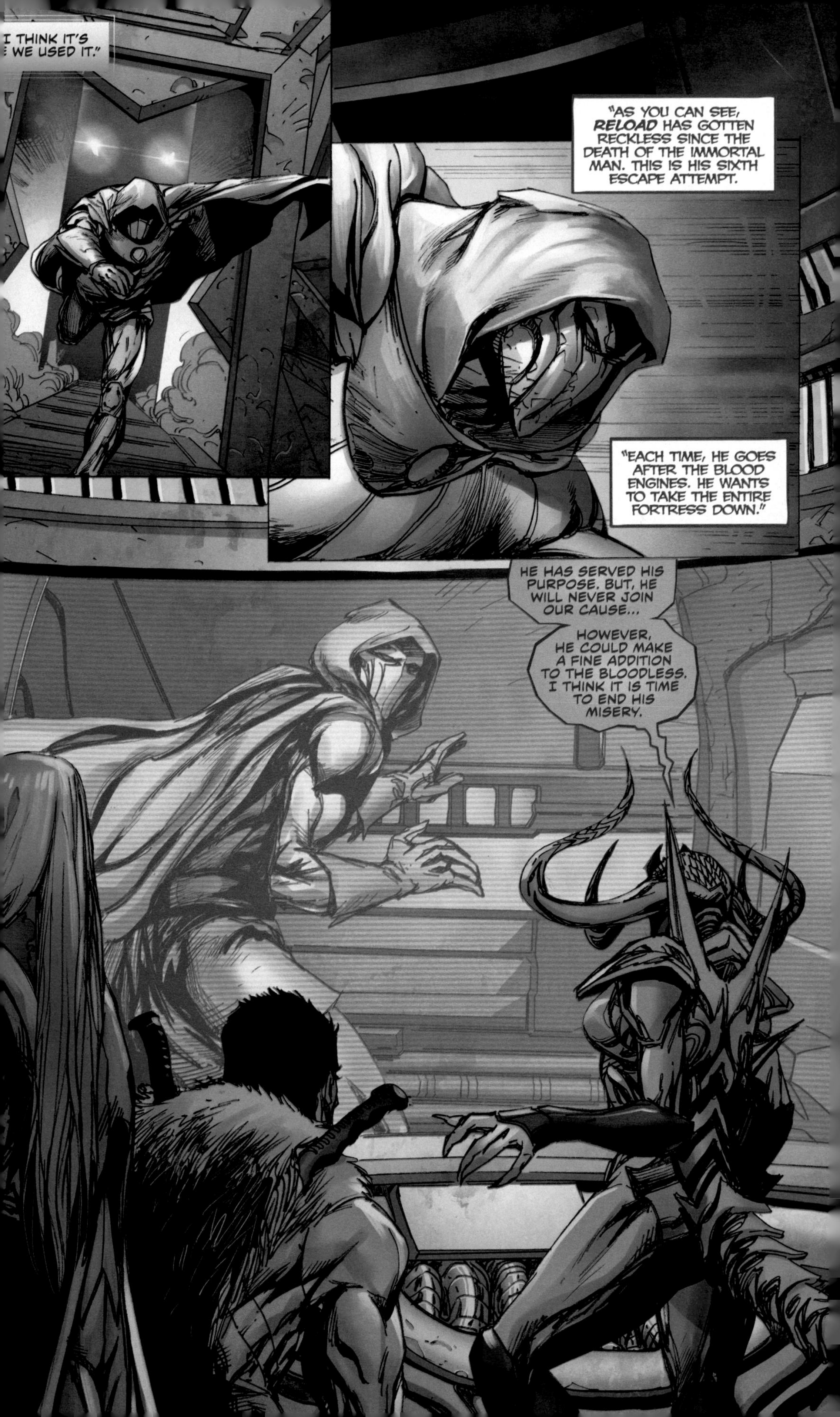
I THINK IT'S
E WE USED IT."
"AS YOU CAN SEE, RELOAD HAS GOTTEN RECKLESS SINCE THE DEATH OF THE IMMORTAL MAN. THIS IS HIS SIXTH ESCAPE ATTEMPT.
"EACH TIME, HE GOES AFTER THE BLOOD ENGINES. HE WANTS TO TAKE THE ENTIRE FORTRESS DOWN."
HE HAS SERVED HIS PURPOSE. BUT, HE WILL NEVER JOIN OUR CAUSE...
HOWEVER, HE COULD MAKE A FINE ADDITION TO THE BLOODLESS. I THINK IT IS TIME TO END HIS MISERY.

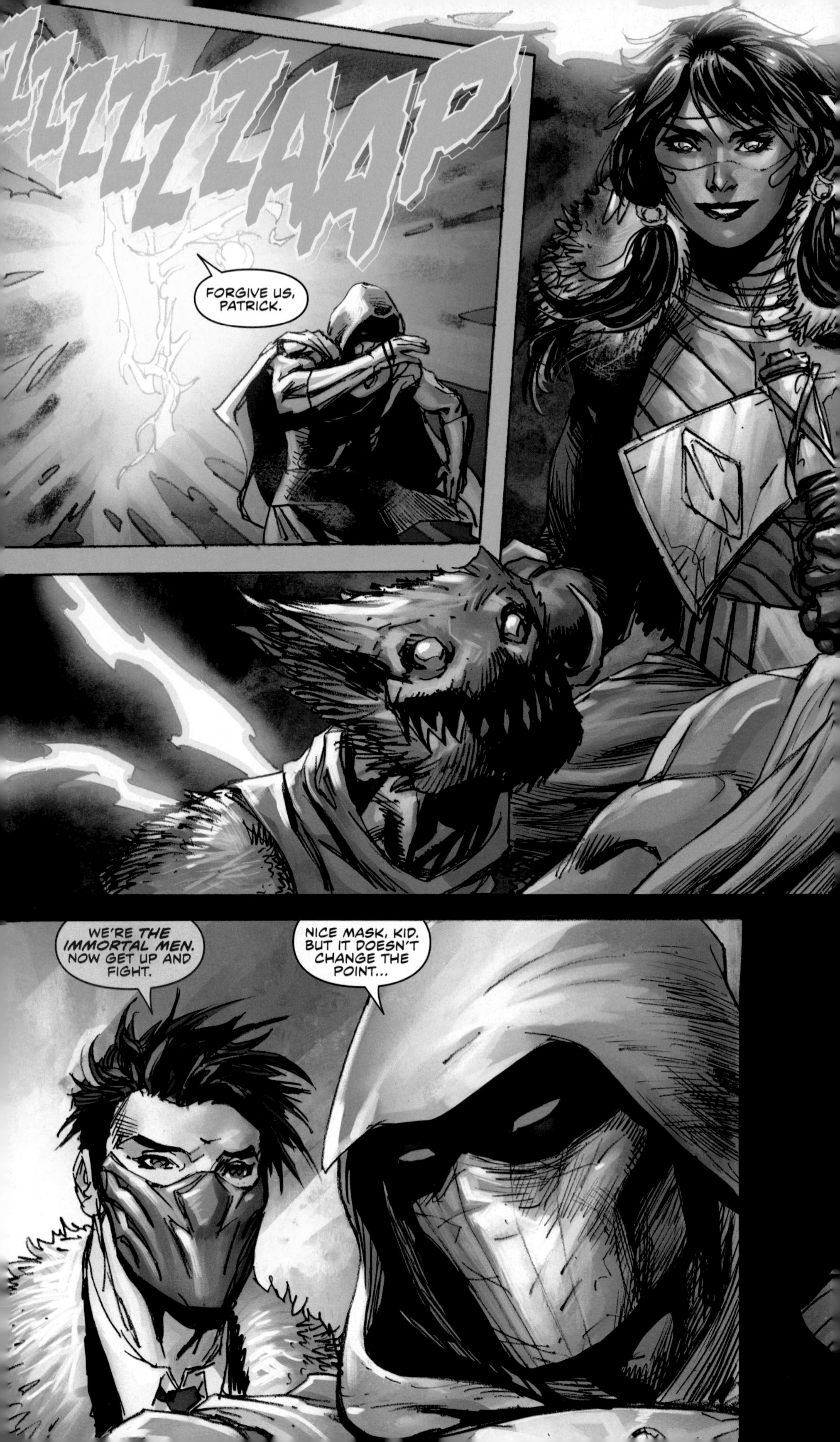
ZZZZZZAAP
FORGIVE US, PATRICK.
WE'RE *THE IMMORTAL MEN.* NOW GET UP AND FIGHT.
NICE MASK, KID. BUT IT DOESN'T CHANGE THE POINT...

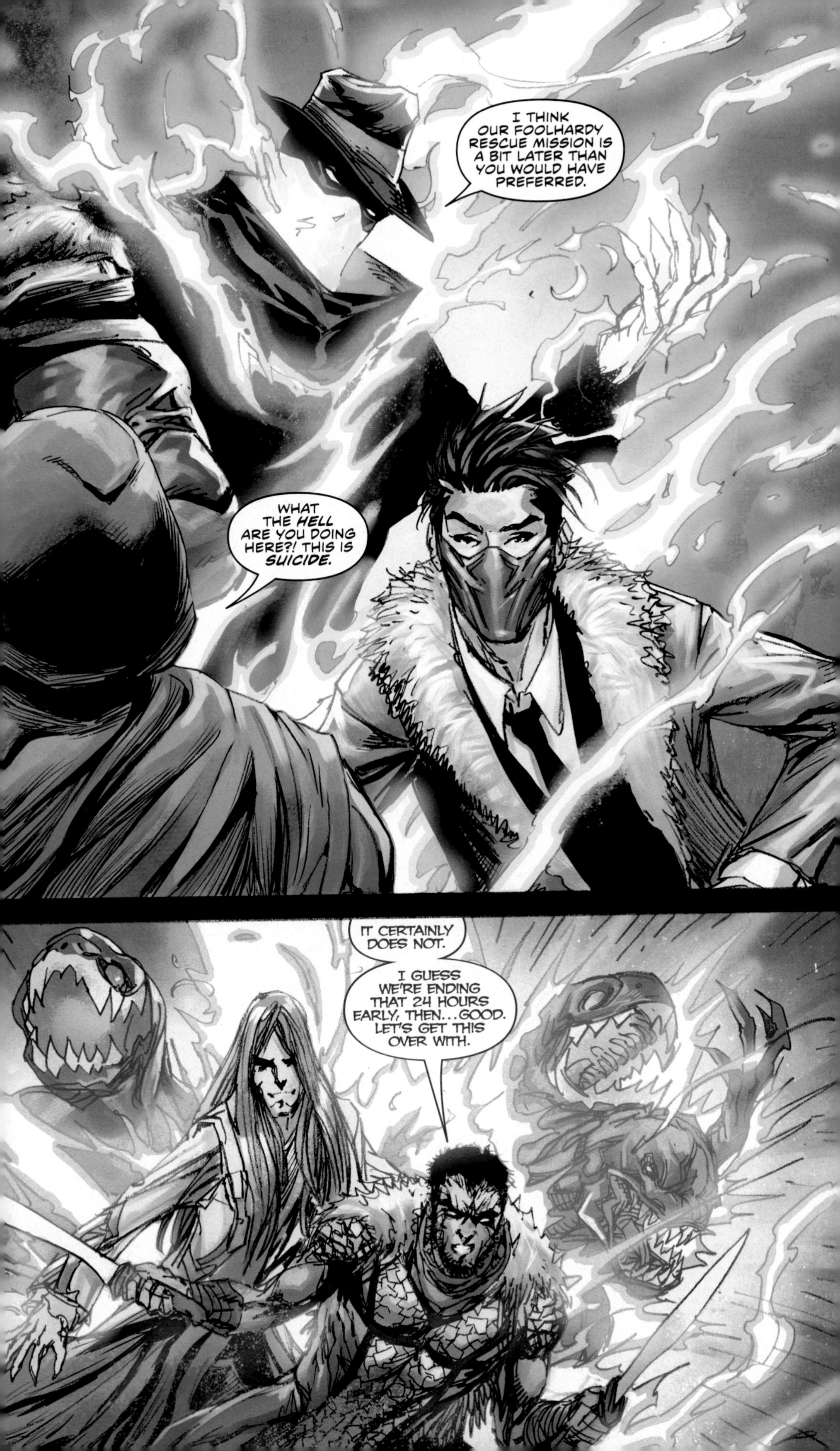
I THINK OUR FOOLHARDY RESCUE MISSION IS A BIT LATER THAN YOU WOULD HAVE PREFERRED.
WHAT THE *HELL* ARE YOU DOING HERE?! THIS IS *SUICIDE.*
IT CERTAINLY DOES NOT.
I GUESS WE'RE ENDING THAT 24 HOURS EARLY, THEN...GOOD. LET'S GET THIS OVER WITH.

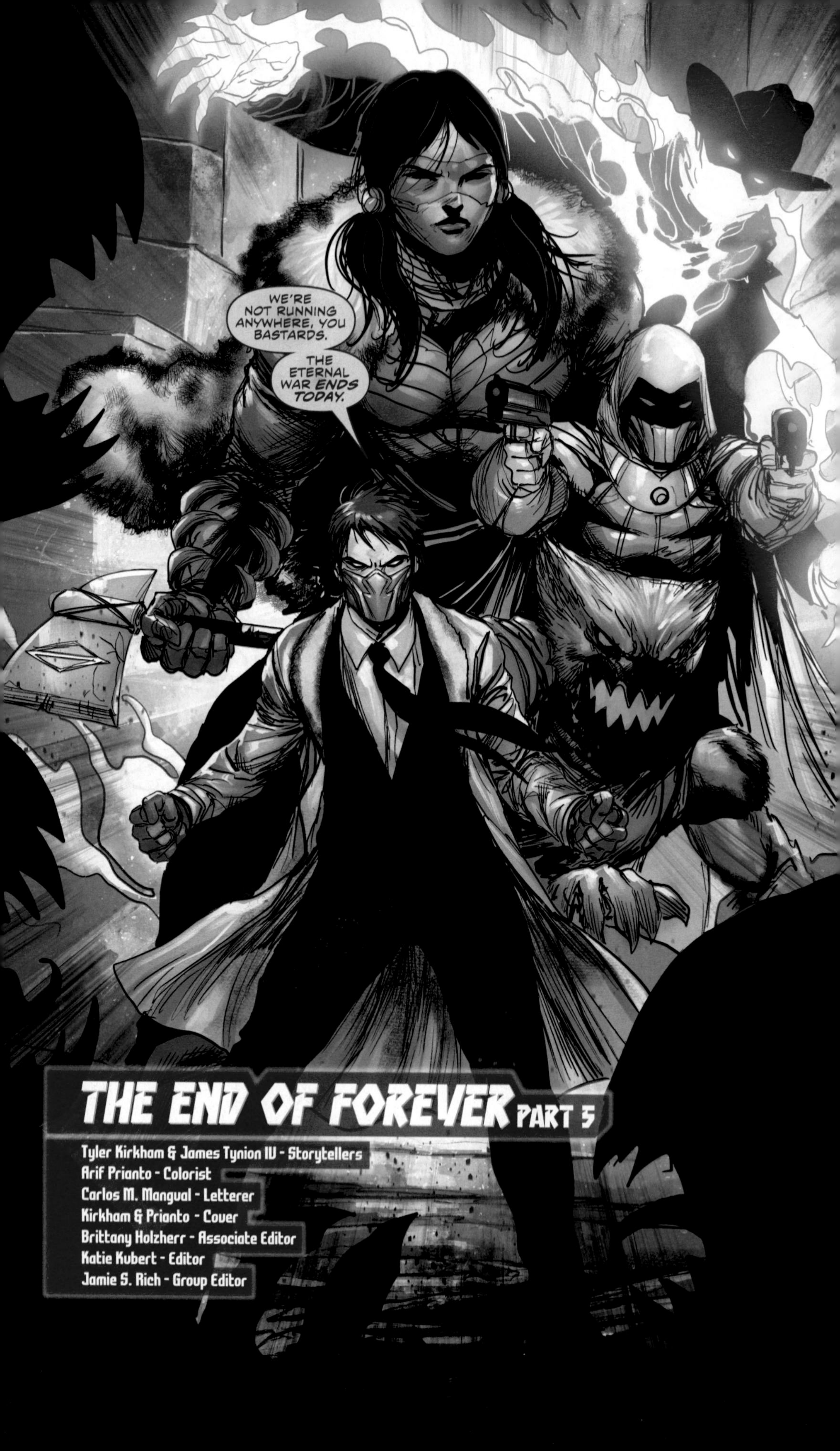
WE'RE NOT RUNNING ANYWHERE, YOU BASTARDS.
THE ETERNAL WAR ENDS TODAY.
THE END OF FOREVER PART 3
Tyler Kirkham & James Tynion IV - Storytellers
Arif Prianto - Colorist
Carlos M. Mangual - Letterer
Kirkham & Prianto - Cover
Brittany Holzherr - Associate Editor
Katie Kubert - Editor
Jamie S. Rich - Group Editor

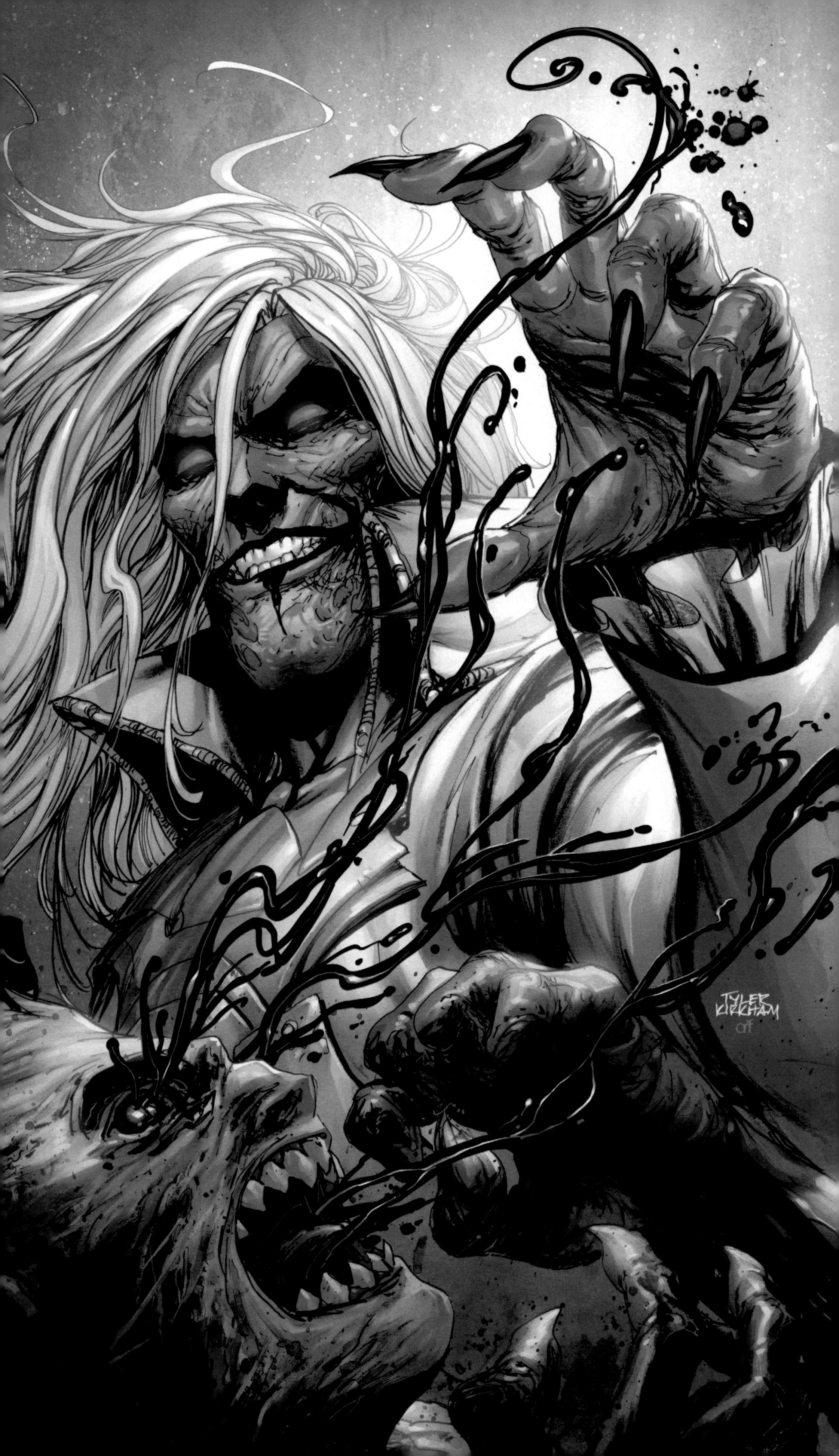
TYLER KIRKHAM
art

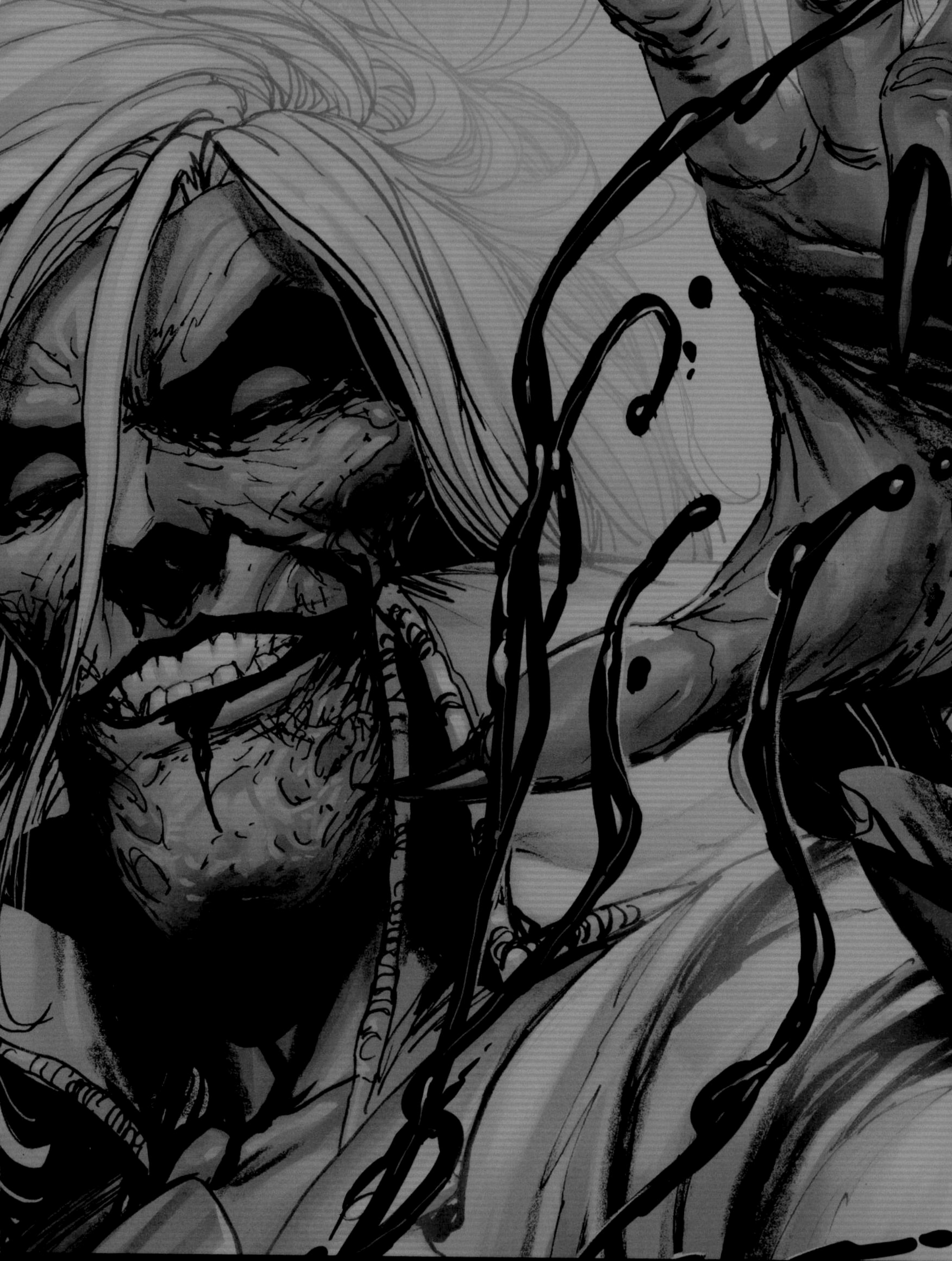

THE
IMMORTAL MEN
#6

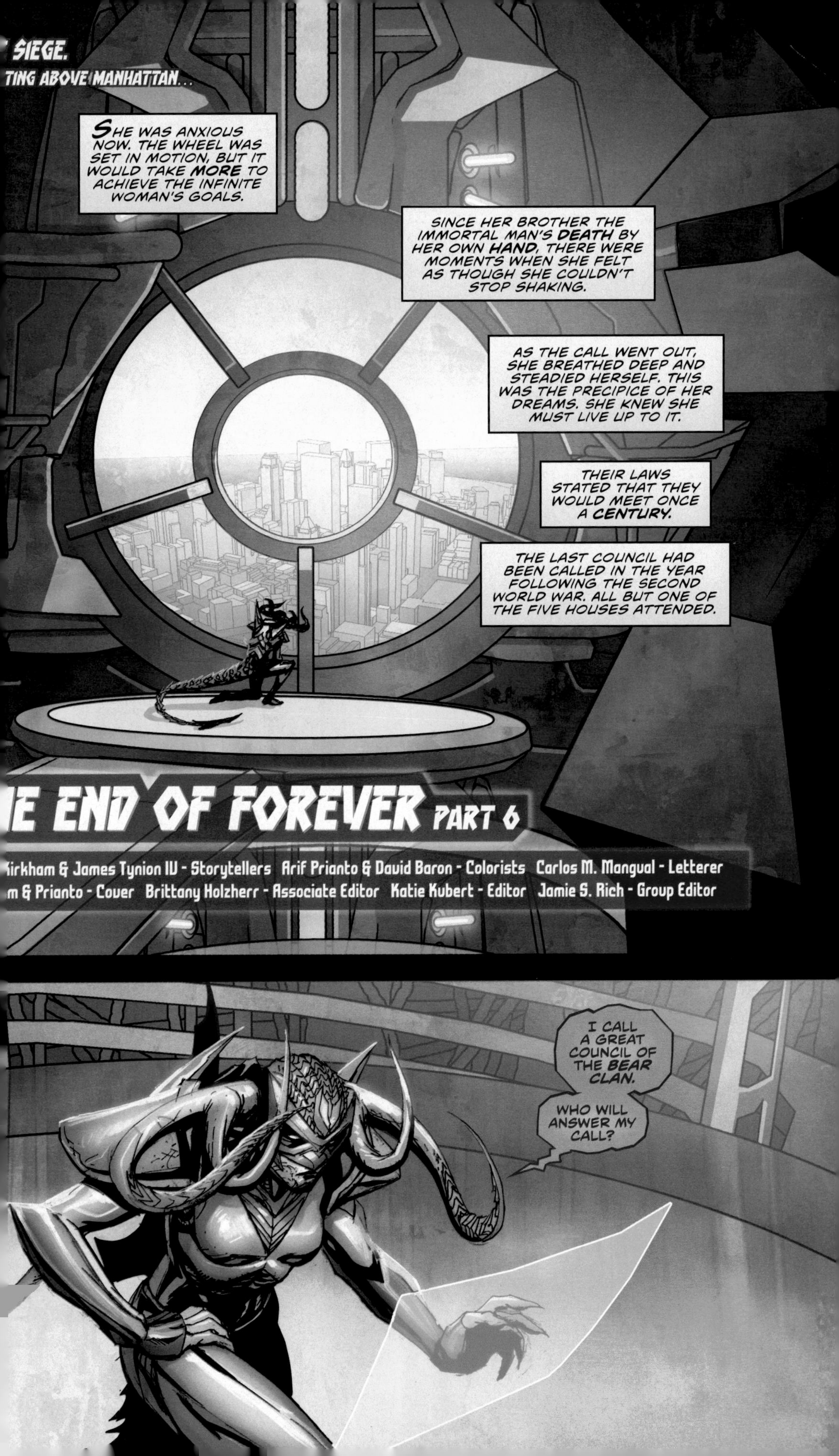

SIEGE.
TING ABOVE MANHATTAN...
SHE WAS ANXIOUS NOW. THE WHEEL WAS SET IN MOTION, BUT IT WOULD TAKE MORE TO ACHIEVE THE INFINITE WOMAN'S GOALS.
SINCE HER BROTHER THE IMMORTAL MAN'S DEATH BY HER OWN HAND, THERE WERE MOMENTS WHEN SHE FELT AS THOUGH SHE COULDN'T STOP SHAKING.
AS THE CALL WENT OUT, SHE BREATHED DEEP AND STEADIED HERSELF. THIS WAS THE PRECIPICE OF HER DREAMS. SHE KNEW SHE MUST LIVE UP TO IT.
THEIR LAWS STATED THAT THEY WOULD MEET ONCE A CENTURY.
THE LAST COUNCIL HAD BEEN CALLED IN THE YEAR FOLLOWING THE SECOND WORLD WAR. ALL BUT ONE OF THE FIVE HOUSES ATTENDED.
E END OF FOREVER PART 6
irkham & James Tynion IV - Storytellers Arif Prianto & David Baron - Colorists Carlos M. Mangual - Letterer
m & Prianto - Cover Brittany Holzherr - Associate Editor Katie Kubert - Editor Jamie S. Rich - Group Editor
I CALL A GREAT COUNCIL OF THE BEAR CLAN.
WHO WILL ANSWER MY CALL?

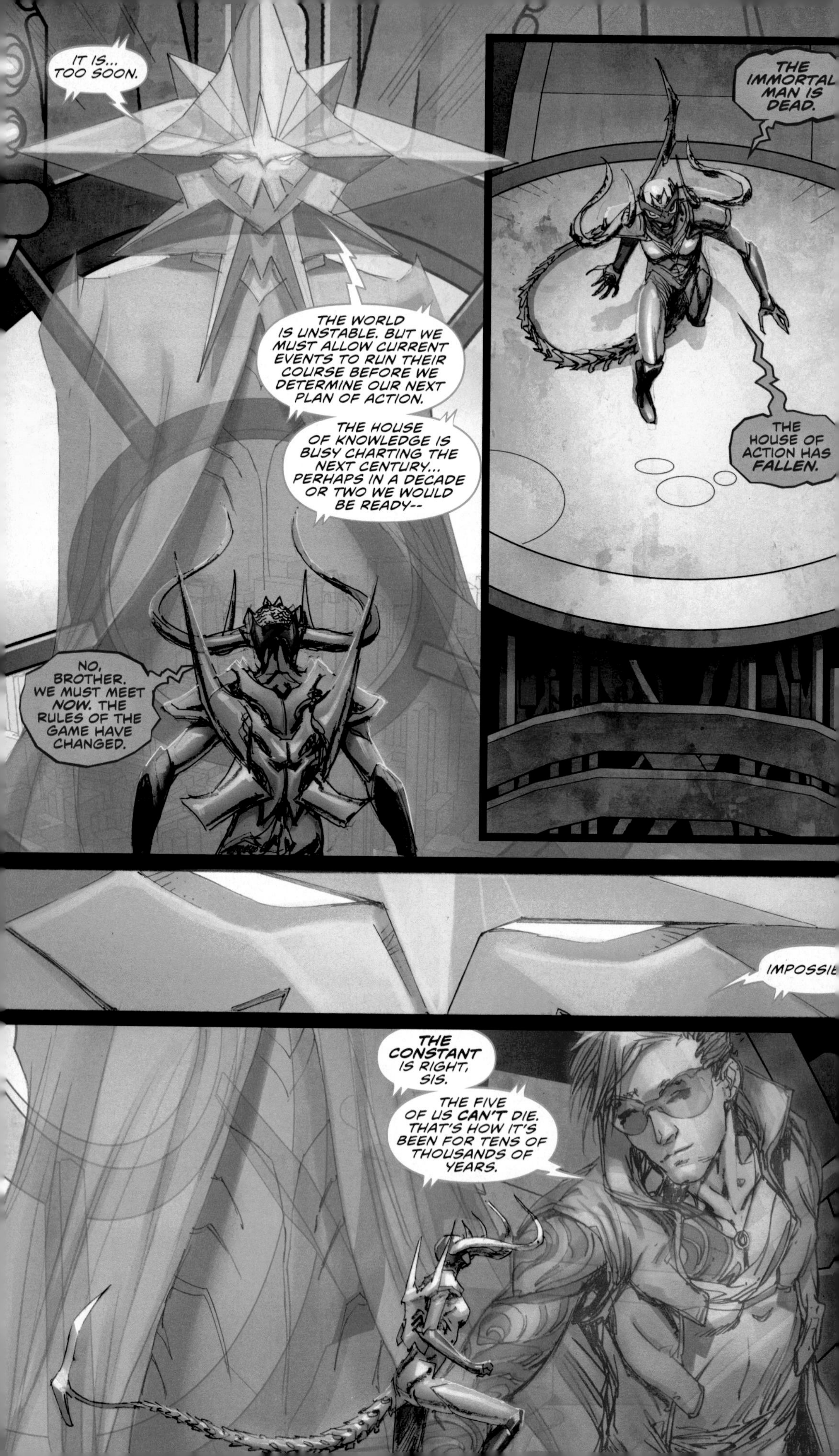
IT IS... TOO SOON.
THE WORLD IS UNSTABLE. BUT WE MUST ALLOW CURRENT EVENTS TO RUN THEIR COURSE BEFORE WE DETERMINE OUR NEXT PLAN OF ACTION.
THE HOUSE OF KNOWLEDGE IS BUSY CHARTING THE NEXT CENTURY... PERHAPS IN A DECADE OR TWO WE WOULD BE READY--
NO, BROTHER. WE MUST MEET NOW. THE RULES OF THE GAME HAVE CHANGED.
THE IMMORTAL MAN IS DEAD.
THE HOUSE OF ACTION HAS FALLEN.
IMPOSSIB
THE CONSTANT IS RIGHT, SIS.
THE FIVE OF US CAN'T DIE. THAT'S HOW IT'S BEEN FOR TENS OF THOUSANDS OF YEARS.

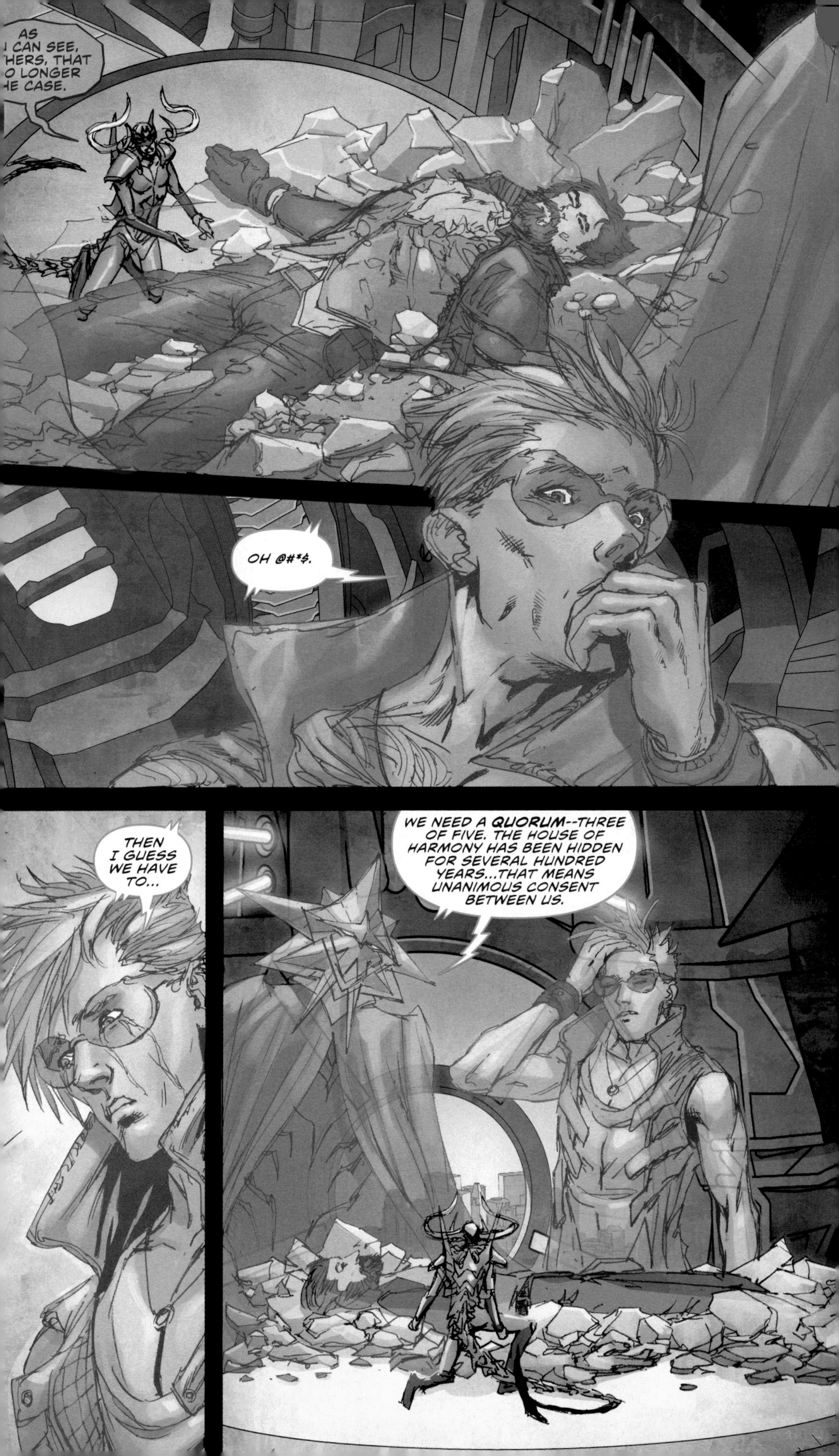
AS
CAN SEE,
HERS, THAT
O LONGER
HE CASE.
OH @#*$.
THEN I GUESS WE HAVE TO...
WE NEED A QUORUM--THREE OF FIVE. THE HOUSE OF HARMONY HAS BEEN HIDDEN FOR SEVERAL HUNDRED YEARS...THAT MEANS UNANIMOUS CONSENT BETWEEN US.

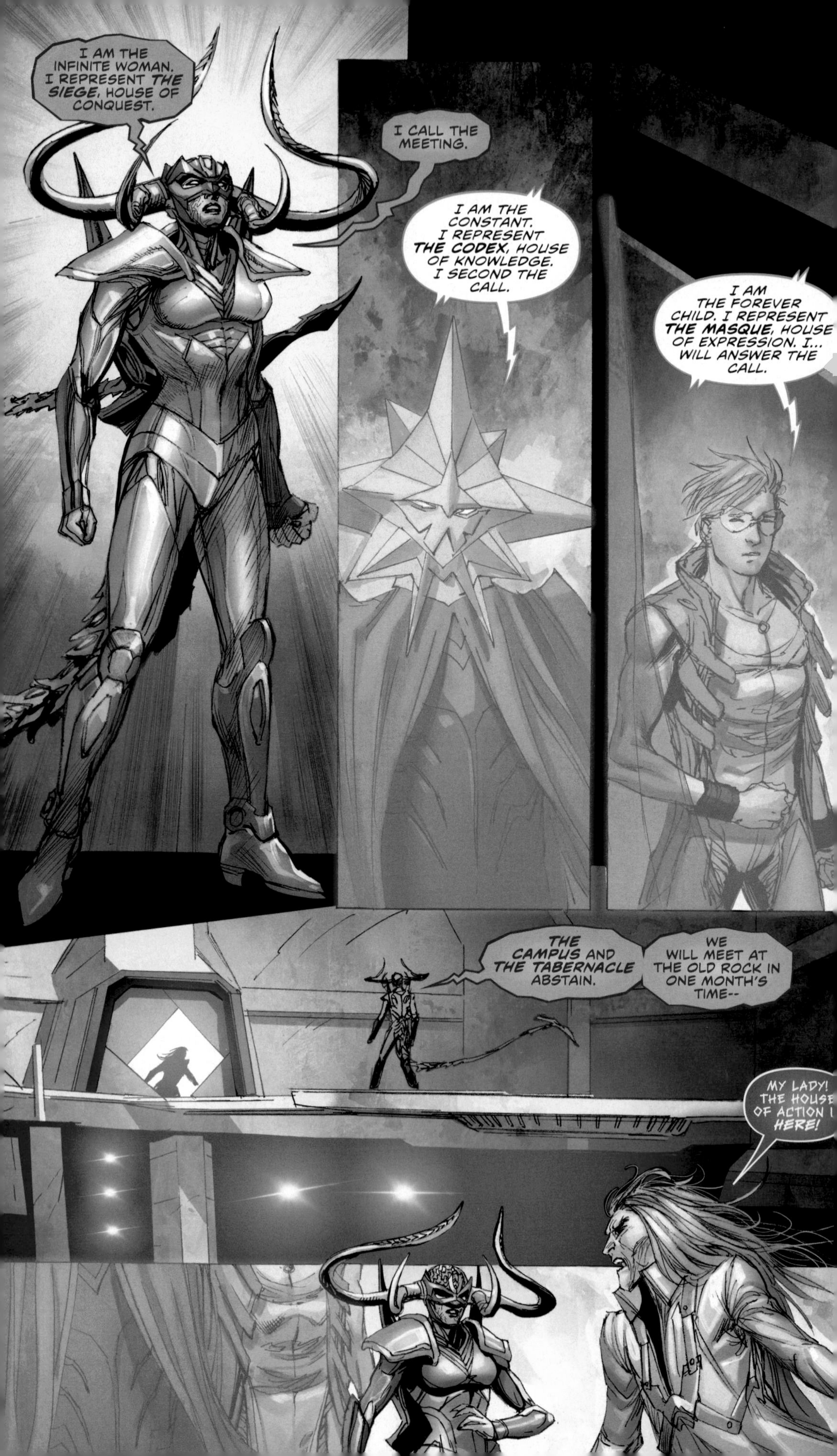
I AM THE INFINITE WOMAN. I REPRESENT THE SIEGE, HOUSE OF CONQUEST.
I CALL THE MEETING.
I AM THE CONSTANT. I REPRESENT THE CODEX, HOUSE OF KNOWLEDGE. I SECOND THE CALL.
I AM THE FOREVER CHILD. I REPRESENT THE MASQUE, HOUSE OF EXPRESSION. I... WILL ANSWER THE CALL.
THE CAMPUS AND THE TABERNACLE ABSTAIN.
WE WILL MEET AT THE OLD ROCK IN ONE MONTH'S TIME--
MY LADY! THE HOUSE OF ACTION I HERE!

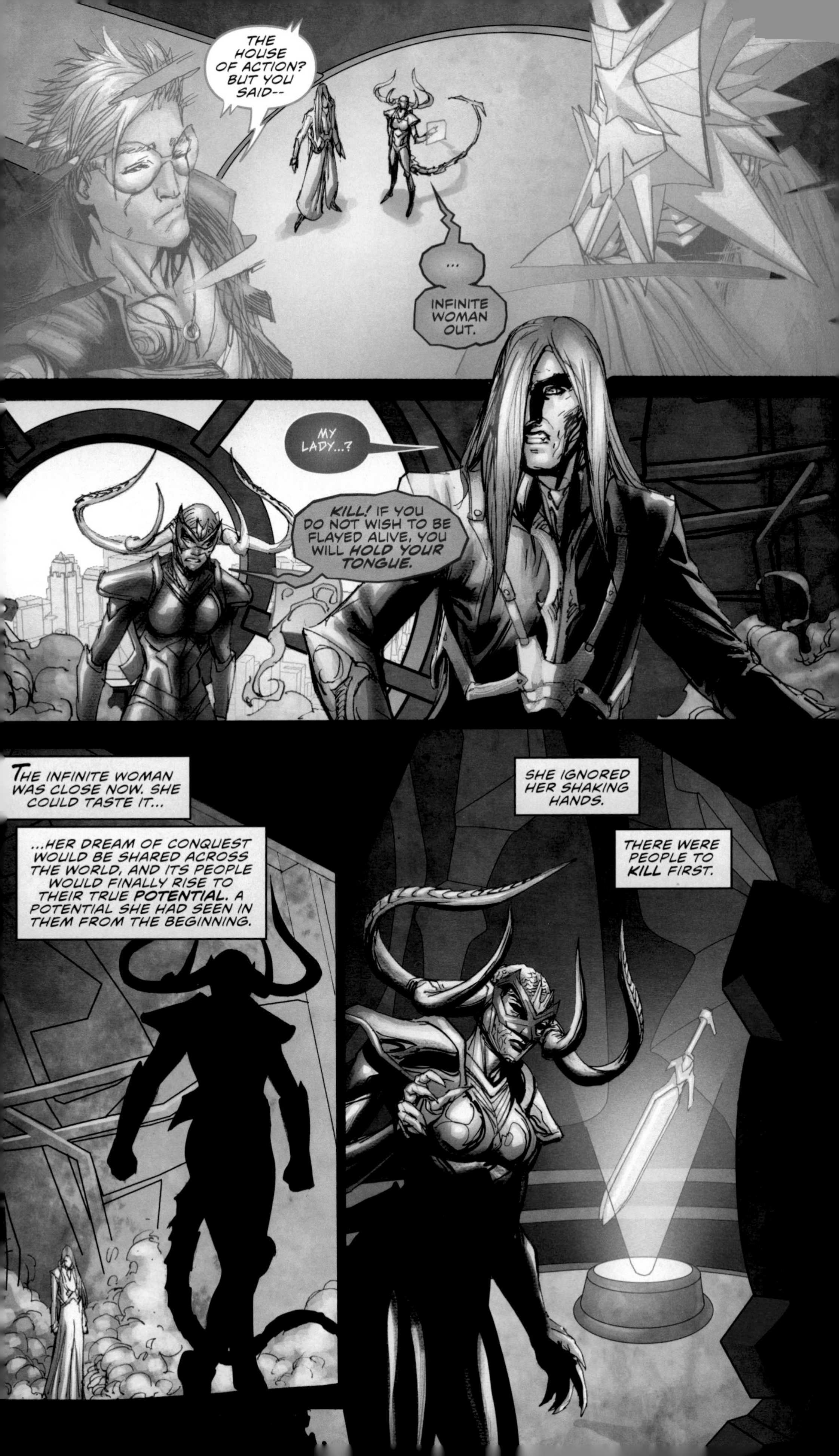
THE HOUSE OF ACTION? BUT YOU SAID--
...
INFINITE WOMAN OUT.
MY LADY...?
KILL! IF YOU DO NOT WISH TO BE FLAYED ALIVE, YOU WILL HOLD YOUR TONGUE.
THE INFINITE WOMAN WAS CLOSE NOW. SHE COULD TASTE IT...
...HER DREAM OF CONQUEST WOULD BE SHARED ACROSS THE WORLD, AND ITS PEOPLE WOULD FINALLY RISE TO THEIR TRUE POTENTIAL. A POTENTIAL SHE HAD SEEN IN THEM FROM THE BEGINNING.
SHE IGNORED HER SHAKING HANDS.
THERE WERE PEOPLE TO KILL FIRST.

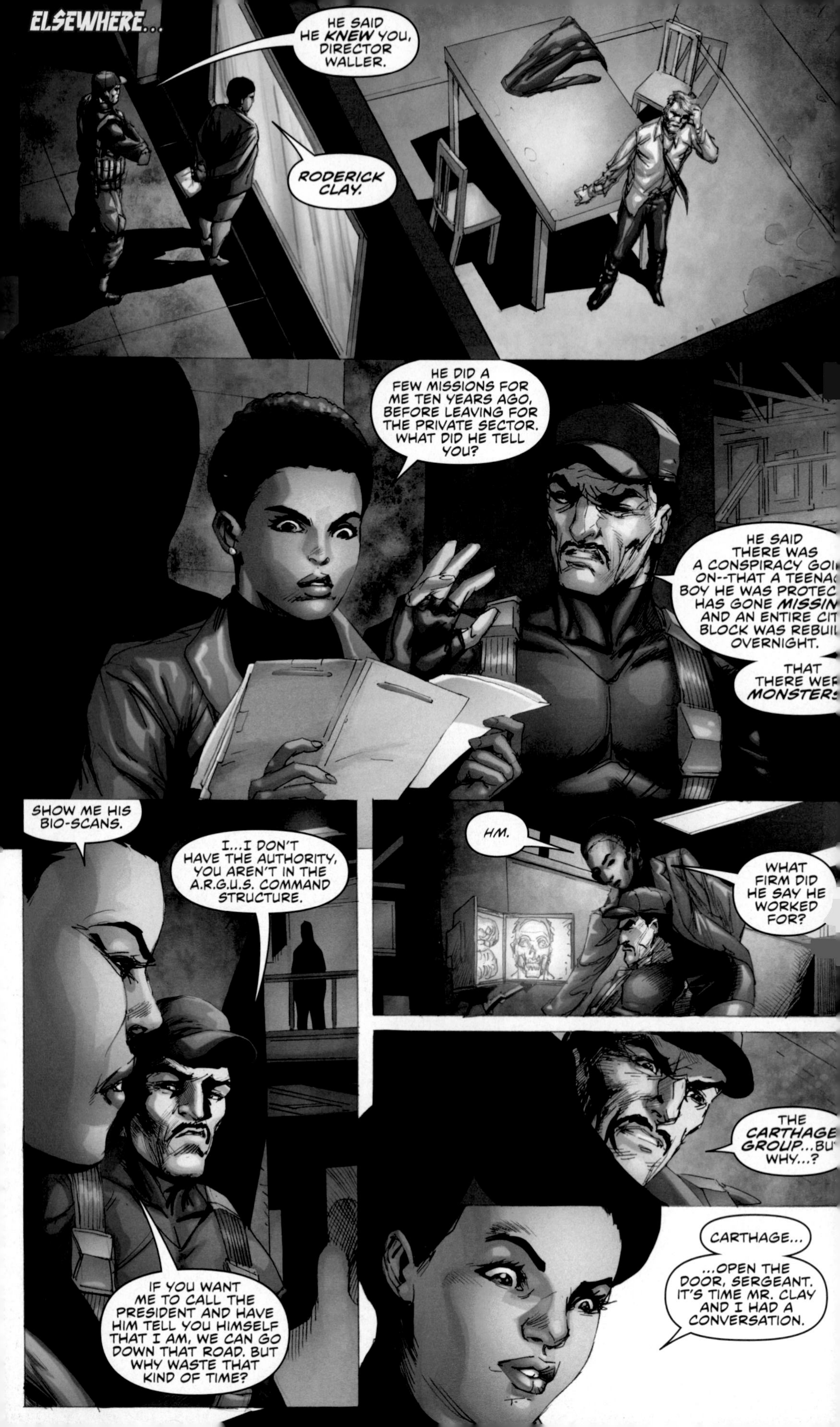
ELSEWHERE...
HE SAID HE KNEW YOU, DIRECTOR WALLER.
RODERICK CLAY.
HE DID A FEW MISSIONS FOR ME TEN YEARS AGO, BEFORE LEAVING FOR THE PRIVATE SECTOR. WHAT DID HE TELL YOU?
HE SAID THERE WAS A CONSPIRACY GOI ON--THAT A TEENA BOY HE WAS PROTEC HAS GONE MISSIN AND AN ENTIRE CIT BLOCK WAS REBUI OVERNIGHT.
THAT THERE WER MONSTERS
SHOW ME HIS BIO-SCANS.
I...I DON'T HAVE THE AUTHORITY. YOU AREN'T IN THE A.R.G.U.S. COMMAND STRUCTURE.
IF YOU WANT ME TO CALL THE PRESIDENT AND HAVE HIM TELL YOU HIMSELF THAT I AM, WE CAN GO DOWN THAT ROAD. BUT WHY WASTE THAT KIND OF TIME?
HM.
WHAT FIRM DID HE SAY HE WORKED FOR?
THE CARTHAGE GROUP...BU WHY...?
CARTHAGE...
...OPEN THE DOOR, SERGEANT. IT'S TIME MR. CLAY AND I HAD A CONVERSATION.

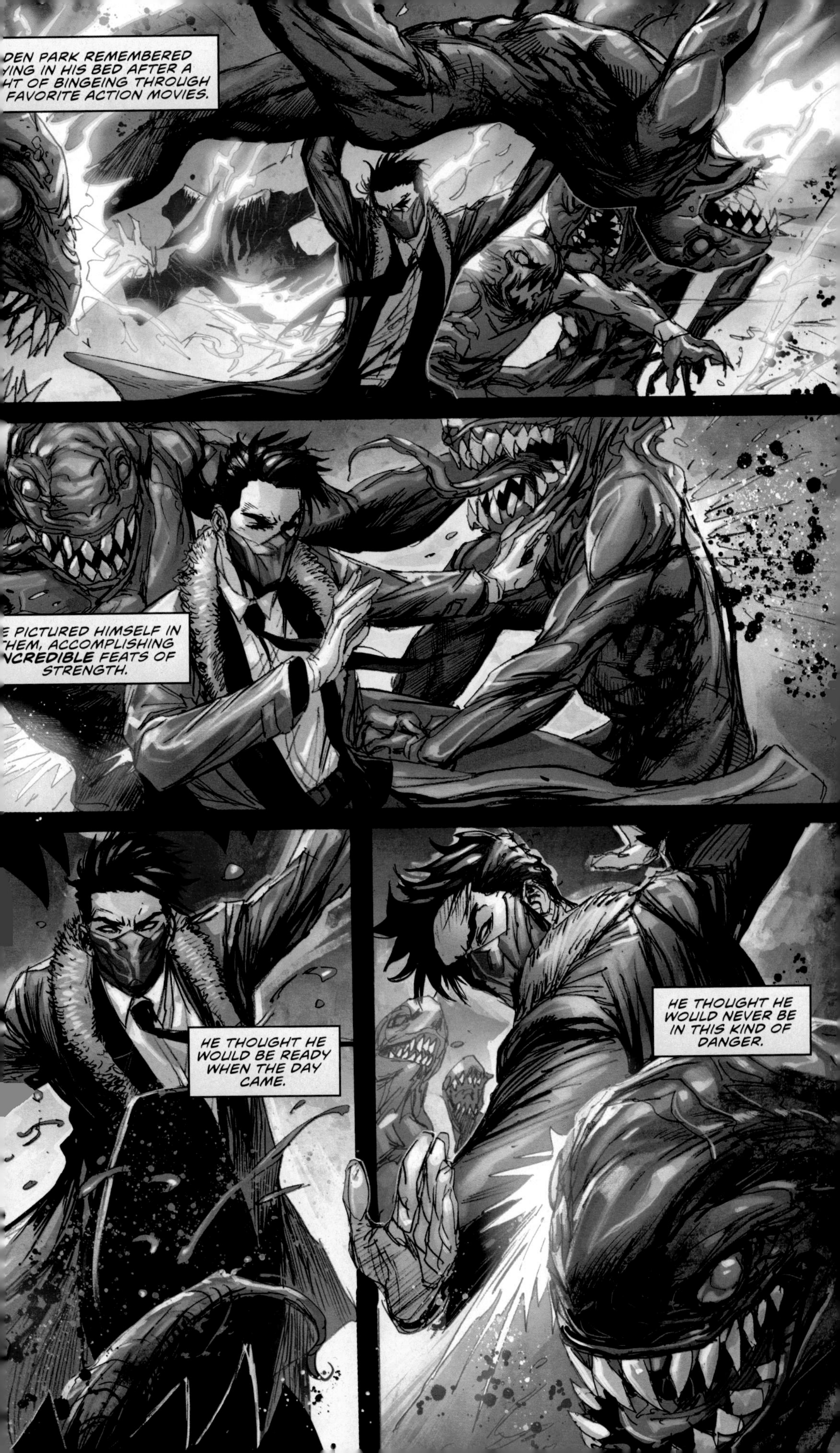

DEN PARK REMEMBERED
YING IN HIS BED AFTER A
HT OF BINGEING THROUGH
FAVORITE ACTION MOVIES.
E PICTURED HIMSELF IN
THEM, ACCOMPLISHING
NCREDIBLE FEATS OF
STRENGTH.
HE THOUGHT HE
WOULD BE READY
WHEN THE DAY
CAME.
HE THOUGHT HE
WOULD NEVER BE
IN THIS KIND OF
DANGER.

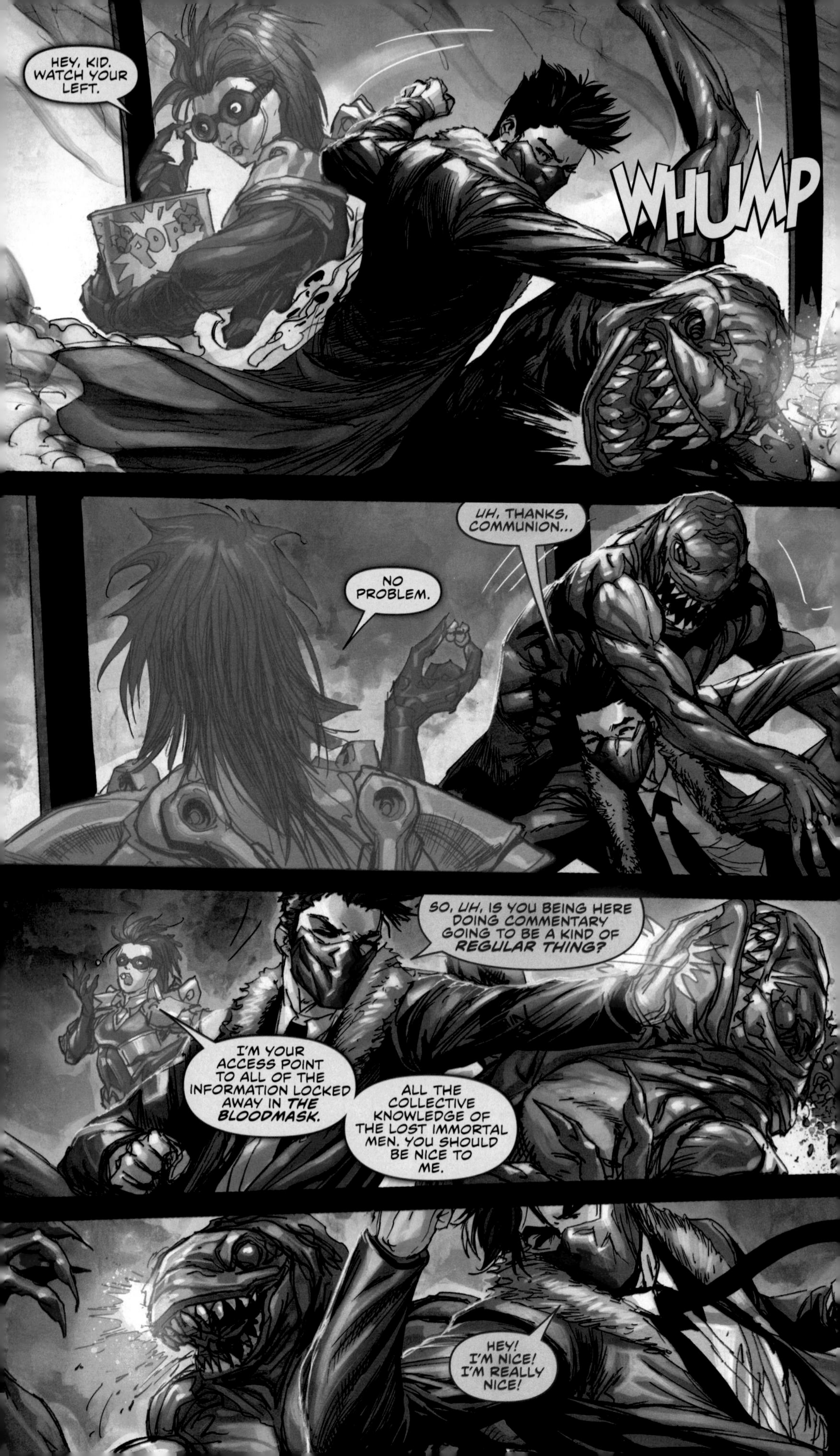
HEY, KID. WATCH YOUR LEFT.
POP
WHUMP
UH, THANKS, COMMUNION...
NO PROBLEM.
SO, UH, IS YOU BEING HERE DOING COMMENTARY GOING TO BE A KIND OF REGULAR THING?
I'M YOUR ACCESS POINT TO ALL OF THE INFORMATION LOCKED AWAY IN THE BLOODMASK.
ALL THE COLLECTIVE KNOWLEDGE OF THE LOST IMMORTAL MEN. YOU SHOULD BE NICE TO ME.
HEY! I'M NICE! I'M REALLY NICE!

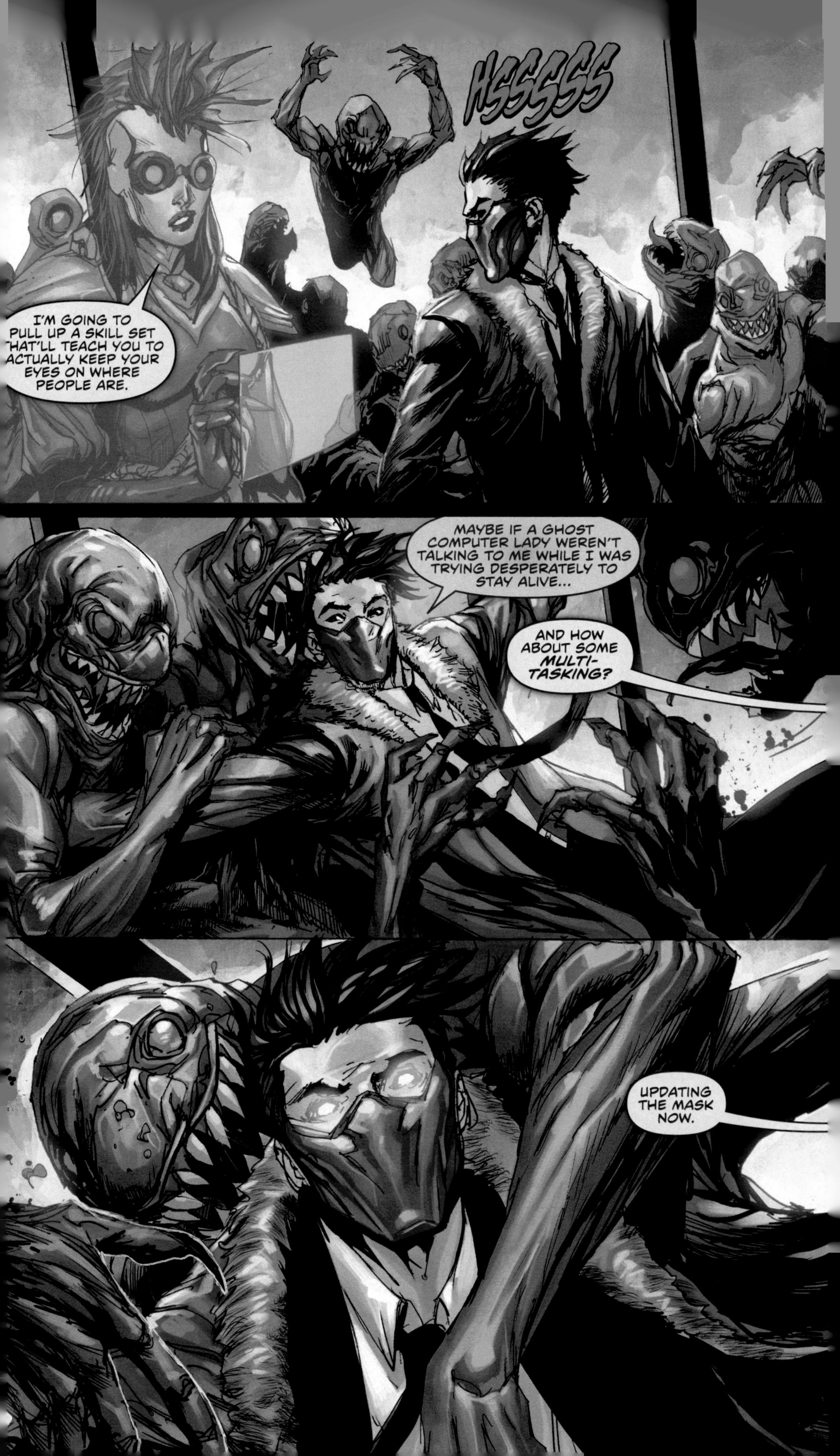
HSSSSS
I'M GOING TO PULL UP A SKILL SET THAT'LL TEACH YOU TO ACTUALLY KEEP YOUR EYES ON WHERE PEOPLE ARE.
MAYBE IF A GHOST COMPUTER LADY WEREN'T TALKING TO ME WHILE I WAS TRYING DESPERATELY TO STAY ALIVE...
AND HOW ABOUT SOME *MULTI-TASKING?*
UPDATING THE MASK NOW.

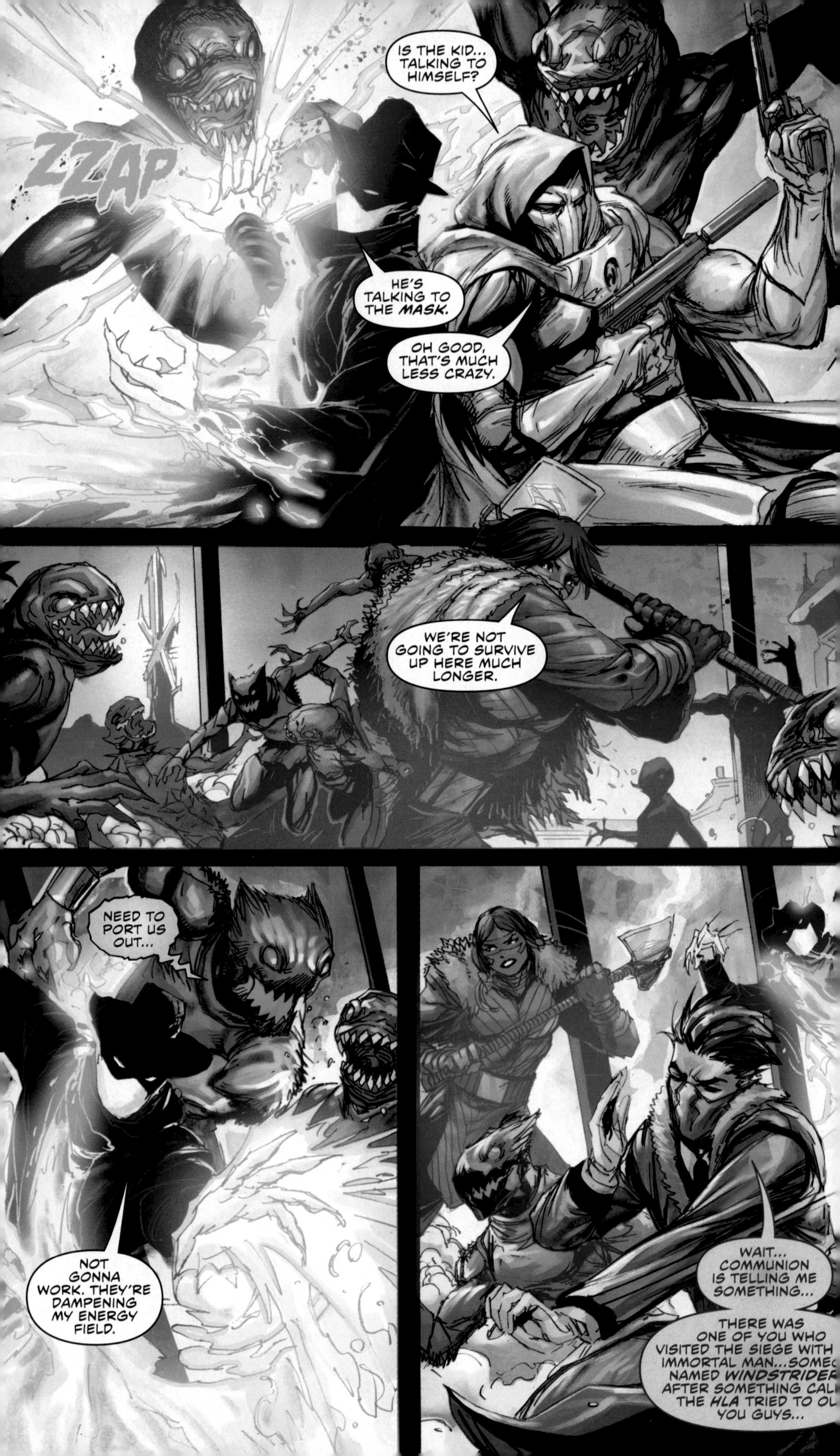
ZZAP
IS THE KID... TALKING TO HIMSELF?
HE'S TALKING TO THE *MASK*.
OH GOOD, THAT'S MUCH LESS CRAZY.
WE'RE NOT GOING TO SURVIVE UP HERE MUCH LONGER.
NEED TO PORT US OUT...
NOT GONNA WORK. THEY'RE DAMPENING MY ENERGY FIELD.
WAIT... COMMUNION IS TELLING ME SOMETHING...
THERE WAS ONE OF YOU WHO VISITED THE SIEGE WITH IMMORTAL MAN...SOME NAMED *WINDSTRIDER* AFTER SOMETHING CAL THE *HLA* TRIED TO OU YOU GUYS...

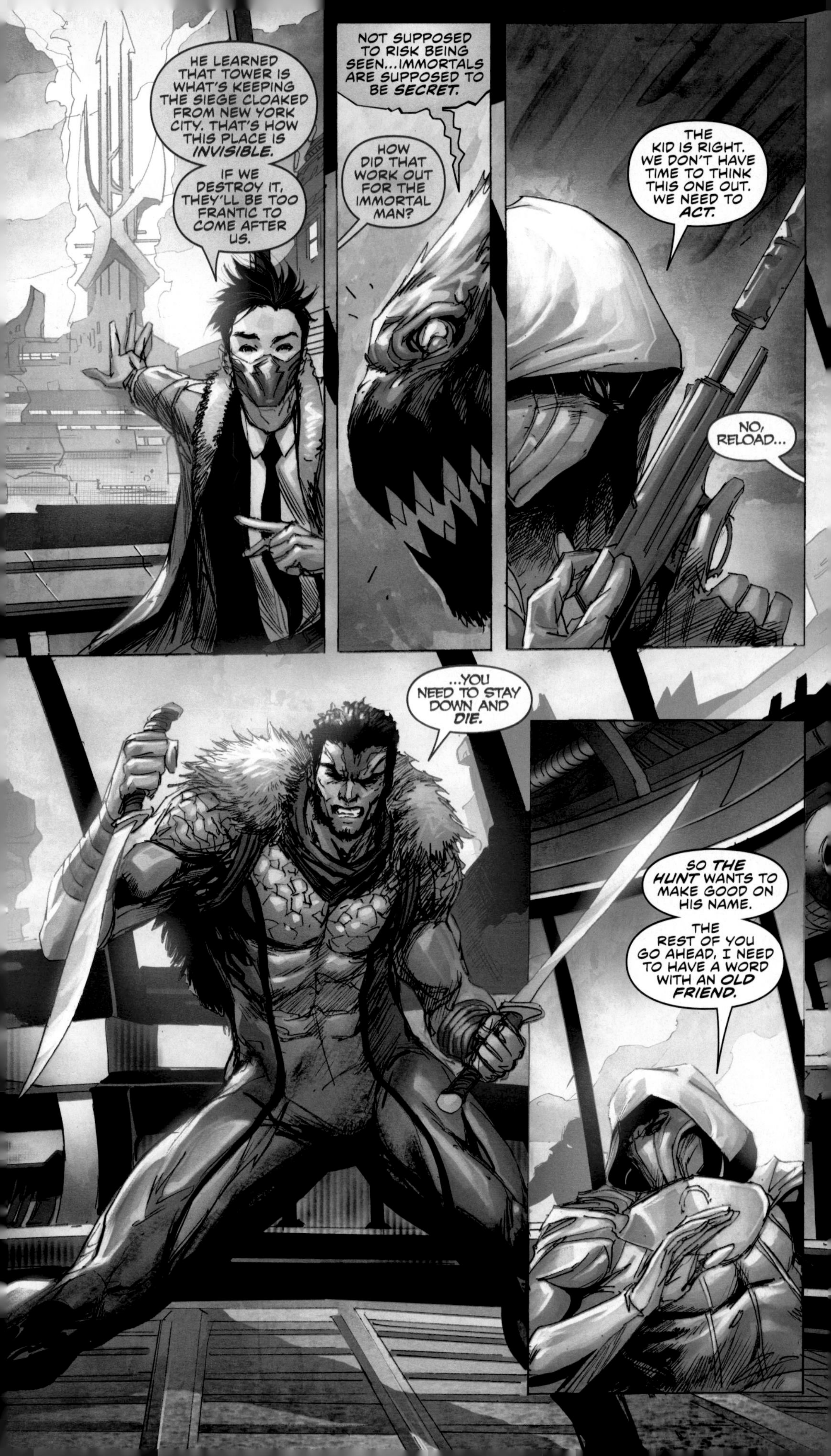

HE LEARNED THAT TOWER IS WHAT'S KEEPING THE SIEGE CLOAKED FROM NEW YORK CITY. THAT'S HOW THIS PLACE IS *INVISIBLE.*
IF WE DESTROY IT, THEY'LL BE TOO FRANTIC TO COME AFTER US.
NOT SUPPOSED TO RISK BEING SEEN...IMMORTALS ARE SUPPOSED TO BE *SECRET.*
HOW DID THAT WORK OUT FOR THE IMMORTAL MAN?
THE KID IS RIGHT. WE DON'T HAVE TIME TO THINK THIS ONE OUT. WE NEED TO *ACT.*
NO, RELOAD...
...YOU NEED TO STAY DOWN AND *DIE.*
SO *THE HUNT* WANTS TO MAKE GOOD ON HIS NAME.
THE REST OF YOU GO AHEAD. I NEED TO HAVE A WORD WITH AN *OLD FRIEND.*

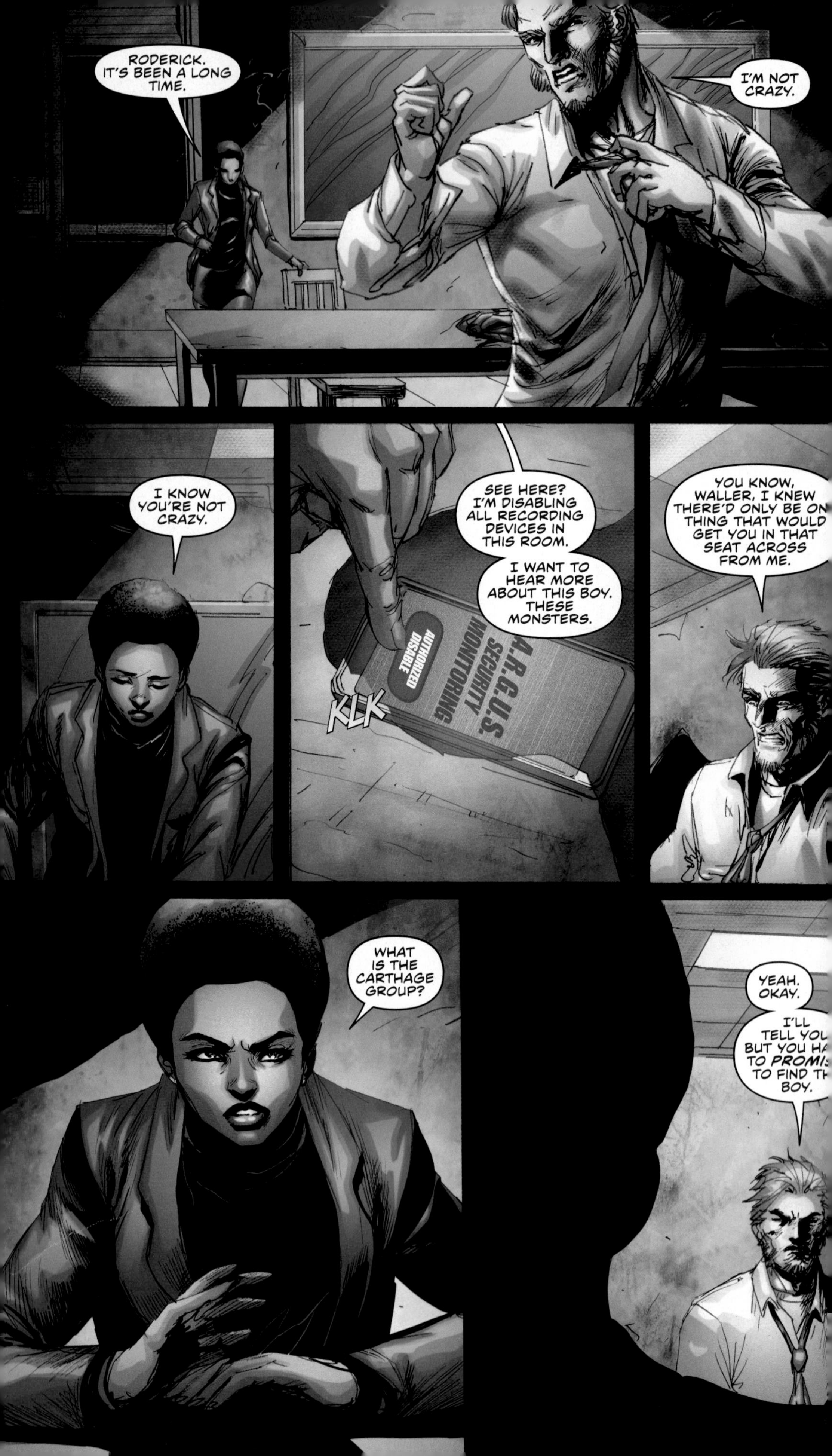
RODERICK. IT'S BEEN A LONG TIME.
I'M NOT CRAZY.
I KNOW YOU'RE NOT CRAZY.
SEE HERE? I'M DISABLING ALL RECORDING DEVICES IN THIS ROOM.
I WANT TO HEAR MORE ABOUT THIS BOY. THESE MONSTERS.
A.R.G.U.S. SECURITY MONITORING
AUTHORIZED DISABLE
KLK
YOU KNOW, WALLER, I KNEW THERE'D ONLY BE ON THING THAT WOULD GET YOU IN THAT SEAT ACROSS FROM ME.
WHAT IS THE CARTHAGE GROUP?
YEAH. OKAY.
I'LL TELL YOU BUT YOU HA TO PROMIS TO FIND TH BOY.

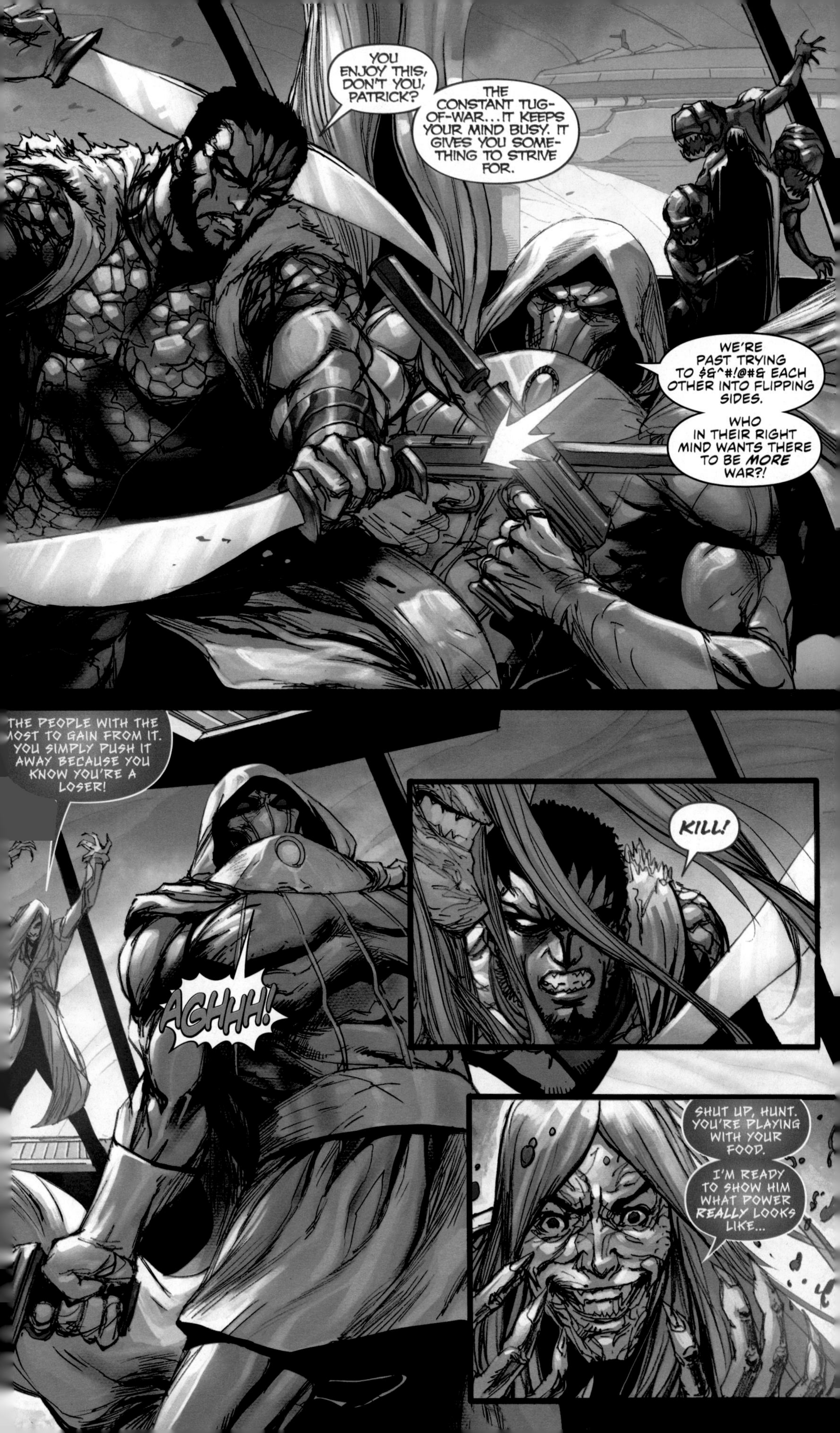

YOU ENJOY THIS, DON'T YOU, PATRICK?
THE CONSTANT TUG-OF-WAR...IT KEEPS YOUR MIND BUSY. IT GIVES YOU SOMETHING TO STRIVE FOR.
WE'RE PAST TRYING TO $&^#!@#& EACH OTHER INTO FLIPPING SIDES.
WHO IN THEIR RIGHT MIND WANTS THERE TO BE MORE WAR?!
THE PEOPLE WITH THE MOST TO GAIN FROM IT. YOU SIMPLY PUSH IT AWAY BECAUSE YOU KNOW YOU'RE A LOSER!
AGHHH!
KILL!
SHUT UP, HUNT. YOU'RE PLAYING WITH YOUR FOOD.
I'M READY TO SHOW HIM WHAT POWER REALLY LOOKS LIKE...

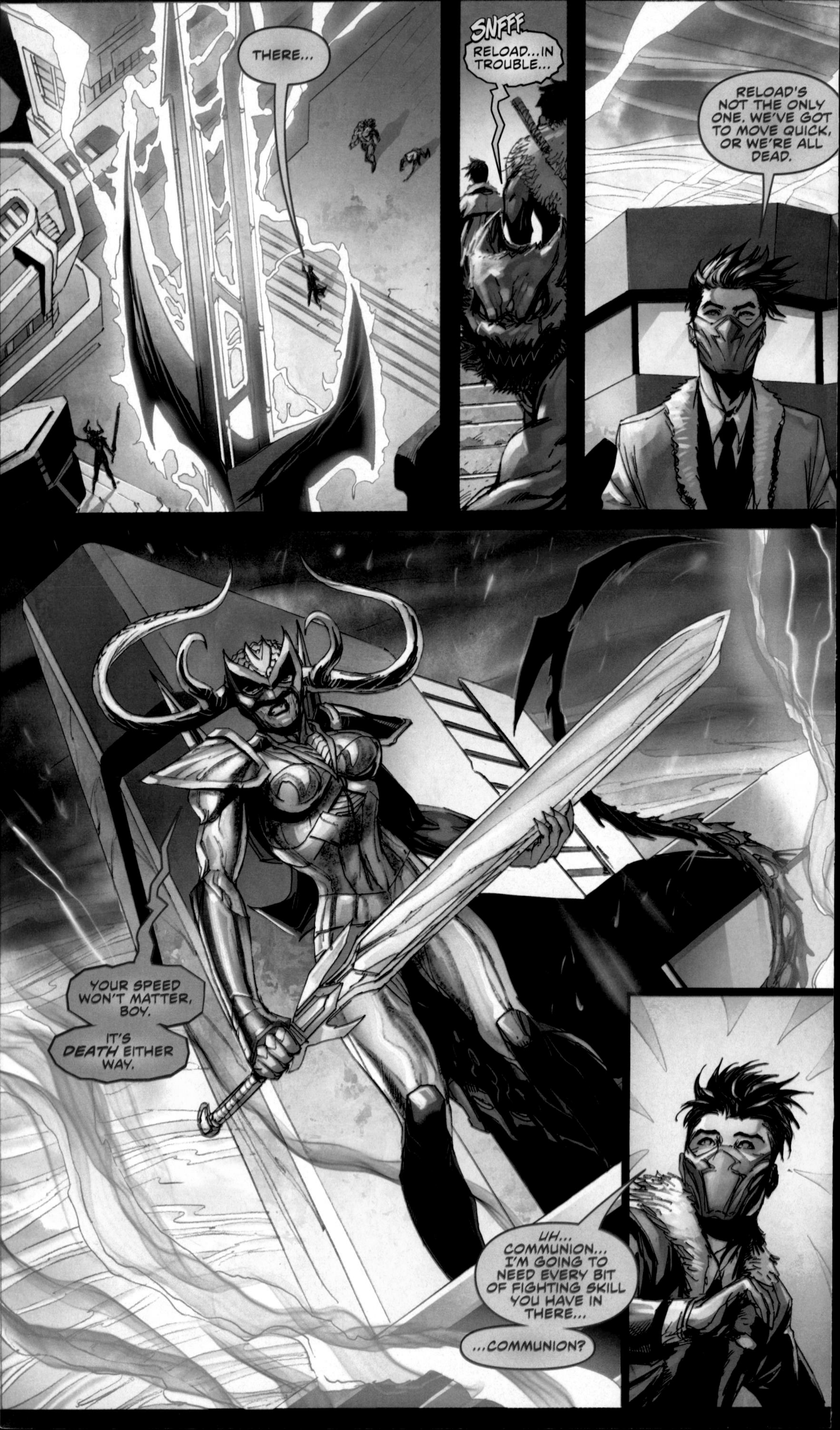
THERE...
SNFFF
RELOAD...IN TROUBLE...
RELOAD'S NOT THE ONLY ONE. WE'VE GOT TO MOVE QUICK, OR WE'RE ALL DEAD.
YOUR SPEED WON'T MATTER, BOY.
IT'S DEATH EITHER WAY.
UH... COMMUNION..., I'M GOING TO NEED EVERY BIT OF FIGHTING SKILL YOU HAVE IN THERE...
...COMMUNION?

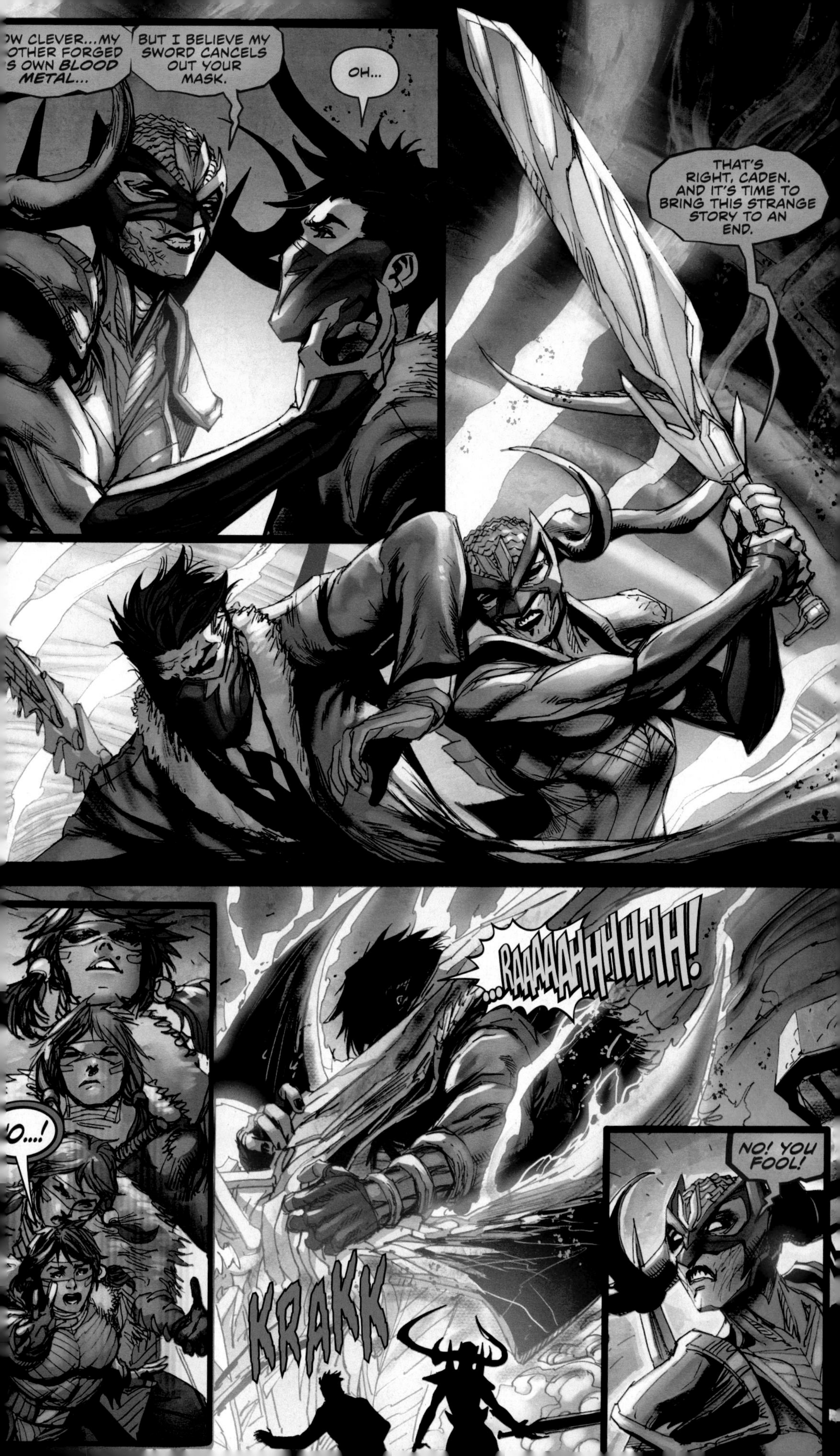

OW CLEVER...MY OTHER FORGED 'S OWN BLOOD METAL...
BUT I BELIEVE MY SWORD CANCELS OUT YOUR MASK.
OH...
THAT'S RIGHT, CADEN. AND IT'S TIME TO BRING THIS STRANGE STORY TO AN END.
...RAAAAAHHHHHH!
O...!
NO! YOU FOOL!
KRAKK

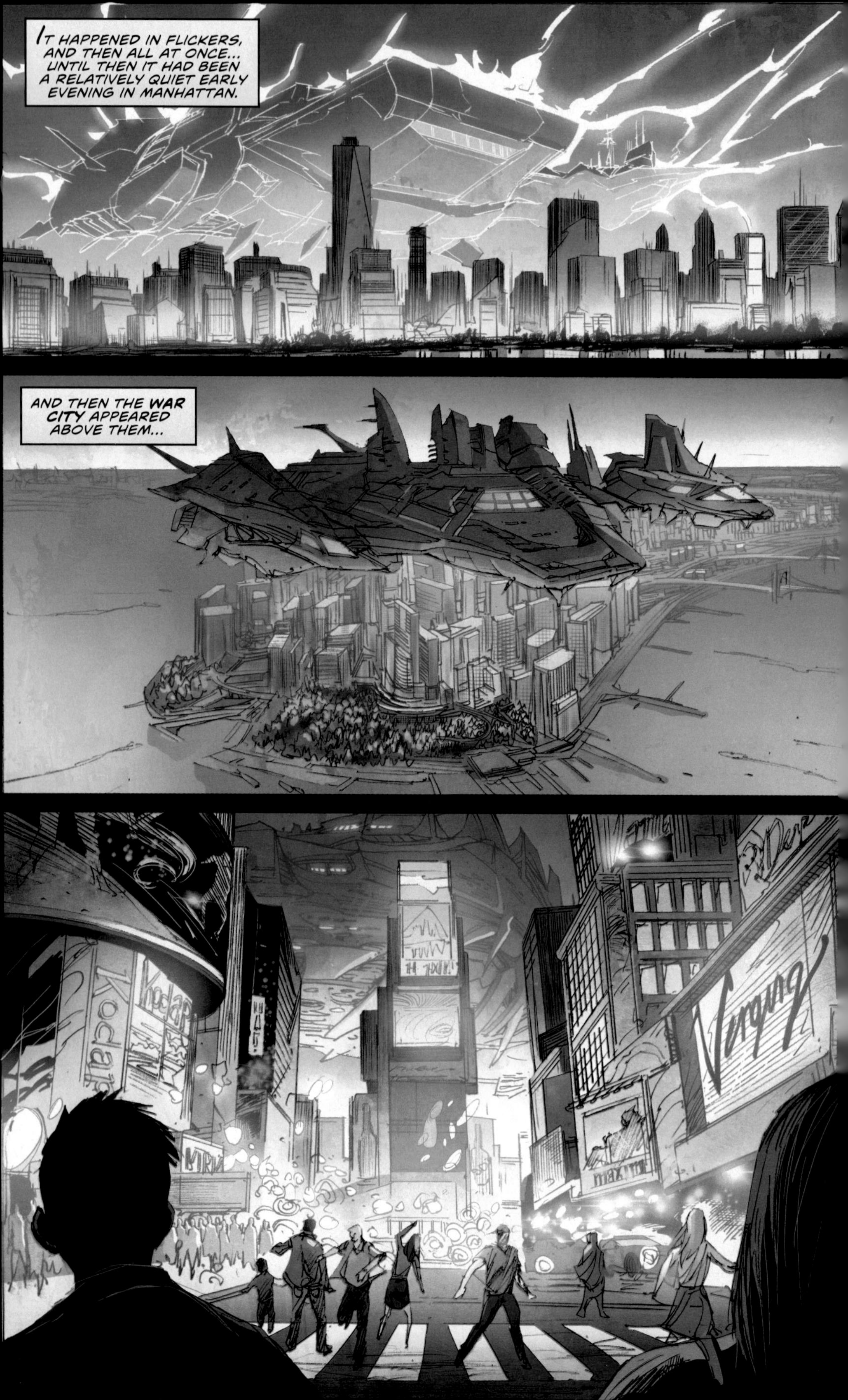
IT HAPPENED IN FLICKERS, AND THEN ALL AT ONCE... UNTIL THEN IT HAD BEEN A RELATIVELY QUIET EARLY EVENING IN MANHATTAN.
AND THEN THE WAR CITY APPEARED ABOVE THEM...

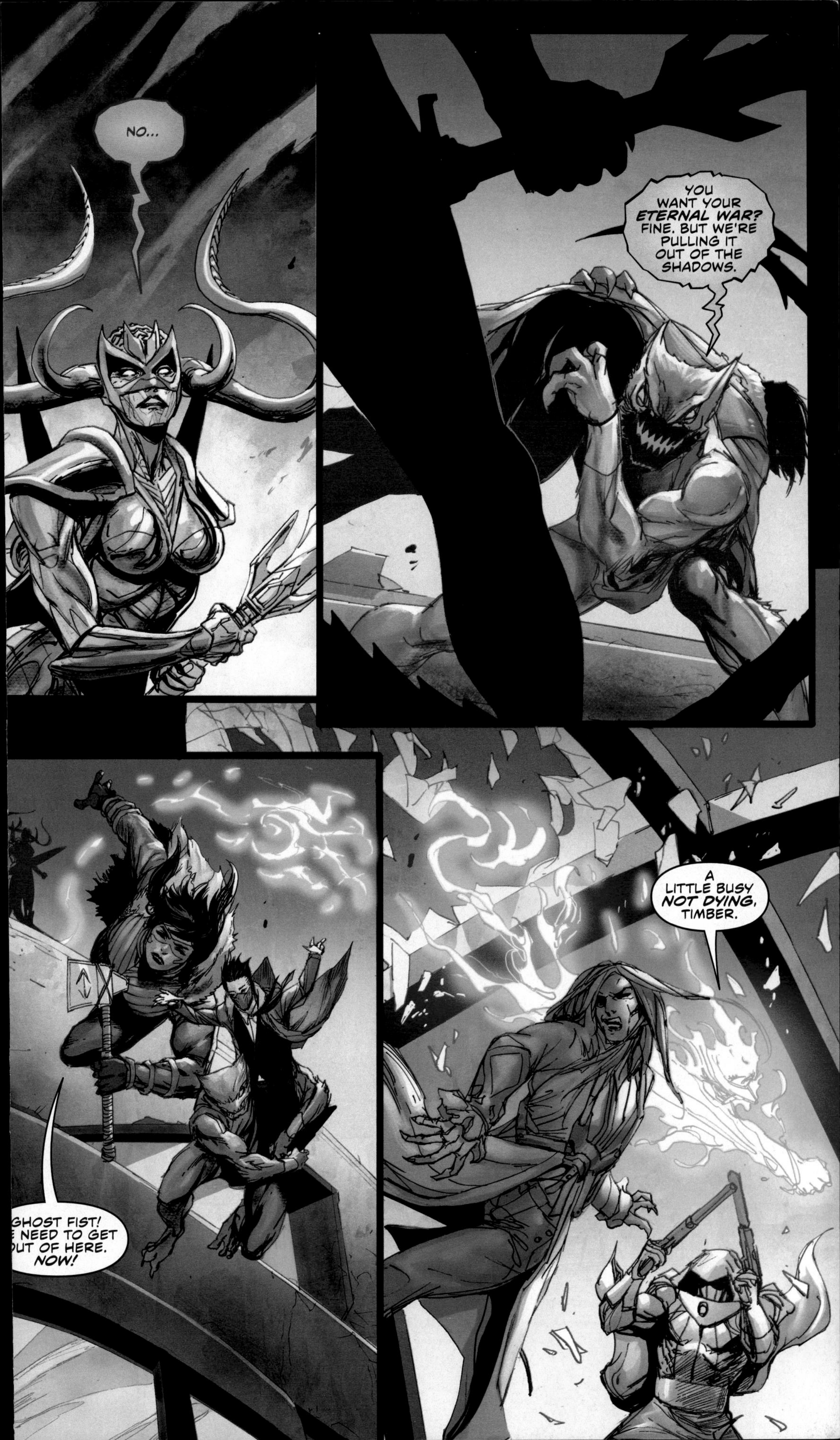
NO...
YOU WANT YOUR ETERNAL WAR? FINE. BUT WE'RE PULLING IT OUT OF THE SHADOWS.
GHOST FIST! E NEED TO GET UT OF HERE. NOW!
A LITTLE BUSY NOT DYING, TIMBER.

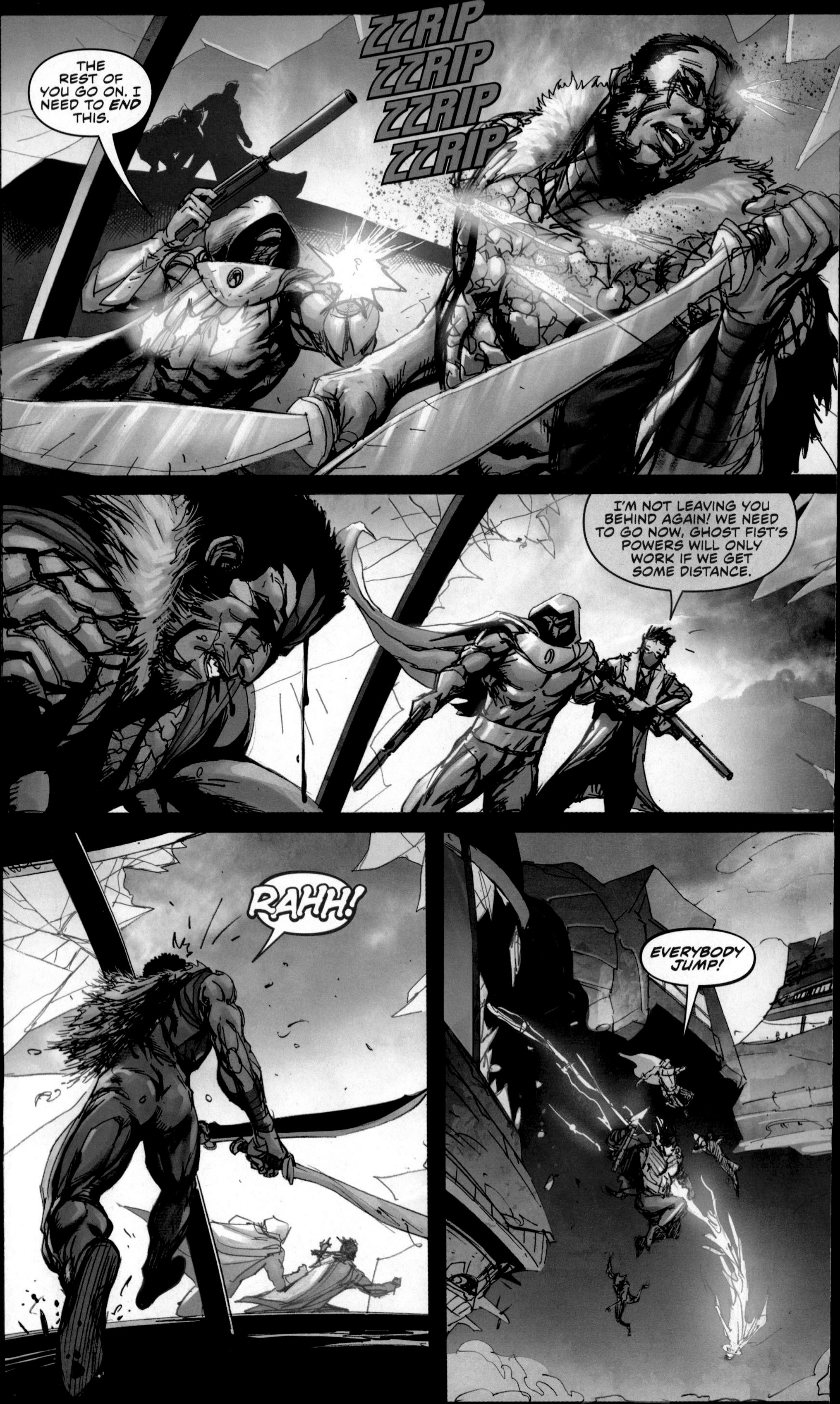
THE REST OF YOU GO ON. I NEED TO END THIS.
ZZRIP ZZRIP ZZRIP ZZRIP
I'M NOT LEAVING YOU BEHIND AGAIN! WE NEED TO GO NOW, GHOST FIST'S POWERS WILL ONLY WORK IF WE GET SOME DISTANCE.
RAHH!
EVERYBODY JUMP!

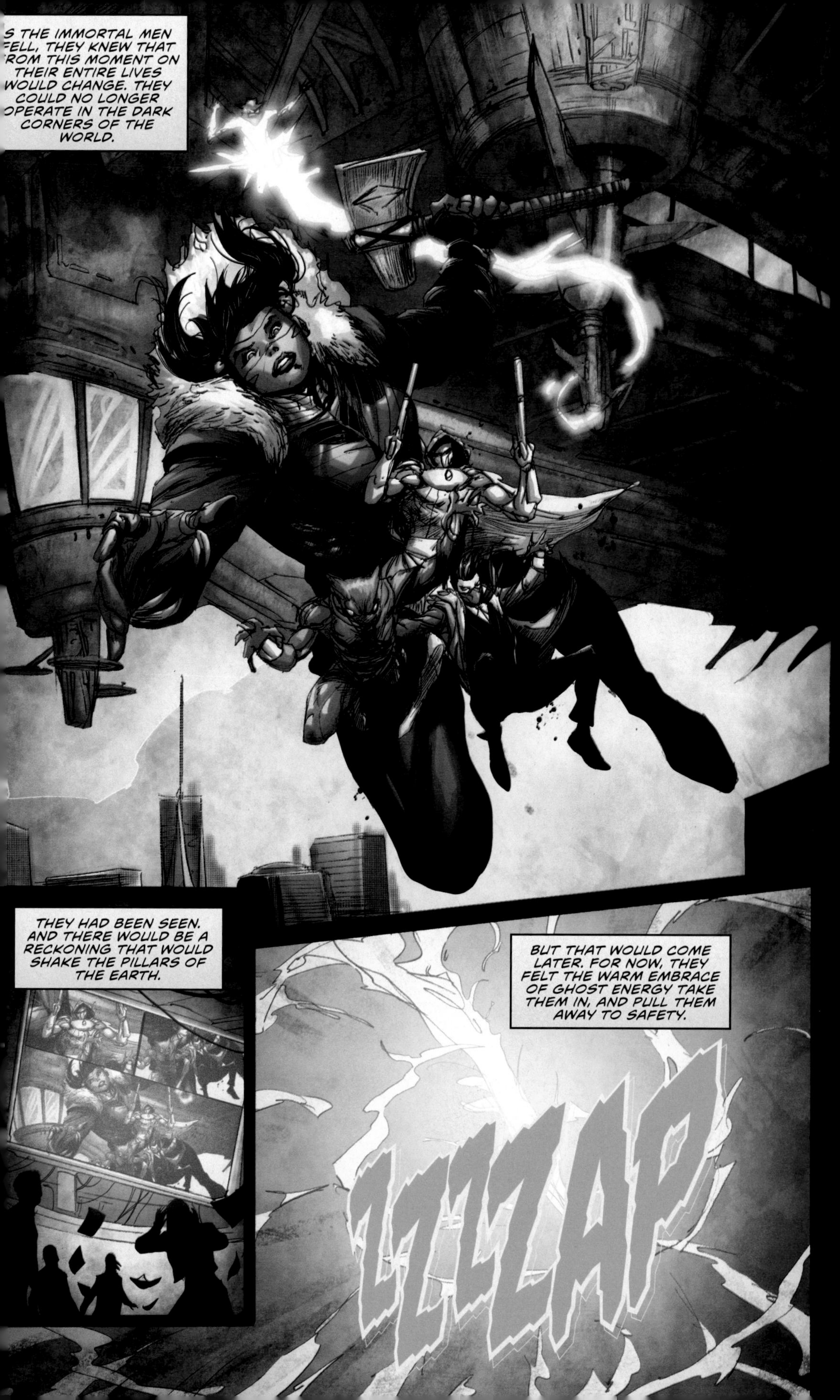
S THE IMMORTAL MEN FELL, THEY KNEW THAT FROM THIS MOMENT ON THEIR ENTIRE LIVES WOULD CHANGE. THEY COULD NO LONGER OPERATE IN THE DARK CORNERS OF THE WORLD.
THEY HAD BEEN SEEN. AND THERE WOULD BE A RECKONING THAT WOULD SHAKE THE PILLARS OF THE EARTH.
BUT THAT WOULD COME LATER. FOR NOW, THEY FELT THE WARM EMBRACE OF GHOST ENERGY TAKE THEM IN, AND PULL THEM AWAY TO SAFETY.
ZZZZAP

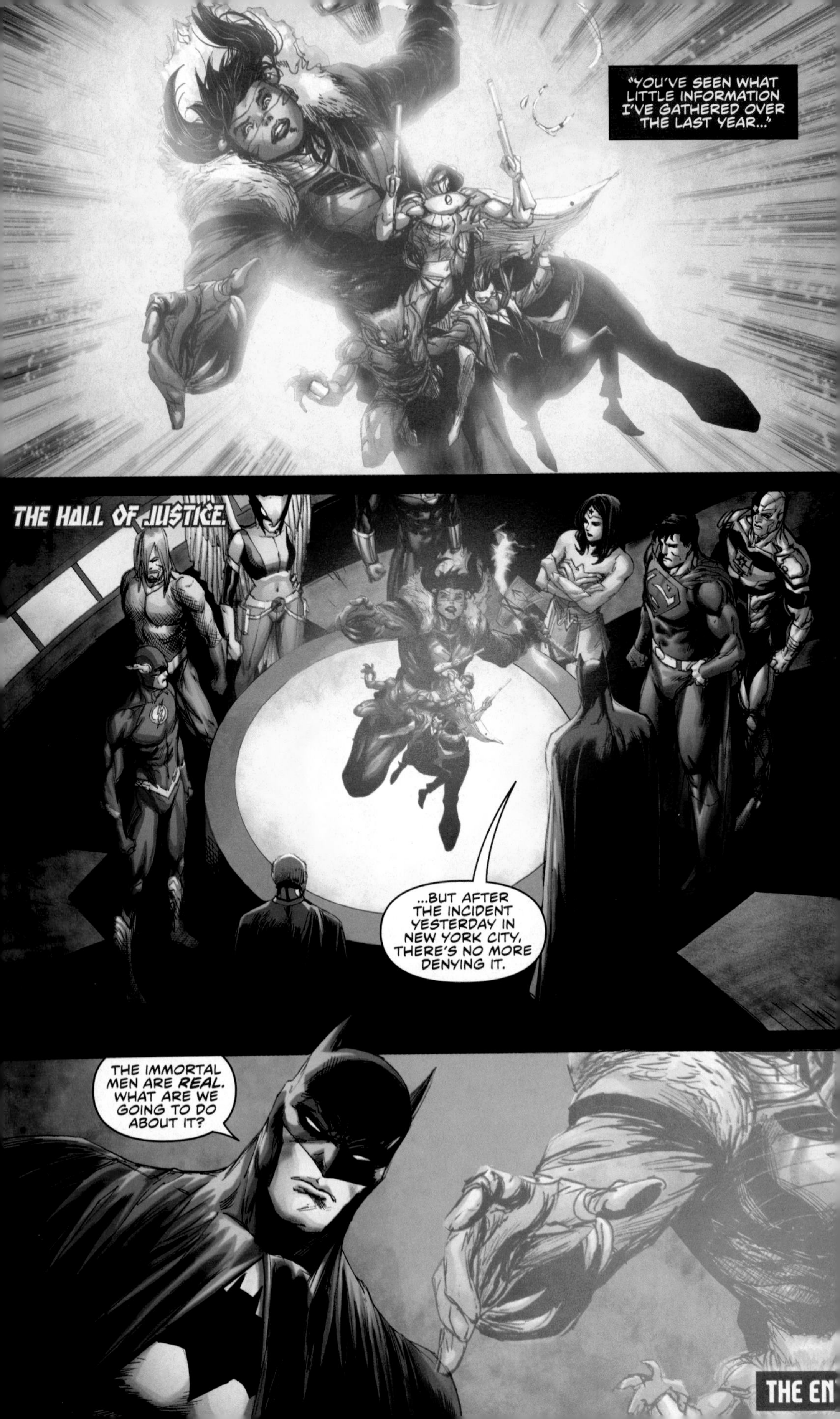
"YOU'VE SEEN WHAT LITTLE INFORMATION I'VE GATHERED OVER THE LAST YEAR..."
THE HALL OF JUSTICE.
...BUT AFTER THE INCIDENT YESTERDAY IN NEW YORK CITY, THERE'S NO MORE DENYING IT.
THE IMMORTAL MEN ARE *REAL*. WHAT ARE WE GOING TO DO ABOUT IT?
THE EN

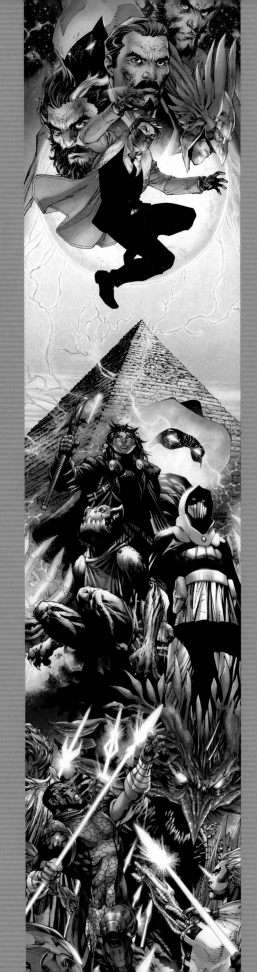

THE IMMORTAL MEN #1 full triptych cover

by Jim Lee, Scott Williams and Alex Sinclair

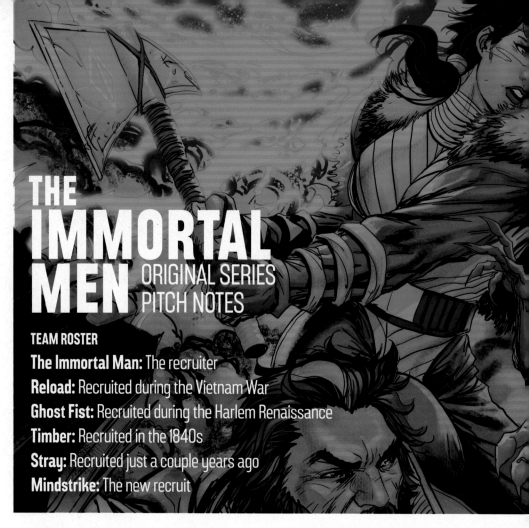

THE IMMORTAL MEN
ORIGINAL SERIES PITCH NOTES

TEAM ROSTER

The Immortal Man: The recruiter
Reload: Recruited during the Vietnam War
Ghost Fist: Recruited during the Harlem Renaissance
Timber: Recruited in the 1840s
Stray: Recruited just a couple years ago
Mindstrike: The new recruit

HISTORY

There is a secret history to the DC Universe—a secret history of secret heroes who have protected humanity from the shadows since the dawn of time. A TEAM of young heroes, each of whom can live forever. A team that wages a battle no one knows about, kept secret from even the mightiest heroes in the DCU.

The IMMORTAL MEN: Metahuman heroes from throughout time, granted immortality and tasked with preserving the peaceful evolution of all humankind.

At the dawn of mankind's history, five siblings were made immortal through their communion with a mysterious substance known as Nth metal. Each sibling represents a different aspect of humanity's collective soul: Action, Conquest, Expression, Wisdom and Harmony. Since that fateful day, Conquest has sought to cull the human herd using violence and war, and only Action, a.k.a. the Immortal Man, has stood in her way. Both sides gained followers and sought elite soldiers in a fight that would rage for centuries.

The deal is simple: join a secret war to save not just a few lives, but ALL lives. To fight not just for a few years while their bodies are at their peak but fight for CENTURIES. In exchange, they just need to leave their old lives behind. They will NEVER be celebrated for their achievements, but they can make a difference on the world like few others in humankind's history.

POWERS & WEAPONS

The Immortal Man is team leader and one of the origina[l] five siblings made immortal through their contact with Nth metal. Possesses superhuman strength and limited telekinetic abilities.

Mindstrike a.k.a. Caden Park is a telepath who has barely begun to understand the extent of his abilities. Cade[n] see the history of anyone through tactile contact. It is theor[i] he will one day replace the Immortal Man and lead the team victory over Conquest.

Reload can subtract time from an object—if he fires all the bullets in his gun, he can reverse the time of the object to w[hen] it was fully loaded. Infinite ammunition.

Ghost Fist draws energy out of the air that crackles as g[reen] lightning from his fingertips when he fights.

Timber can increase her size to over one hundred feet tall.

Stray transforms into a giant humanoid cat-creature whe[n] angered, but can't fully transform back into a human.

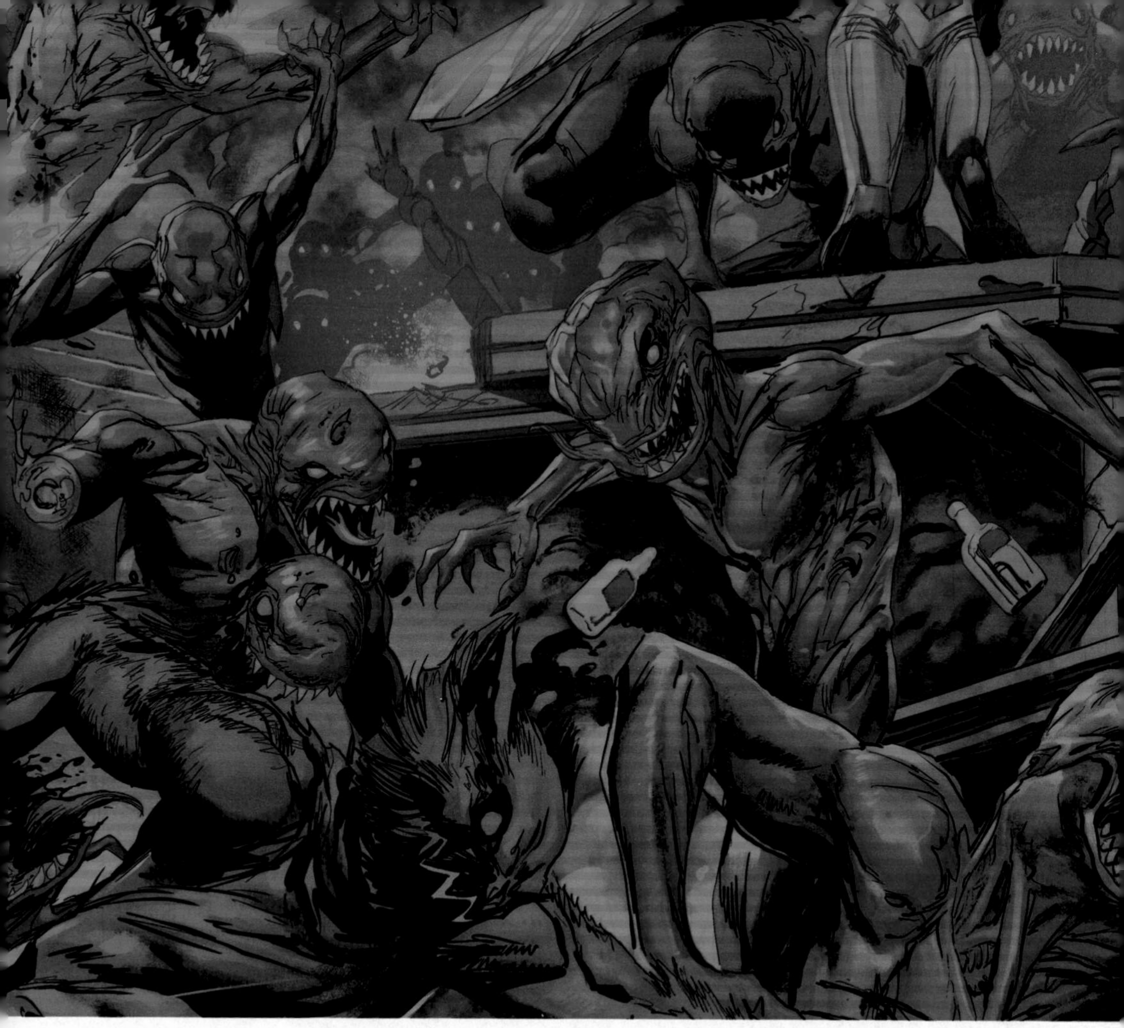

The Immortal Houses

- Five siblings, all members of the Bear Tribe at the dawn of man, all altered forever by a piece of impossible Nth metal. All made IMMORTAL. They are invulnerable to harm, and have not aged since that moment. They made a decision, millennia ago, to help shape humankind's destiny. To ensure its survival. But they disagreed on what form that help should take. Each of the five oversees a specific realm of influence in the world, and there is a standing agreement that none of the siblings will interfere with the others' realms.
  - **Action** assembles heroes, the special people willing to sacrifice everything for the cause.
  - **Conquest** fuels warfare to encourage humanity toward innovation and progress.
  - **Expression** was once a patron of the arts but sold out long ago.
  - **Wisdom** values knowledge and information, hoarding it rather than sharing.
  - **Harmony** encouraged the creation each of the major world religions and lost her faith in humankind as a result of how humanity warped them.

- The Campus (base of operations for the Immortal Men, where Action brings his heroes to train)
  - The original campus, located near Philadelphia, PA, was destroyed in THE IMMORTAL MEN #1 and a new facility is under construction.
- The University (Wisdom's secret base of operations where scholar monks study everything about the world without ever interacting with it)

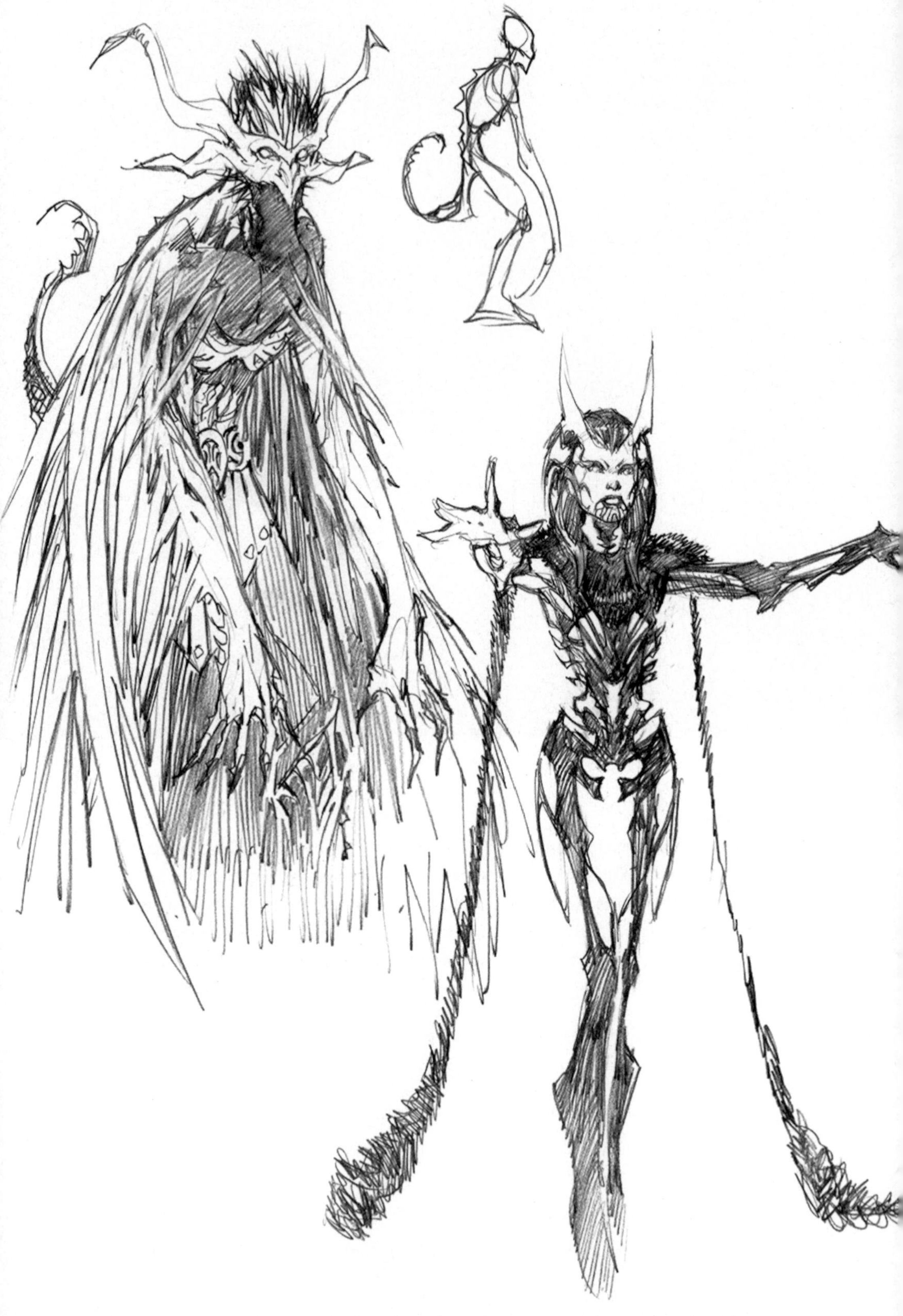

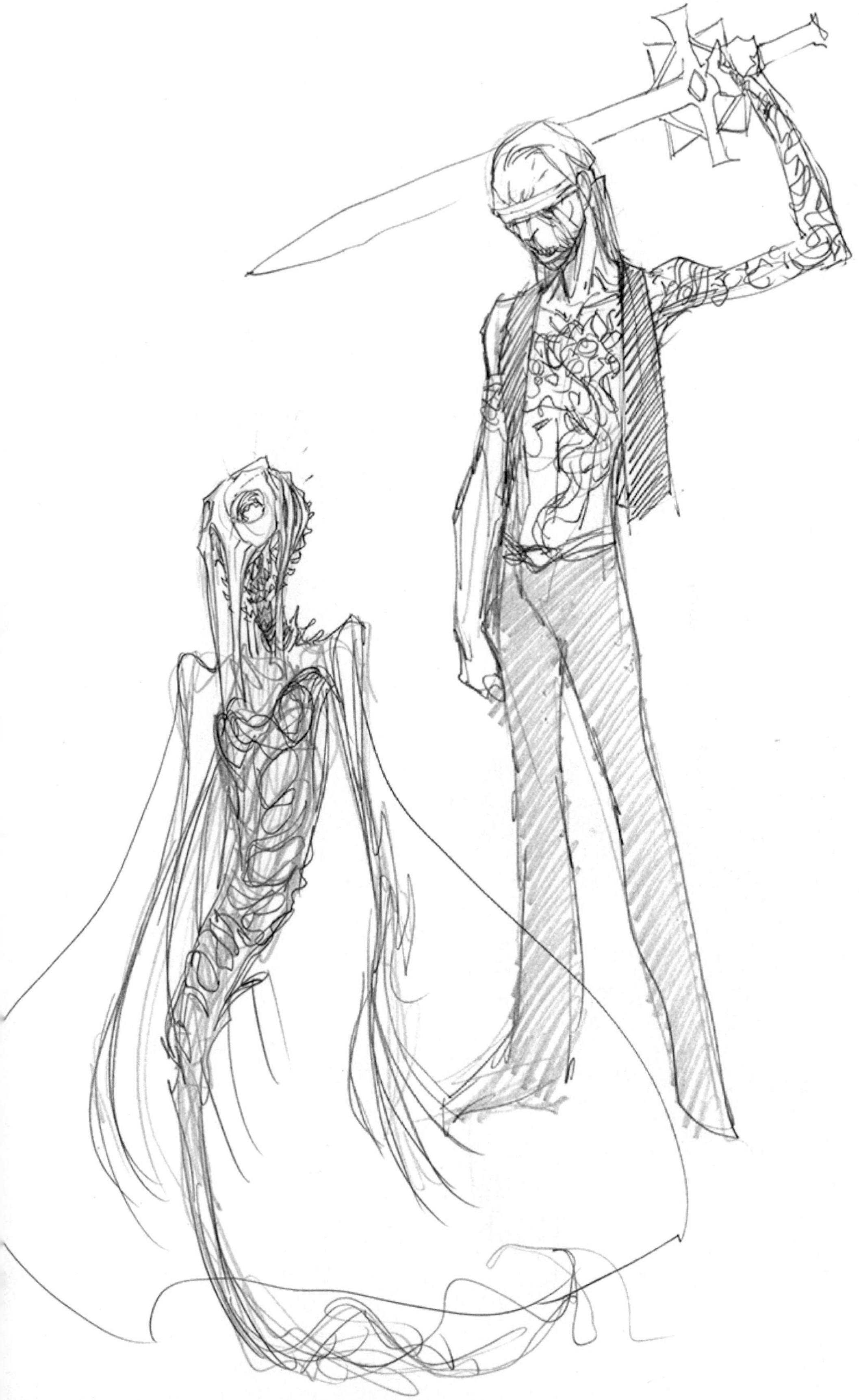

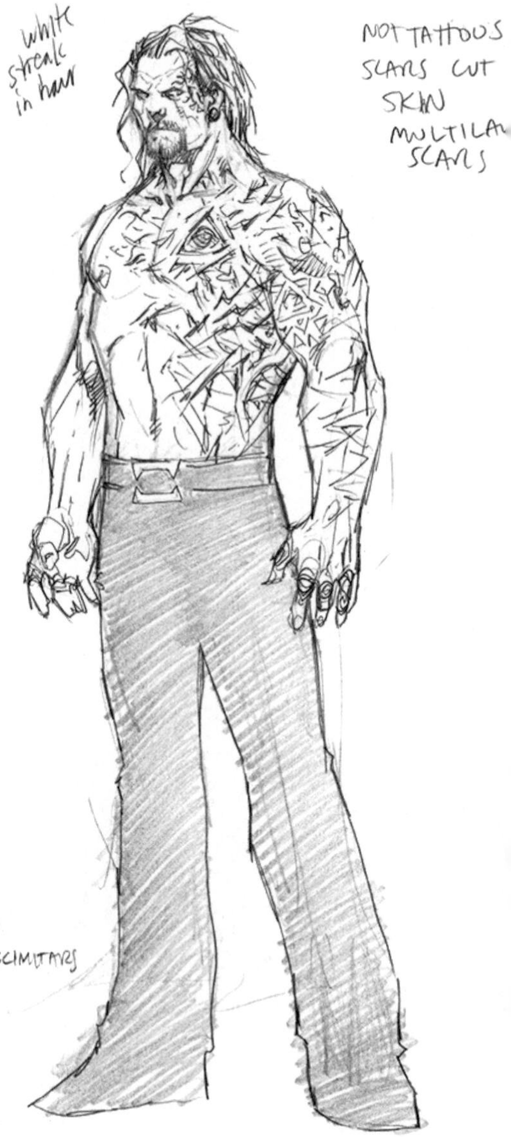
white streak in hair
NOT TATTOOS
SCARS CUT
SKIN
MULTILA
SCARS

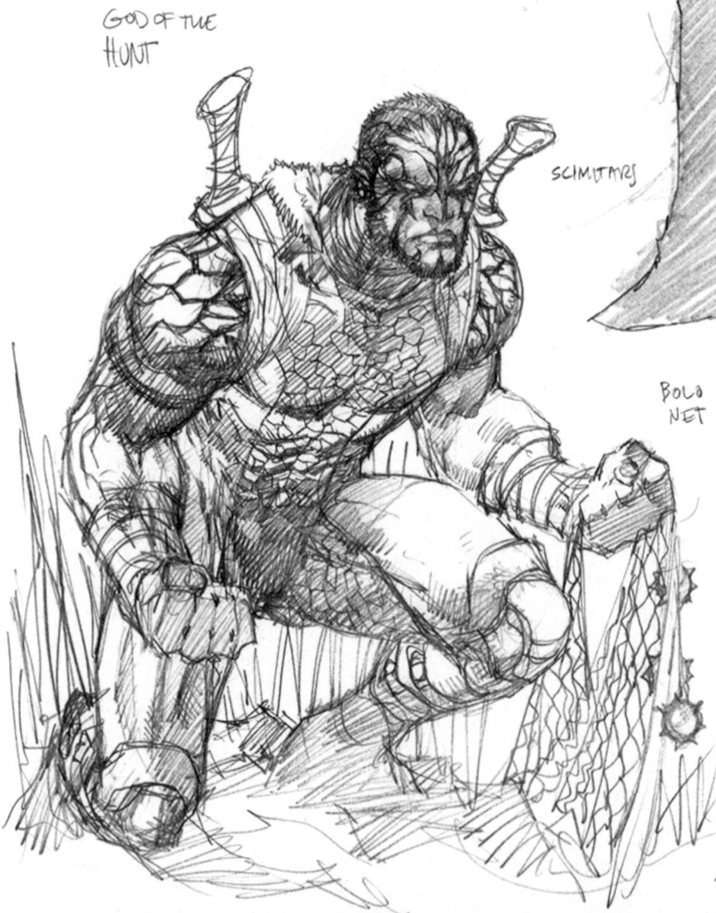
GOD OF THE
HUNT
SCIMITARS
BOLO
NET

THE HUNT CHARACTER SKETCH
AND THE IMMORTAL MAN EARLY CHARACTER DESIGN BY JIM LEE

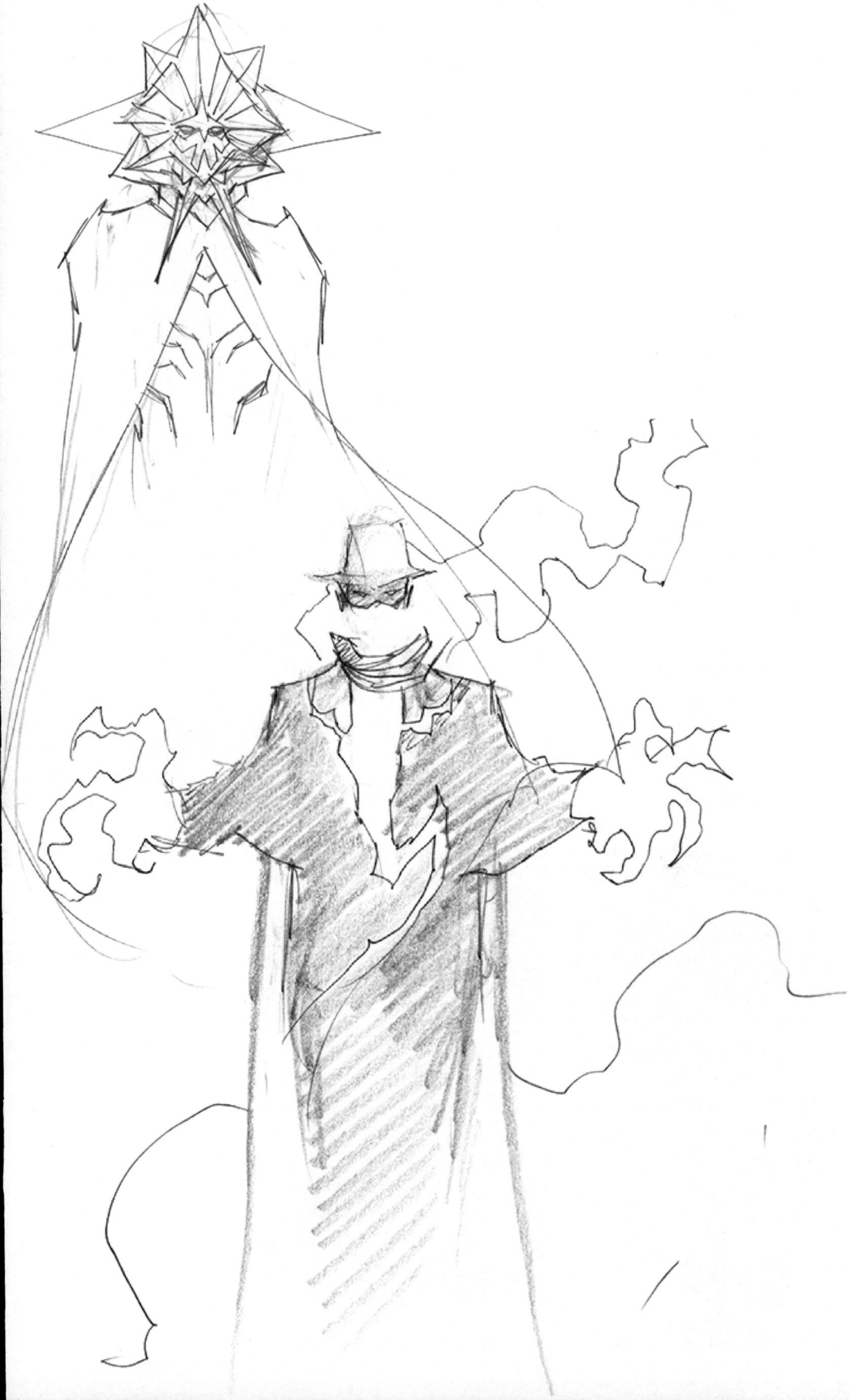

THE CONSTANT AND GHOST FIST CHARACTER SKETCHES BY JIM LEE

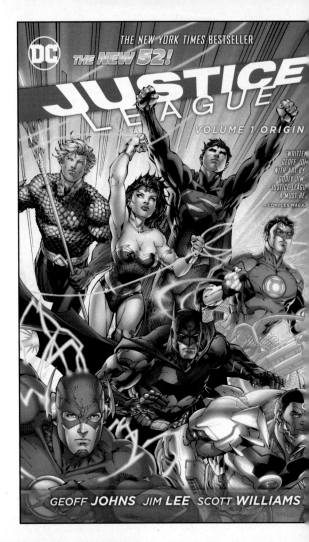

THE NEW YORK TIMES BESTSELLER

THE NEW 52!

JUSTICE LEAGUE

VOLUME 1 ORIGIN

"WRITTEN
GEOFF JOH
WITH ART BY
GODLY JIM
JUSTICE LEAGU
A MUST RE:
— COMPLEX MAGA2

GEOFF **JOHNS**   JIM **LEE**   SCOTT **WILLIAMS**

"Welcoming to new fans looking to get into superhero comics for the first time and old fans who gave up on the funny-books long ago."
– SCRIPPS HOWARD NEWS SERVICE

JUSTICE LEAGUE

VOL. 1: ORIGIN
GEOFF JOHNS and JIM LEE

JUSTICE LEAGUE
VOL. 2: THE VILLAIN'S JOURNEY

JUSTICE LEAGUE
VOL. 3: THRONE OF ATLANTIS

READ THE ENTIRE

JUSTICE LEAGUE
TI

JUSTICE LEAGUE
FOREVER I

JUSTICE LEAGUE
INJUSTICE I

JUSTICE LEAGUE
DARKSEID WAR

JUSTICE LEAGUE
DARKSEID WAR